365
DAILY DEVOTIONALS
- FROM THE -
Doctrine & Covenants

Women Read Scripture

365 DAILY DEVOTIONALS
– FROM THE –
Doctrine & Covenants

MARIANNA RICHARDSON, MBA, EdD, JD
CHRISTINE THACKERAY,
DRU HUFFAKER & GANEL-LYN CONDIE

© 2024 Marianna Richardson, Christine Thackeray, Ganel-Lyn Condie, and Dru Huffaker
All rights reserved.

No part of this book may be reproduced in any form whatsoever, whether by graphic, visual, electronic, film, microfilm, tape recording, or any other means, without prior written permission of the publisher, except in the case of brief passages embodied in critical reviews and articles.

This is not an official publication of The Church of Jesus Christ of Latter-day Saints. The opinions and views expressed herein belong solely to the author and do not necessarily represent the opinions or views of Cedar Fort, Inc. Permission for the use of sources, graphics, and photos is also solely the responsibility of the author.

Paperback ISBN 13: 978-1-4621-4751-9
Ebook ISBN 13: 978-1-4621-4839-4

Published by CFI, an imprint of Cedar Fort, Inc.
2373 W. 700 S., Suite 100 Springville, UT 84663
Distributed by Cedar Fort, Inc., www.cedarfort.com

Library of Congress Control Number: 2024944994

Cover design by Shawnda Craig
Cover design © 2024 Cedar Fort, Inc.

Printed in the United States of America

10 9 8 7 6 5 4 3 2 1

Printed on acid-free paper

We dedicate this book to the early Saints for their belief, sacrifice, and dedication to The Church of Jesus Christ of Latter-day Saints.
We also dedicate this book to the Prophet Joseph Smith, the prophet of the Restoration, and our current prophet, who continues to reveal the words of the Lord to the world.
Lastly, we dedicate this book to the Saints of today who stay faithful amidst the swirling attitudes and philosophies that pull people away from the truth that Jesus is our Savior and through Him we can do all things!

Introduction

President Joseph Fielding Smith described the Doctrine and Covenants as "distinctly peculiar" (*Church History and Modern Revelation*, 1:252). The Greek word translated as "peculiar" in the New Testament means to be preserved or possessed (1 Peter 2:9f). Throughout our study of the Doctrine and Covenants, we should preserve the words of these revelations in our hearts and possess them in our minds. As we live these teachings, we will become preserved and possessed by the Lord.

That is our purpose—to become the Lord's peculiar treasure by incorporating the wealth of knowledge and truth found in the Doctrine and Covenants.

Marianna has felt the powerful words of the Doctrine and Covenants fortify her testimony of prophets and strengthen the role of personal revelation in her own life.

Christine loves how the Doctrine and Covenants answers questions, setting an example of how to find answers to the many complex questions in our hearts and lives.

Dru is grateful for the restoration of truths, powers, and ordinances necessary to bring about the salvation of men and women and that teach her how to stand as a witness of Jesus Christ.

Ganel-Lyn appreciates how the study and application of modern-day scriptures foster greater faith and hope for the future.

The four of us have strong testimonies of the truthfulness of the Doctrine and Covenants. Thank you for joining us on this journey of discovery.

Doctrine and Covenants 1:6

My preface unto the book of my commandments, which I have given them to publish unto you, O inhabitants of the earth.

The Lord's Preface

After I finish writing a book, I write the preface that describes my thoughts about why I wrote the book and my inspiration for doing it. I also like to acknowledge those who supported me in my writing journey. In contrast, a foreword is written by a different person from the author. The purpose of a foreword is to write independent commentary and to add credibility to the book.

But the Lord does not need a foreword written by someone else to establish credibility. In section 1, the Lord states emphatically that this is a preface written by the author (and not a foreword). The Prophet Joseph Smith's nephew President Joseph Fielding Smith bore a strong witness that the preface "was not written by Joseph Smith, but was dictated by Jesus Christ, and contains his and his Father's word to the Church and to all the world" (*Church History and Modern Revelation*, 1:252).

By reading the Doctrine and Covenants, we can know the Savior, His words, His laws, and His promises given to us through His living prophets. We can receive confirmation from the Holy Spirit that these are the Savior's and His Father's words, not the words of man.

—Marianna

> "A prophet does not stand between you and the Savior. Rather, he stands beside you and points the way to the Savior."
>
> Neil L. Anderson
> "The Prophet of God," Apr. 2018

Doctrine and Covenants 1:4

And the voice of warning shall be unto all people, by the mouths of my disciples, whom I have chosen in these last days.

Direction for Life

Once, while driving to speak at a Young Women camp, I totally lost my GPS signal. I was without cell coverage. The directions I had been given were vague and limited. As the dark increased, so did my anxiety. Praying for help, I heard a quiet whisper: "Follow the rainbow." Off in the distance, I saw a lovely rainbow.

I continued through the canyon and then along a highway. The farther I drove, the closer the rainbow got. I kept praying that I could trust the earlier prompting. Joyfully, I arrived safely and on time at the camp. I testified to the girls that the rainbow was a sign from God. Could God really direct me safely just like He had with Noah? God uses His prophets and disciples to help guide, warn, and instruct His people.

Heeding the warning voice of God calls for a believing and trusting heart. Sometimes we will be told to stop or start things. Potholes and detours may be avoided simply because of our obedience. Faith is not always knowing the *why* of a commandment. I am grateful for a living prophet on earth. He is a GPS for life.

—Ganel-Lyn

> "Pray to your Heavenly Father. This is His sacred work. He will guide you in what to do. He will open doors, remove roadblocks, and help you overcome obstacles."
>
> Neil L. Andersen
> "It's a Miracle," Apr. 2013

Doctrine and Covenants 1:12

Prepare ye, prepare ye for that which is to come, for the Lord is nigh.

Divine Warning

Some years ago while being set apart in the Primary presidency, I received a divine warning. The bishop counseled through his blessing that I should get my food storage organized. He didn't even say a word about serving children! It was so odd that I listened. Church leaders have been teaching about food storage for a while, but I'd never felt I had the resources.

The next day I rolled up my sleeves and set up a shelf in the basement. Using our meager savings, I bought canned and dried goods, did the math, and made a list of menus for one year with all the ingredients stored. It took most of the summer.

A few months later I got very sick and couldn't shop or cook for about a year. My teenage son took on that responsibility and never had to worry about what to prepare. This allowed my husband to work without interruption to provide for our family. We felt the Lord was nigh, or near us. This inspired warning allowed us to be prepared so we could face a challenging trial with gratitude.

—Christine

> "A loving Father in Heaven and His Son . . . have provided us scriptures and prophets to prepare us, warn us about dangers, and give us guidance to prepare and protect us."
>
> Quentin L. Cook
>
> "Be Peaceable Followers of Christ," Oct. 2023

Doctrine and Covenants 1:16

But every man walketh in his own way, and after the image of his own god, whose image is in the likeness of the world.

The Image of His Own God

My husband, Steve, was offered a new position in Seattle, Washington, and I did not want to go. We were living in a suburb of Washington, DC, and I loved it there. I had finished building and decorating my home; it was perfect. I had dear friends who looked up to me. I was involved at a prestigious university that admired my scholarship. Life was good—for me.

But my husband was not happy because he did not like his job. I enjoyed the image of my life, and I did not want to see his pain. I was walking in my way rather than seeking what the Lord wanted for my family and my husband. The image of my god had become my world rather than thinking celestial. I had to humble myself, to fall on my knees to find the right path. Finally, I was ready to hear the Lord's answer. He wanted us to move. Months later, I realized the move was for me, too. I found happiness and fulfillment in our new home.

To understand the preface of the Doctrine and Covenants, we should read it with humility. The Lord's words are direct, bold, and even fear-inducing when talking about His righteous judgment. Preparation for His coming might mean major changes in our personal lives. To comply, we must be humble enough to give up our image of what our life should be and allow the Lord to shape it.

—Marianna

"The Lord's perspective transcends your mortal wisdom. His response to your prayers may surprise you and will help you to think celestial."

Russell M. Nelson

"Think Celestial!" Oct. 2023

Doctrine and Covenants 1:32

Nevertheless, he that repents and does the commandments of the Lord shall be forgiven.

Satan Is a Liar

When I became a mother, I wanted my children to avoid living life with a lens of perfectionism. Perfectionists often see everything with an all-or-nothing perspective. Such does not leave much room for the messiness of mortality.

Consider the premortal council when the adversary suggests an all-or-nothing plan. It is no wonder that he is still trying to use those same tactics today. One of Satan's top lies is that if we sin, all is lost. He makes us believe we can't be forgiven. The good news of the gospel is that all can be redeemed by the Savior. The enemy encourages us to hide the truth. God is truth. He celebrates when we come to Him and joyfully repent.

When my kids came home from school, I would ask them what mistakes they made that day. I wanted them to know that making mistakes brings meaning. Being perfect was never part of the Father's plan. It is through Jesus that repentance and becoming perfected is always possible. Don't believe the big liar. Talk with God every day. As I do with my own children, He loves watching us learn, even when we make mortal mistakes.

—Ganel-Lyn

> "Satan will try to make us believe that our sins are not forgiven because we can remember them. Satan is a liar; he tries to blur our vision and lead us away from the path of repentance and forgiveness."
>
> Dieter F. Uchtdorf
>
> "Point of Safe Return," Apr. 2007

Doctrine and Covenants 1:34

And again, verily I say unto you, O inhabitants of the earth: I the Lord am willing to make these things known unto all flesh.

The Need to Know

I grew up in challenging circumstances, living in a crime-ridden, low-income neighborhood where my parents worked long hours to earn a living. Our home wasn't always a happy place. It was often overshadowed by sadness and fear, and I often felt lost and alone. In the midst of these difficulties, my mother clung to her faith in Jesus, which provided a source of strength and hope for our family.

Once a week, on Sunday and again on Wednesday nights, we attended a little community church in the heart of Phoenix, Arizona. I yearned to know who Jesus was and how He could save me, not just from sin and death but also from the scary and uncertain situation I was living in.

In time, I was taught the gospel by two young Utah missionaries and joined The Church of Jesus Christ of Latter-day Saints. I had found the truth, and the truth had set me free in ways I could never have imagined. I had not been lost. The Savior knew me. He came to my rescue.

—Dru

> "The Savior will help you see and understand the vision He has for you. You are His beloved daughters."
>
> **Elaine S. Dalton**
> "Press Forward and Be Steadfast," Apr. 2003

Doctrine and Covenants 1:38

My word shall not pass away, but shall all be fulfilled, whether by mine own voice or by the voice of my servants, it is the same.

Is He Worthy?

We moved to a new area, and I made quick friends with a sweet neighbor who was disappointed with our local Church leader. I truly felt this man had been called for a reason, but my friend was simply waiting for him to be released. My husband told me it didn't matter who was called, she wouldn't like him. I disagreed in support of my friend.

Surprisingly, shortly after this conversation, that brother was released, and my husband was called to fill that position. My family and my friend's family had been very close, but within a few weeks, there was distance between us. I heard through the grapevine that my friend was extremely disappointed with my husband's choices. My husband was right. When we speak ill of one Church leader, it is easy to start looking for negatives. And we will find them!

It is good to remember that our Church leaders do not have to be perfect; no one is. They only need to be worthy. As we support them, they will grow and be inspired by the Spirit. Through this process, we also grow in patience and faith. In contrast, when we reject our leaders, we reject the Lord.

—Christine

"Disrespect for ecclesiastical leaders has caused many to suffer spiritual weakening and downfall. We should look past any perceived imperfections . . . and uphold the office which they hold."

James E. Faust
"Called and Chosen," Oct. 2005
Quoted by Henry B. Eyring, "The Lord Leads His Church," Oct. 2017

> **Joseph Smith—History 1:6**
> *Priest contending against priest, and convert against convert . . . all their good feelings . . . were . . . lost in a strife of words.*

Facebook Friends and Movie Debates

The summer blockbuster movie *Barbie* created quite a stir. People dressed up and posted pictures on social media. Parties were planned around the theme of this movie. It triggered strong emotions and opinions.

There wasn't really a neutral zone when it came to this film. Friends and families debated the messages of the movie. Thought leaders even weighed in. The meaning behind the script was debated. I had a full one-hour discussion about this pink movie with the women I am assigned to minister to. There were online arguments and meme wars about the value of this theatrical creation.

Like politics or religion, when people start posting about personal opinions, they rarely change someone else's point of view. A young Joseph Smith understood what it feels like to live in a world filled with wars of words. Consider that constantly contending and commenting will rarely convert anyone to your way of thinking. Instead, consider being more of a peacemaker and less of a protagonist.

—Ganel-Lyn

> "In situations that are highly charged and filled with contention, I invite you to remember Jesus Christ. As we follow the Prince of Peace, we will become His peacemakers."
>
> **Russell M. Nelson**
> "Peacemakers Needed," Apr. 2023

Joseph Smith—History 1:12

Never did any passage of scripture come with more power to the heart of man than this did at this time to mine.

Scripture Power

The power of the Word is real and may include a physical side effect. Sometimes I feel a warm glow that radiates throughout my body. Other times I feel tightness, as if loving arms are enfolding me. These physical manifestations may feel different for different people, and each person may use different words to describe them. But the spiritual power of the Lord's words has physical power that changes us.

Joseph had a question to which he sincerely wanted an answer. He turned to the scriptures to figure out what he should do. After reading James 1:5, Joseph felt the power of those words with "great force into every feeling of [his] heart" (Joseph Smith–History 1:12).

When I read the scriptures with a question in my mind, the words and phrases possess a deeper significance for me. They seem to pop up off the page and sink into my soul.

In times of trouble, I turn to scripture power to heal my doubts, problems, fears, and heartaches.

—Marianna

> "Scriptures can calm an agitated soul, giving peace, hope, and a restoration of confidence in one's ability to overcome the challenges of life. They have the potent power to heal emotional challenges when there is faith in the Savior. They can accelerate physical healing."
>
> Richard G. Scott
> "The Power of Scripture," Oct. 2011

Joseph Smith—History 1:13

I at length came to the determination to "ask of God," concluding that if he gave wisdom to them that lacked . . . I might venture.

Taking a Chance

When I was sixteen, a young Latter-day Saint boy asked me out on a date. At the time, I was an active member of another faith, but for years I had struggled with questions that seemed to have no answers. According to family guidelines lovingly provided by his parents, the young man could only go out with a non-member if he took her to a Church event. So, he invited me to attend a play called *A Vision of Love* with his family. I held his two-year-old brother on my lap, and tears streamed down my cheeks as I heard the story of a young boy who was also searching for truth and answers. Then I heard the words that would change my life forever: "This is my Beloved Son. Hear Him" (Joseph Smith–History 1:17).

My heart was completely consumed with the Spirit. Like Joseph, I have the ability to pray. I have the ability to hear God's voice, understand His will for me, and serve so as to complete a mighty work for Him.

I will be forever grateful for a young man who was brave enough to share the message of the Restoration and point me toward the Savior.

—Dru

"Our Father knows that when we are surrounded by uncertainty and fear, what will help us the very most is to hear His Son."

Russell M. Nelson
"Hear Him," Apr. 2020

Joseph Smith—History 1:16

I saw a pillar of light exactly over my head, above the brightness of the sun, which descended gradually until it fell upon me.

Light Always Wins

If I wake up in a room other than my own, like in a hotel or a tent, I get disoriented easily, especially if it is really dark. Having a small night-light helps dispel the dark. I feel calmer when I can orient myself with even a glimmer of illumination. It doesn't take a lot of light to beat back the dark.

When Joseph went to the grove of trees near his home, he was attacked with darkness and despair. According to the record, at the moment when he nearly lost hope, he saw a pillar of light over his head. The fourteen-year-old boy almost "abandoned [himself] to destruction" (Joseph Smith–History 1:16).

Have you ever found yourself disoriented by extreme darkness, depression, or doubt? Create your own sacred grove spaces and places. It will give you access to God's strength and power. Remember, a little light always wins. Continue to call upon God, hourly and daily, to receive the needed strength to overcome the adversary.

—Ganel-Lyn

> "He was seized by the power of the enemy. . . . He called upon God, and the evil power left him. There is great power in prayer. . . . Pray to God in the name of Jesus Christ for strength."
>
> Boyd K. Packer
>
> "The Standard of Truth Has Been Erected," Oct. 2003

Joseph Smith—History 1:17

One of them spake unto me, calling me by name and said, pointing to the other—This is My Beloved Son. Hear Him!

Selective Hearing

I inherited selective hearing from my mother. It has been both a gift and a curse. If I am really into a good book, the world could end and I may not notice. More than once, a toddler has climbed into my lap and grabbed both my cheeks before I realized I was being summoned. According to modern psychologists, this is a talent, not a disorder. My children would disagree.

At the Mount of Transfiguration, when Christ appeared after His Resurrection in the Americas, and later when God the Father and Jesus Christ came to Joseph Smith, the Father introduced His "Beloved Son" and expressed the plea, "Hear Him!"

When it comes to the words of Christ, selective hearing will not do. The Father has made it clear; our most important job during mortality is listening to Christ's words. We do that by reading scriptures, listening to His authorized servants, and inviting the whisperings of the Holy Ghost into our hearts, because those promptings are "the words of Christ" (see 2 Nephi 32:3). May our ears and hearts be open and ready.

—Christine

"Our world, our challenges, our circumstances will not get quieter, but we can and must hunger and thirst after the things of Christ to 'hear Him' with clarity."

Bonnie H. Cordon
"Never Give Up an Opportunity to Testify of Christ," Apr. 2023

Joseph Smith—History 1:18

My object in going to inquire of the Lord was to know which of all the sects was right, that I might know which to join.

Finding a Sacred Grove Answer

My son was getting into the wrong crowd at school, and I was beside myself with worry. I didn't know what to do. Feeling that I was losing him, I tried becoming involved in his school, talking to his teachers, and spending more time with him individually, but none of these things were working.

I knew I needed the Lord's help and found a quiet place where I could be alone—my sacred grove—to pour out my heart to God. The words came out swiftly, accompanied by many tears. Then, I waited. I sat in silence and let my mind become open to what the Lord had to say. The thought popped into my mind: "homeschool." I had never considered homeschooling him. My answer was very specific to me, my situation, and the needs of my son.

In 1820, Joseph Smith found a quiet spot to ask his question. He knew he would do whatever the Lord asked him to do. The Lord's answer surprised Joseph. It was something he had never thought about before. Joseph followed the Lord's sacred grove answer, showing his real intent and commitment to obey the Lord's command—no matter what He asked Joseph to achieve, organize, or accomplish.

—Marianna

> "To access information from heaven, one must first have a firm faith and a deep desire. . . . 'Real intent' means that one really intends to follow the divine direction given."
>
> **Russell M. Nelson**
> "Ask, Seek, Knock," Oct. 2009

Joseph Smith—History 1:25

I have actually seen a vision; and who am I that I can withstand God, or why does the world think to make me deny what I have actually seen?

Do You Really Know Brad Wilcox?

I am often asked if I really know Brother Brad Wilcox. I do. We have had the opportunity to work and travel together. More than anything, I am grateful to call him my friend. On more than one occasion, I have reached out to Brother Brad to ask for advice or help. He is one of the most generous people I know.

When people ask me what Brad is really like, I say, "He is as nice as you think he is. More kind than you can imagine. And a true disciple of Christ." When we meet people who know other people personally, we get a better sense of who those people really are.

Because of the First Vision and Joseph's testimony, we know who God the Father and the Savior are. But we should not solely bank on the spiritual experiences of the prophets, apostles, and general Church leaders. Through personal revelation, every child of God can come and see and come and know for themselves who God really is.

—Ganel-Lyn

> "We know who God is; we know who the Savior is, because we have Joseph, who went into a grove of trees as a boy, seeking forgiveness for his sins."
>
> M. Russell Ballard
>
> "Praise to the Man," Oct. 2023

Joseph Smith—History 1:29

For I had full confidence in obtaining a divine manifestation.

Answers Come

Not all prayers are the same. The words and intensity vary dramatically with the circumstances of life. Sometimes I whisper, giving heartfelt thanks for the blessings bestowed on me and those I love. In other settings, with tear-filled eyes and a broken heart, I cry out in desperation and despair, pleading for healing, intervention, or a miracle.

One thing I know for certain is that Heavenly Father cares deeply and loves us. He listens and answers every prayer according to His infinite wisdom. The scriptures teach us, "For your Father knoweth what things ye have need of, before ye ask him," and He "knoweth all things, for all things are present before [His] eyes" (Matthew 6:8; Doctrine and Covenants 38:2).

Sometimes worthy desires do not come to fruition the way we had hoped. Our job is to trust in the answers and guidance God provides. He sees the big picture and knows what lies ahead. When it's difficult to wait on the Lord, know He is answering your prayer in His way and timing. He hears you and is behind the scenes, working things out for your good.

—Dru

> "[Your prayers] are always answered at the time and in the way an omniscient and eternally compassionate parent should answer them."
>
> **Jeffrey R. Holland**
>
> "Waiting on the Lord," Oct. 2020

Joseph Smith—History 1:28–29

I frequently fell into foolish errors . . . and the foibles of human nature. . . . In consequence of these things, I often felt condemned.

The Foible Chain

For my eighth birthday, I chose to go to the Barnum & Bailey Circus. Of all the wonders there, I was most fascinated by the elephants. Each had a little chain around its right front ankle. On the way home, I asked my father why. He told me that when baby elephants are trained, they are tied to a pole with a large chain. As the animal fights to escape, it realizes it is trapped. As the elephant grows, the large chain is replaced with smaller and smaller ones. As long as the elephant has a chain on its leg, it remembers its earlier experience and believes it cannot get free—even if it is tied to nothing at all.

Like the elephant, each of us carries small chains of guilt that hold us down. Though they may only be made of the tiny foibles of humanity, sometimes we carry them as though they are much heavier and more debilitating than they need to be.

Like Joseph, when our foible chains become unwieldy, we need to turn to our Savior in prayer or go to His holy temple. More than once, I've felt the Lord lift that chain off my ankle or open my eyes to see how small it really was. Remember, it is Satan who wants you to feel trapped. Through Christ, we are made free.

—*Christine*

"This mighty change of heart brings us a feeling of freedom, trust, and peace."

Eduardo Gavarret

"A Mighty Change of Heart," Apr. 2022

Joseph Smith—History 1:33

He called me by name, and said unto me that . . . my name should be had for good and evil among all . . . people.

Your Name

I was named after my great-grandmother Ganel. My mom's middle name is Ganel. It hasn't always an easy name to bear. It has been mispronounced in more ways than I can count. A few years ago, I discovered that Ganel means garden of God. Knowing that changed how I felt about having a name that rarely is said correctly.

I know that God knows my name and will know how to pronounce it when I meet Him again someday.

Can you imagine what the young Joseph must have felt when he heard God call him by name? Then he met the angel Moroni, who told him some of what his mission would be and gave him instructions and specific directions about the coming forth of the Book of Mormon.

Not all of us will be called to serve in such significant stewardship, but we can all play a part in building the kingdom of God on earth. God knows our personal strengths and struggles. He knows our name. And He will help us as He helped the Prophet Joseph to do a great and marvelous work.

—*Ganel-Lyn*

"Each of you has a part to play in this great and marvelous work. The Savior will help you. He will lead you by the hand. He knows you by name."

Elaine S. Dalton

"He Knows You by Name," Apr. 2005

Joseph Smith—History 1:34
He also said that the fulness of the everlasting Gospel was contained in it, as delivered by the Savior to the ancient inhabitants.

Eighty-Five Days

I am the author of multiple books. Both my online and printed books are written for and measured by profit margins. Writing is my second language, although sometimes it can be a struggle to compose my thoughts and feelings on paper.

It's impressive that "Joseph Smith translated the Book of Mormon at the rate of about 10 pages per day, completing the task in about 85 days!" (Russell M. Nelson, "A Testimony," Oct. 1999). The success of the Book of Mormon isn't calculated by the volumes sold but by the number of souls touched. It was written anciently for our day and contains the fulness of the gospel.

The authors of the Book of Mormon never received awards or accolades. They were stewards of the stories of their time. Sharing their perspectives powerfully changes our perspectives today.

If you open the pages of this sacred record, you may be sanctified while studying. I am so grateful for all that the Prophet Joseph did to help give us the Book of Mormon.

—Ganel-Lyn

> "The Book of Mormon . . . was written anciently for our day. It reveals the endless Lordship of Jesus Christ . . . preserved for the benefit of us who live in this dispensation of the fulness of times."
>
> **Russell M. Nelson**
> "A Testimony of the Book of Mormon," Oct. 1999

Joseph Smith—History 1:36

After telling me these things, he commenced quoting the prophecies of the Old Testament.

Prophesying of Truth

When I read the Old Testament, especially the words of Isaiah, Zedekiah, Joel, and Malachi, I am impressed that many of the prophecies are about the latter days rather than the times in which these prophets lived. They were blessed to understand the truth, or the way things are, were, and will be.

These Old Testament prophets were inspired by the Lord to tell us what mankind has to look forward to in the days leading up to the Second Coming of our Savior. This vision is not restricted to people living in the years 800 BC, 500 BC, AD 1830, or even AD 2024. All mankind in every age needs to know how to prepare to participate in the millennial day.

Joseph Smith was instructed by the angel Moroni about what these prophets said. The prophecies had not changed, but the translation and re-translations over the centuries had left out some important words and concepts.

As I gain a testimony of the truth of these prophecies, I don't need to worry about if or when these events will happen. Instead, I only need to worry about my spiritual preparation and my understanding of these prophecies.

—Marianna

> "Later prophets, such as Jeremiah, Isaiah, and Malachi, left equally indelible testimonies throughout their ministries, prophesying of the coming Messiah and His infinite Atonement."
>
> Stephen B. Oveson
>
> "Appreciating the Counsel of Those Who Are Bowed with Years," Apr. 2005

Joseph Smith—History 1:38–39

And he shall plant in the hearts of the children the promises made to the fathers.

Bring Them Home

As a four-year-old, I went on a family trip to visit our relatives who lived in the hills and hollers of western Tennessee. Granddaddy had bought a shaggy, old pony and named her Fatty. And yes, she definitely lived up to her name! One day, all of the cousins were invited to come over and ride her. As we set out to round her up, climbing over several fences and passing through various gates along the way, I suddenly realized I had to go to the bathroom. I was told to run back to the house and return to the pasture when I was done. It sounded simple, but in the process, I became hopelessly lost.

I wandered for several miles down the dusty country roads. As I approached an old house, a bunch of yappy, fierce dogs came toward me. I began to cry and scream. An old man came out of the house and asked if I was lost. Thankfully, he knew Granddaddy and offered to drive me back to his home.

In the spirit world, billions of people are waiting for someone to find them and help them return to their heavenly home. The Lord knows and loves each one, and He will keep His promises to them through our efforts to seek them, find them, and perform saving ordinances on their behalf.

—Dru

> "That is a central focus of the plan of our Heavenly Father: uniting family for this life and for eternity."
>
> **Benjamin De Hoyos**
>
> "The Work of the Temple and Family History—One and the Same Work," Apr. 2023

Doctrine and Covenants 2:1–2

Elijah . . . shall plant in the hearts of the children the promises made to the fathers, and the hearts of the children will turn to their fathers.

Prophecy Fulfilled

Each Passover, covenant Jews set an extra place at their table for the prophet Elijah. Malachi prophesied Elijah would return and turn the hearts of the children to their fathers, awakening those promises made to the fathers lest the earth be smitten with a curse (see Malachi 4:5–6).

Moroni quoted this scripture to the young Joseph Smith when he appeared in Joseph's bedroom. Guess who came thirteen years later, on the day the first temple of this dispensation was dedicated?

Elijah!

He restored the sealing keys to Joseph Smith. When we are sealed to our families, our hearts turn to our ancestors. We feel the need to do their work and know that they are part of us, that we will be with them again.

One of the coolest parts of Elijah's return was that he came on April 3, 1836, which was Passover. Thousands of Jews around the world had Elijah's place open at their tables, ready for his return.

—Christine

> "With access to the sealing power, our hearts naturally turn to those who have gone before. The latter-day gathering into the covenant crosses through the veil."
>
> D. Todd Christofferson
> "The Sealing Power," Oct. 2023

Doctrine and Covenants 3:1–4

The works, and the designs, and the purposes of God cannot be frustrated, neither can they come to naught.

The Work of God Continues Forward

At church, a friend came to me in amazement and said, "Look at the temple where one of my family names was recently baptized. Kyiv, Ukraine!" I was so surprised that when I returned home I looked up the temple information. The Kyiv Ukrainian Temple was open, and I could make an appointment on Wednesday if I wanted to take a trip over there.

The temple was closed on February 24, 2022, because of the war with Russia but reopened on October 16, even though the war was still raging. A Church spokesperson said, "The Church of Jesus Christ of Latter-day Saints has carefully evaluated the current circumstances and decided to resume—on a limited basis—the sacred religious ceremonies in the temple" (Church Newsroom, Oct. 16, 2022).

The Lord's work cannot be frustrated! Neither wars, nor pandemics, nor human frailties, nor individual sin can stop His work and His glory from coming to pass. It will happen despite what men do. What a wonderful promise to remember!

—Marianna

> "I assure you that opposition to our cause testifies of its divinity. Would satanic powers combine against us if we were not posing a threat to such powers?"
>
> Carols E. Asay
>
> "The Sealing Power," Oct. 1981

Doctrine and Covenants 3:8

Yet you should have been faithful; and he would have extended his arm and supported you against all the fiery darts of the adversary.

Nerf Darts

During an EFY (now FSY) presentation, I was teaching the principle of trusting God no matter what is thrown at us. I decided to illustrate the faith of Samuel the Lamanite by bringing one of my son's many Nerf guns.

I told the youth that "Sam the man" stood on the wall while fiery darts whizzed by his face. It must have been distracting and discouraging to feel the fire of testimony on the inside but not able to convince the people to repent on the outside. No matter what was thrown at him, Sam was not deterred from his mission. God protected him as he stood on that wall.

I then loaded the Nerf gun and fired the spongy darts into the audience. (Don't worry—no one was hurt.) It is easy to feel afraid while the adversary fires darts at us. But, just like my demonstration showed, God will support us and protect us in times of trouble. The darts may appear nasty, but in reality, they are just made of foam.

—Ganel-Lyn

> "By the shield of our faith in Jesus Christ, we become peacemakers, quenching—meaning to calm, cool, or extinguish—all the fiery darts of the adversary."
>
> Neil L. Andersen
>
> "Following Jesus: Being a Peacemaker," Apr. 2022

Doctrine and Covenants 3:20
Rely upon the merits of Jesus Christ.

Enough?

As a brand-new mom, I felt overwhelmed by the weight of my inexperience and insecurities. Being the youngest in my own family, I felt utterly unprepared to care for the precious baby girl that had been entrusted to me. Day in and day out, when I was alone, her cries seemed never-ending. Yet, when my husband would cradle her in his arms after returning home from work, she found solace and calm. In those moments, doubt crept in. I remember thinking, "What's wrong with me? I'm a terrible mom. She deserves so much more than I can ever give."

Over time, I turned to the Lord, my heart tender with discouragement and frustration. As I sincerely sought His guidance through prayer, He patiently taught me that nurturing a family should not rest solely on my shoulders. Through Jesus Christ's merciful Atonement, I found strength to face the demands of motherhood. Christ's enabling power gave me the ability to carry my burdens and encouraged me along the path to becoming a more confident and capable mom.

—Dru

"We are not and never need be alone. We can press forward in our daily lives with heavenly help."
David A. Bednar
"Bear Up Their Burdens with Ease," Apr. 2014

Doctrine and Covenants 4:1–3

For behold, a marvelous work is about to come forth. . . . Therefore, if ye have desires to serve God ye are called to the work.

Desires to Serve God

The first time a boy broke my heart in college I decided to go on a mission. I wanted to escape, go someplace exotic, and have success. Serving the Lord was a side benefit.

In the MTC, I learned that section 4 goes perfectly to the tune of the hymn "We Are All Enlisted." I sang it often during the first months of my mission. The line that always pricked me was "If ye have desires to serve God, ye are called to the work." I struggled because although I loved my service, I believed my initial motivation wasn't well founded.

My companion and I were teaching a sweet woman who was dating a member of the ward. One night, she called in tears. We hurried to her home and found her devastated. He had dumped her, and she was wondering whether to continue in the faith.

My feelings were still raw from my own dating experience, and we cried, hugged, and prayed together. That night both our hearts started healing, and she felt the comforting peace of the Spirit for the first time. Soon after, she was baptized.

When I left the area, I knew the Lord was aware of me and had put me there for a reason. From that time forward my desire to serve Him increased. At times, the true desire comes along the way.

—Christine

"Of all the qualifications, a desire to serve may be the most important."

Russell M. Nelson

"Senior Missionaries and the Gospel," Oct. 2004
Quoted by Ronald A Rasband, "How Great Will Be Your Joy," Oct. 2023

Doctrine and Covenants 4:2

See that ye serve him with all your heart, might, mind and strength that ye may stand blameless before God at the last day.

Unto the Least of These

Years ago, two elderly twin sisters lived in our ward. One reminded me so much of my mom, who lives far away, that I felt an instant connection. The other sister was born with severe physical challenges, including the inability to walk or speak.

I decided to visit these women and see if I could help. As time went on, we became close friends. My children and I looked forward to our visits. We'd spend hours chatting, laughing, and listening to stories from their childhood. Though they lived with little, we never left their home empty-handed. They insisted we leave with mini candy bars and treats for my kids. Although our initial intention was to serve them, the joy and warmth they brought into our lives were immeasurable. They became like family to us, and we will always cherish the precious times we had together.

The impact of compassion, kindness, and service is immeasurable. Blessings come to both the giver and receiver. Hearts are touched, friendships are forged, and lives are changed for the better as we do our best to love and serve God's children.

—Dru

"We have a life of devoted discipleship to give in demonstrating our love of the Lord."

Jeffrey R. Holland

"The First Great Commandment," Oct. 2012

Doctrine and Covenants 4:5

And faith, hope, charity and love, with an eye single to the glory of God, qualify him for the work.

Bifocals

After a certain age, glasses often become necessary. I remember reading my scriptures after putting on my first pair of glasses. It was amazing. I had no idea how bad my vision had become until things were brought into better focus.

Having an eye single to serving and loving God becomes a lens for life. I've learned that this lens is like bifocals. Bifocals have two levels. When I wear them, I can read small print more easily and see the speaker at the pulpit at church more clearly. They clarify both the up-close and distant views. We are both called and qualified to do the work when we keep the focus on God. The work may be acting on an impression to bring flowers to a neighbor, calling a friend to say hello, or taking dinner to a new mom. We aren't in this work alone. Because of God, we are qualified, and we begin to see everything as it really is. It is more than a formal Church calling or a mission badge that builds Zion. It is the simple everyday acts of faith, hope, and charity that bring about the greatest results.

—Ganel-Lyn

"Only when things begin to come into focus 'with an eye single' do we see 'things as they really are!'"

Neal A. Maxwell

"Settle This in Your Hearts," Oct. 1992

Doctrine and Covenants 4:7

Ask and ye shall receive; knock, and it shall be opened unto you, Amen.

Ask the Right Questions

Recently, I had to decide between doing two good things. I was in turmoil because they were both worthy activities, but I knew I only had enough time to do one of them. I kept asking the Lord, and I kept getting no for an answer. One night, as I was praying about this problem, the thought came to my mind, "You are asking the wrong question. You should be asking if neither is right because of all that you are already doing." I changed my question, and I immediately knew the answer. The Lord wanted me to do other things.

In February 1829, Joseph Smith Sr. visited Joseph and Emma in Harmony, Pennsylvania, because they had been going through such a difficult time with the death of their first son. During his visit, the Lord gave Joseph's father this revelation.

Often, we read section 4 as only relating to missionary work. But this section includes a list of qualities that we all need to acquire to be a part of the Lord's work. The final verse of the section is the key to finding out what we need to work on in this lineup of Christlike attributes. Pray and ask the question, What does Thou want me to work on? Then listen to the answer. Ask and ye shall receive.

–Marianna

> "Every Latter-day Saint may merit personal revelation. The invitation to ask, seek, and knock for divine direction exists because God Lives and Jesus is the Living Christ."
>
> **Russell M. Nelson**
> "Ask, Seek, Knock," Oct. 2009

Doctrine and Covenants 6:7

Seek not for riches but for wisdom, . . . and then shall you be made rich. Behold, he that hath eternal life is rich.

Zimbabwe

My son was called to serve as a full-time missionary in the beautiful African country of Zimbabwe. One of the first things he realized was that the people often go without some of the temporal comforts of life. Even though food and money are scarce, happiness and faith are found in abundance. They are the happiest of people. Believing in God is the norm.

As soon as Cameron landed in America, he knew he wasn't in Africa anymore. People had their heads down and were focused on their phones instead of looking up and smiling at passersby. How could a country that had so little, offer so much? I believe it is because the humble Zimbabweans discovered the truth. Riches are fleeting, but faith in God is the essence of eternal happiness.

—Ganel-Lyn

> "Each of us has the responsibility to seek that goodly pearl, the kingdom of heaven, which is, according to the Savior's parable, the pearl of great price."
>
> Delbert L. Stapley
>
> "The Path to Eternal Glory," Apr. 1973

Doctrine and Covenants 6:22–23

Cast your mind upon the night you cried unto me in your heart. . . . Did I not speak peace to your mind? What greater witness can you have than from God?

Anchoring Your Testimony

One windy day, we went camping at Lake Henry. I was curious how the dock was built to be safe despite the choppy water. A common method uses anchors, some as heavy as six hundred pounds. Then strong cables are cast from the dock to the anchor to allow for some movement while giving the platform stability. Often when docks fail, it isn't the anchors that give but the cables connected to them.

When a friend turned from the gospel, I asked about her spiritual anchors. She said she knew the Book of Mormon was true and loved the temple, but she couldn't be associated with a church she disagreed with. Her cables were weak. Like Oliver Cowdery, she just couldn't "cast her mind" that far.

Part of the purpose of daily scripture study and prayer is casting our minds to our spiritual anchors. As we ponder and pray, we strengthen the cables that connect us to our Father and increase our sensitivity to the Spirit's influence. Let's keep our anchors sure and our cables strongly connected to the true anchor, Jesus Christ.

—Christine

"We realize that as evil increases in the world, our spiritual survival, and the spiritual survival of those we love, will require that we more fully nurture, fortify, and strengthen the roots of our faith in Jesus Christ."

Neil L. Andersen
"Drawing Closer to the Savior," Oct. 2022

Doctrine and Covenants 6:33, 36

Fear not to do good, my sons, for whatsoever ye sow, that shall ye also reap; . . . Look unto me in every thought; doubt not, fear not.

Reap Good

We never know when someone is watching us. We may be sowing good (or evil) and affecting others' lives without realizing it.

I was in Costco with my preschool daughters, Clara and Deborah. It was holiday time, so all twelve of my children were coming home and I needed lots of food. I had a hand truck full of goodies when Deborah decided she was done. She started screaming, and there was nothing I could do to stop her. I hugged, I coaxed, I even offered her a part of a banana, but I handled the situation with love and kept my cool.

The next fast Sunday, a man in our ward stood to bear his testimony. He said that he was watching me at Costco and was so impressed with the way I had lovingly handled a screaming child that it caused him to be more patient with his children.

I was amazed! I had no idea that I was being watched. I was so thankful that I had handled that situation in a patient, loving way (because that was not always the case).

If we look to the Lord in every thought, then the actions we sow will touch the lives of those around us for good.

—Marianna

> "If we are steadfast and immovable in doing good, our customs will be in accordance with the principles of the gospel."
>
> Refael E. Pino
>
> "Let Doing Good Be Our New Normal," Oct. 2022

Doctrine and Covenants 8:2

Yea, behold, I will tell you in you mind and in your heart, by the Holy Ghost, which shall come upon you and . . . dwell in your heart.

A New Language

While sitting on a beach in Hawaii, I overheard a family speaking a language I didn't recognize. Based on their gestures, I could tell that they were discussing the beautiful blue water, the kids playing in the sand, and the warmth of the sun. I thought they were speaking Italian or Portuguese but wasn't sure. So, I boldly said hello and asked where they were from.

They said they now lived in the United States, but they were immigrants from Ukraine and spoke Ukranian. I had never heard of Ukrainian.

I love learning about new people and places, religions, and races. But it takes time and patience to really understand who someone is and communicate effectively.

The way the Spirit speaks to you is a type of language. The Holy Ghost may speak more to you in dreams or images. Or you might hear God in music and feelings. My son shared with me that it wasn't until his mission that he realized that the Spirit spoke to him with joy, not with tears. Learn how the Spirit speaks to you. Be patient, like you would be when learning to speak Ukrainian or any other language. The way the Spirit speaks to you is a new language.

—Ganel-Lyn

> "The Spirit speaks to different people in different ways, and He may speak to the same person in different ways at different times."
>
> David P. Homer
>
> "Hearing His Voice," Apr. 2019

Doctrine and Covenants 9:6

Do not murmur, my son, for it is wisdom in me that I have dealt with you after this manner.

Trusting God's Wisdom

For a short time, I was called as the ward organist. I never made it through a hymn without hitting at least one sour note, despite practicing for hours. The funny thing was, the woman who led the music played the organ beautifully, but our bishop said he felt I should play. I said yes, but I knew I was so much better at leading the music and may have murmured a little—or a lot-tle!

I imagine my feelings were much like Oliver Cowdery when he was stuck simply transcribing rather than doing the fun work of translating. Oliver was a teacher and later a lawyer. He was brilliant and certain he could do a better job translating than the poorly educated young prophet, Joseph Smith.

At last, the Lord gave him a chance to try, and Oliver could not do it. He wasn't meant to. We don't know the reason, only that it was God's wisdom. Then Oliver was told, "Stand fast in the work wherewith I have called you . . . and you shall be lifted up at the last day" (Doctrine and Covenants 9:14).

As a result of my stint on the organ, I am not a better organist, but I have lost any reserve of doing whatever I'm called to do. I'll even volunteer, if I feel it's the Lord's will. I may not be great, but now I'm always willing.

—Christine

> "Our willingness is directly proportionate to the amount of time we commit to be in holy places."
>
> Kevin W. Pearson
>
> "Are You Still Willing," Oct. 2022

Doctrine and Covenants 9:7

Behold, you have not understood; you have supposed that I would give it unto you, when you took no thought save it was to ask me.

So Many Questions

When kids turn two or three years old, the most common word in their vocabulary tends to be *why*. Parents around the world can attest to the constant questions coming from their children.

Why is the moon in the sky? Why do I have to eat my peas? Why do I have to go to bed or brush my teeth? The questions are how children learn about the world around them and discover their place in it.

At a certain point, it can be easy to stop asking questions. Adults may mistakenly assume that they know everything. But the pattern of learning hasn't changed much from the age of two. God loves our questions. The Restoration was opened because a fourteen-year-old boy went to a grove of trees and asked a question.

What question do you need to ask today? Study it out in your mind and go to God in prayer. He is ready and willing to give you access to His power and grace.

—Ganel-Lyn

"Understanding what we must do to access God's power in our lives is not easy, but I have found it is doable by studying it out in out minds and praying for the Holy Ghost to enlighten us."

Kelly R. Johnson
"Enduring Power," Oct. 2020

Doctrine and Covenants 9:8

But, behold, I say unto you, that you must study it out in your mind; then you must ask me if it be right.

At the Crossroads

I stood at a crossroads in my career, torn between a tempting job offer promising financial gain and another job offer aligned with my values. Seeking guidance, I turned to prayer, pouring out my concerns about the impact on my family and future. Through quiet reflection, I found clarity, feeling a renewed commitment to prioritize principles over immediate gains.

Trusting in the answers I received, I turned down the lucrative offer and chose a path aligned with my convictions. This decision brought me peace and unexpected blessings, reinforcing my belief that prayers are answered and guidance is given when we seek help from our Heavenly Father.

When faced with tough decisions such as choosing between a tempting job offer or sticking to our values, it helps if we take time to think about the impact of each option and turn to prayer for guidance. By talking to our Heavenly Father about our worries and what matters most to us, we will find the clarity we're looking for.

—Dru

> "Our prayers need to be 'All I want is what you want. Thy will be done.'"
> Henry B. Eyring
> "Our Constant Companion," Oct. 2023

Doctrine and Covenants 10:4

Do not run faster or labor more than you have strength . . . but be diligent unto the end.

The Race

Two summers ago, my daughter-in-law asked me to sign up for a moonlight half-marathon—a 13.1–mile race that begins in the middle of a canyon and twists its way through the foothills until it ends at a city park. This particular race had a fun little twist. Instead of crowning the fastest runner, the grand prize went to whoever finished closest to midnight, with no timing devices allowed and a flexible start time.

This challenge was way out of my comfort zone. Finding time and motivation to exercise regularly wasn't easy in my busy life. My husband still jokes that my preparation consisted of a last-minute stroll the length of a football field, which isn't too far from the truth. During the race, we maintained a steady pace, resisting the urge to rush as people passed by. I knew pushing too hard would lead to exhaustion and I would be tempted to quit. But guess what? We made it, just minutes before midnight!

This experience taught me a valuable lesson: if I do my best, persevere, and stay on course, I will be victorious in the end.

—Dru

"Slow down a little, proceed at the optimum speed for our circumstances, focus on the significant, lift up your eyes, and truly see the things that matter most."

Dieter F. Uchtdorf

"Of Things That Matter Most," Oct. 2010

Doctrine and Covenants 10:5

Pray always, that you may come off conqueror; yea, that you may conquer Satan.

Let's Raise Our Ebenezer

One of my favorite hymns is "Come Thou Fount of Every Blessing." The second verse reads, "Here I raise my Ebenezer / Here by Thy great help I've come" (Wyeth, 1813).

Ebenezer is mentioned in 1 Samuel 5:1 and 7:12. The people of Israel had lost the ark of the covenant in a battle with the Philistines. Samuel encouraged the people to turn to the Lord in their time of need: "Prepare your hearts unto the Lord and serve him only" (1 Samuel 7:3). As Israel changed their hearts and served only the Lord, the ark was returned to its sacred place, and the Philistines were vanquished because of a thunderstorm sent by God.

In remembrance of all the Lord had done for them, Samuel put a stone he called "Eben-ezer," which in Hebrew means "stone of help," in a prominent place to remind the people of the Lord's power, grace, and miracles.

When we pray in faith and gratitude, we are raising our Ebenezer and acknowledging the Lord as our stone of help. Praying with added frequency and intensity will remind us of His miracles in our lives and act as a shield against Satan and his servants.

—*Marianna*

"As we pray in faith, we become a vital part in the Lord's work as He prepares the world for His Second Coming."

Henry B. Eyring

"Prayers of Faith," Apr. 2020

Doctrine and Covenants 10:57

Behold, I am Jesus Christ, the Son of God. I came unto mine own, and mine own received me not.

Junior High and Jesus

Right before I started junior high, our family moved to another city. Middle school is difficult enough without being a new student. I remember walking up to a group of teens, trying to figure out how to start a conversation and make friends. I said something awkward involving the gum that was being passed around. As time passed, I found connections with some of my classmates. But even today, forty years later, I can still recall feeling rejection and loneliness.

There is something about the junior high brain that causes us to feel less than, forgotten, or left out, even years later as adults. From the eighty-year-old woman walking into a new Relief Society or the middle-aged woman starting a new job, feelings of rejection from middle school can resurface.

We all, at times, may feel like Jesus did. Our offerings aren't accepted, and our friends may even betray us. When you find yourself cast out, tossed aside, or dismissed, take those feelings to God. Jesus understands. He, too, has come to His own and wasn't received. Ask for grace and His love. He who was rejected will never reject us.

—Ganel-Lyn

> "He was mocked and jeered. He suffered every indignity at the hands of His own people. . . . The Lord 'suffered the pain of all men, that all . . . might repent and come unto him.'"
>
> **Russell M. Nelson**
> "The Atonement," Oct. 1996

Doctrine and Covenants 10:66–67

Whoever repenteth and cometh unto me, the same is my church. Whosoever declareth more or less than this, the same is not of me.

More or Less than This

When I lived in Texas, I visited a house down the street that was for sale. I had no intention of moving but felt I should go. The home had the same pastel curtains that I'd seen in many older Church members' houses. The owner wore her hair in a poof, had an accent that sounded like she was whispering to Primary children, and even had glass grapes on her coffee table, which was popular among members of the Church at the time.

I was shocked. All these clues made me think she was a member of the Church, but I'd never seen her at any meetings. At last, I asked her and found out that she had grown up in Utah but hadn't considered attending since she'd gotten married years earlier.

Today, the cultural clues of Church membership are far more diverse, but they aren't the gospel of Christ. Two years before the Church was organized, Christ revealed that members of His Church only had to repent and come to Him by making and keeping covenants. As we come to Him, He will inspire us to share His word and build His kingdom through service in different areas. He may even prompt you to visit a woman down the street and reawaken memories of the past so you can feel the Spirit together.

—Christine

> "May we enjoy more the spiritual kinship that exists between us and value the different attributes and varied gifts we all have."
>
> Ulisses Soares
>
> "Brothers and Sisters in Christ," Oct. 2023

Doctrine and Covenants 11:3

Behold, the field is white already to harvest; therefore, whoso desireth to reap let him thrust.

Trying

When my children were younger, they made me homemade gifts and breakfast in bed for Mother's Day. Often the breakfast had interesting flavors and tastes, such as a clove and hot dog omelet. The gifts were mostly made from construction paper, glue, and crayons. None of them would ever be considered a museum piece, but it didn't matter how the world would judge these creations. I loved them!

My children gave their best efforts and expressed their good desires to serve me and celebrate me. Now, my adult children will send me flowers and perfume—gifts that they couldn't afford before. The world would think that I would cherish these expensive gifts more than those homemade gifts. But I miss construction paper cards.

When the Lord asks us to accomplish something, our first efforts may look primitive and inept. But the Lord only cares that we try and that our desires are to serve Him. And He loves us for our efforts.

—*Marianna*

> "He looked at me and said, 'Elder Schmeil, you are called for what you can become.' I walked away from that experience pondering about what the Lord wants me to become."
>
> Ciro Schmeil
>
> "Faith to Act and Become," Oct. 2021

Doctrine and Covenants 11:9

Say nothing but repentance unto this generation. Keep my commandments, and assist to bring forth my work . . . and you shall be blessed.

The Personal from the General

Sometimes general conference talks bring us comfort. Other messages and messengers may trigger us. President Harold B. Lee said that the gospel is to comfort the afflicted and to afflict the comfortable (see "The Message," *New Era*, January 1971). Apostles, prophets, and general leaders are called to preach repentance. As a member of the Godhead, the Spirit is called to correct as well as comfort us. So don't be surprised when a trigger becomes a teacher.

When you hear a general message from the pulpit and question the policy or principle behind it, take it to God. Through revelation, you can clarify the personal from the general teaching.

A friend shared how she wrestled with a talk given at general conference. After having a really hard mom week, she heard the speaker say that parents need to do better. Instead of becoming overwhelmed and discouraged, she prayed to know what God wanted her to take from the talk. Journaling the promptings, she found what worked best for her family. It was a personal message from the general. Learn line upon line, and step by step you will become sanctified.

—Ganel-Lyn

> "If we teach by the Spirit and you listen by the Spirit, some one of us will touch on your circumstance, sending a personal prophetic epistle just to you."
>
> Jeffrey R. Holland
>
> "An Ensign to the Nations," Apr. 2011

Doctrine and Covenants 11:21–22

Seek not to declare my word, but first seek to obtain my word, and then shall your tongue be loosed.

Feast on the Words of Christ

One of my greatest joys is teaching institute at Brigham Young University to a large all-freshman class of eager young adults, many of whom are preparing to serve missions or have recently returned home. Each week we come together to learn more about our Savior, Jesus Christ. We strive to increase our faith and deepen our love and appreciation for the unparalleled gift of His Atonement. More than anything else, I pray that the students walk away from each class filled with the Spirit and a greater desire to come unto Christ and to serve Him.

I am not a professor of religion nor a teacher by trade. When I was first called as an instructor, I was overwhelmed and felt completely inadequate. Knowing my fears and doubts, I received comfort and direction from my Heavenly Father as I was set apart. I was promised that if I would consecrate my time to study and prayer, my understanding and ability to teach would expand. I was reassured that I was on the Lord's errand, and with His help, I could fulfill my assignment.

I have learned for myself that this is true when we faithfully and consistently study the words of Christ we will be given in the very hour the words that we should say.

—Dru

> "Become an engaged learner. Immerse yourself in the scriptures to understand better Christ's mission and ministry."
>
> **Russell M. Nelson**
>
> "Christ Is Risen; Faith in Him Will Move Mountains," Apr. 2021

Doctrine and Covenants 12:2

Behold, I am God; give heed to my word, which is quick and powerful, sharper than a two-edged sword.

Sharper than a Two-Edged Sword

My oldest son put a forge in his garage and began making knives. For his wife's birthday, he made a very large and sharp kitchen knife. One day while dicing onions, she inadvertently sliced off the tip of her pinky. The blade was so sharp she didn't feel it at first, but the cut took months to heal.

Soon after Joseph Smith began translating the Book of Mormon, he received three revelations in sections 11, 12, and 14, given to his brother Hyrum, Joseph B. Knight, and David Whitmer. Each revelation proclaims a marvelous work is about to come forth and warns that God's word is quick, powerful, and sharper than a two-edged sword. An issue with two-edged swords is that while they have more cutting power, they have a greater opportunity of harming the person wielding it if they aren't careful.

My daughter-in-law loves her kitchen knife and uses it often, but she learned to be more careful. When we receive, read, or share the word of the Lord, we need to realize its power and take care to treat His words with the respect they deserve or that gift could lead to our detriment.

—Christine

> "Though some may think that mortality is a contest between God and the adversary, a word from the Savior 'and Satan is silenced and banished. . . . It is our strength that is being tested—not God's.'"
>
> Jorg Klebingat
>
> "Valiant Discipleship in the Latter Days," Apr. 2022

Doctrine and Covenants 12:7

Behold, I speak unto you, and also to all those who have desires to bring forth and establish this work.

Educating Our Desires

I often ask my students, "What is the dream? Where do you see yourself in ten or twenty years?" I hear many different answers from being a multi-millionaire by age thirty to having no desires or dreams at all.

We should have desires and dreams that are united with our eternal goals. President Joseph F. Smith taught that the "education . . . of our desires is one of far-reaching importance to our happiness in life" (*Gospel Doctrine*, 297).

Section 12 was given to Joseph Knight Sr., who believed in Joseph Smith as a Prophet of God from the beginning. Father Knight, as he was affectionately called, helped Joseph with the work of translation, providing funds and support. He led the Colesville, New York, branch; he moved with the Saints to Missouri, where his faithful wife, Polly, died; he left Nauvoo with the Saints and died in Iowa at Winter Quarters.

For me, Father Knight's life epitomizes a person who has educated his desires toward righteousness. His life was not successful temporally but spiritually. Yet in Nauvoo, the Prophet Joseph Smith said of Father Knight: "Behold he is a righteous man. . . . It shall be said of him . . . that this man was a faithful man in Israel; therefore his name shall never be forgotten" (HC 5:124–25).

—Marianna

> "In order to have righteous desires, we have to control our thoughts and achieve appropriate feelings."
>
> Dallin H. Oaks
>
> "The Desires of Our Hearts," BYU Speeches, Oct. 8, 1995

Doctrine and Covenants 12:8

And no one can assist in this work except he shall be humble and full of love, having faith, hope, and charity, being temperate in all things.

Garbage Cans

I live in a really windy city. Lehi, Utah is at the mouth of American Fork Canyon, and the wind is intense. We have learned to not put our garbage cans out too early on garbage day. If it starts getting too blustery, a can might topple over and fill the streets with litter and debris. One stormy day, not only was the waste swirling on the streets, but the cans were flying from house to house.

I looked out to see our neighbor trying to rescue and return the right can to the right address. I love living in my corner of Lehi. I have learned a lot about caring for others within our circle of influence by watching my neighbors.

Sometimes it is the little things we do to lift one another that are the best way to follow Jesus. From shoveling a driveway to bringing back a garbage can that blew away, the little things done with love make all the difference—especially when the turbulence of the telestial world continues to torment us.

—Ganel-Lyn

> "Let us humbly put ourselves in a position where Jesus can lift us, lead us, and make the most of our abilities."
>
> Adrián Ochoa
> "Is the Plan Working?," Apr. 2022

Joseph Smith—History 1:68

We . . . went into the woods to pray and inquire of the Lord respecting baptism. . . . A messenger from heaven descended in a cloud of light.

Praying for Baptism

Missionaries pray to find people who are ready to hear the message of the Restoration and be baptized. They become angels of light to people seeking truth, just as John the Baptist was for Oliver and Joseph.

In Brazil, two missionaries were walking down the street when a man called out to them. He was drunk, smoking, and crying. Feeling lost, he asked the missionaries to come back and teach him the next day. When the missionaries returned, they did not think he would even remember them from the day before. To their surprise, the man who answered the door was sober and well groomed, and he kindly invited them into his home.

The missionaries became Edson's angels of light, sharing with him the message of the Restoration. They taught him about faith in Jesus Christ, repentance, baptism, receiving the Holy Ghost, and enduring to the end. With every lesson, Edson looked brighter and cleaner than when the missionaries had first found him as a crying drunk. He gave up drinking and smoking. He was baptized, along with his seventy-five-year-old mother, and he looked forward to receiving the priesthood and going to the temple to receive additional covenants.

—Marianna

> "The Savior invites all to follow Him into the waters of baptism and, in time, to make additional covenants with God in the temple."
>
> Russell M. Nelson
>
> "Come, Follow Me," Apr. 2019

Joseph Smith—History 1:69
I confer the Priesthood of Aaron, which holds the keys of the ministering of angels.

Angels in Our Basement

We host a monthly Preach My Gospel (PMG) group in our home. Teens, college kids, and returned missionaries from all over the valley come and discuss the gospel. We openly discuss subjects like anxiety, addiction, and the Atonement of Christ once a month in our basement. It is amazing to watch these kids sing hymns and share scriptures with one another. They are open and vulnerable. Their honesty invites the Spirit to be present.

Our children started this group ten years ago. It isn't our calling, but it is a sacred privilege. Every time we gather, I feel like I am in the presence of angels.

Many missionaries have gone out in the world from our PMG group. They have become powerful global witnesses and ministers of Christ. Some of them have even started their own PMG groups.

If you want angels in your basement, consider inviting other believers to come teach each other. Have honest conversations, because that is where faith is built.

—Ganel-Lyn

> "In much the same way that angels are authorized messengers sent by God to declare His word and thereby build faith, we who hold the Aaronic Priesthood have been ordained to 'teach, and invite all to come unto Christ.'"
>
> Douglas D. Holmes
>
> "What Every Aaronic Priesthood Holder Needs to Understand," Apr. 2018

Joseph Smith—History 1:69

I confer the Priesthood of Aaron, which holds the keys . . . of the gospel of repentance, and of baptism by immersion for the remission of sins.

Worth the Wait

During the first ten years of our marriage, my husband and I were blessed with five children: four beautiful girls and a strong, handsome boy. Life with our family was awesome, except for one thing—Zack, our only son, longed for a little brother.

After nearly a decade of waiting, Dallin finally arrived! Zack could not have been happier. Despite their age difference, the two boys quickly became inseparable and the best of friends. Dallin became Zack's shadow and tried his best to be just like him.

When Dallin turned eight, he expressed a desire to be baptized and specifically asked Zack to perform the ordinance. As a worthy Aaronic Priesthood holder, Zack gladly accepted the responsibility. I will never forget the look on their faces as the two of them went down into the waters of baptism together to take part in this sacred ordinance. As a mom, my heart was filled with gratitude for the precious gift of my two boys, the love they shared, and their desire to follow the Lord.

—Dru

"Sins are cleansed by the power of Jesus Christ through His atoning sacrifice as we make and keep the baptismal covenant."

Dale G. Renlund

"Jesus Christ Is the Treasure," Oct. 2023

Joseph Smith—History 1:71
While the world was racked and distracted . . . our eyes beheld, our ears heard, as in the 'blaze of day'. . . . We listened, we gazed, we admired!

Eight Exclamation Points!

Oliver Cowdery met Joseph Smith on April 5, 1829, and began transcribing for him two days later. The following spring, only a few weeks before they finished that divine work, the question of baptism emerged. From Oliver, we know the subject arose "after writing the account given of the Savior's ministry" (JS–H 1). When Christ came to the Nephites, one of His first acts was to institute the ordinance of baptism.

Joseph Smith's canonized account accurately describes the events of that day, but in the footnotes, the words of Oliver Cowdery describe his feelings of witnessing John the Baptist's appearance in answer to their prayer and conferring the priesthood so they could enter at the gate that had long since been closed. Oliver's excitement is palpable, as he includes eight exclamation points in one paragraph!

Today, it is easy to become casual about the gospel of Jesus Christ being restored. As we see prophecies being fulfilled and watch this great work rolling forward throughout our families and friends, even to the whole earth, our hearts should also fill with joy, exceeding eight exclamation points!

—*Christine*

"We all shouted for joy in our premortal life when we heard God's plan of happiness, and we continue to shout for joy here as we live according to His plan."

Kevin R. Duncan

"A Voice of Gladness!" Apr. 2023

Joseph Smith—History 1:73–74

Immediately on our coming up out of the water after we had been baptized, we experienced great and glorious blessings from our Heavenly Father.

Great and Glorious Blessings After Baptism

My husband, Steve, and I met a couple learning about the gospel. Although they weren't married, they were in love and wanted a family. Ever since they had started living with each other, they wanted children, but this blessing hadn't happened. Because of their faith in the restored gospel of Jesus Christ, they were married and baptized on the same day.

A few months later, this faithful sister became pregnant. She and her husband were so excited and looked forward to sealing their family in the temple, which they had never thought possible before joining the Church. In tears, she told me, "Becoming a member of the Church was the most important thing that has happened to my family."

Oliver Cowdery and Joseph Smith also received great and glorious blessings after their baptisms. Their minds were enlightened like never before. They said, "We began to have the scriptures laid open to our understandings, and the true meaning and intention of their more mysterious passages revealed unto us in a manner which we never could attain to previously" (Joseph Smith–History 1:74). As baptized members, we, too, should seek for great and glorious blessings for our families and ourselves.

—Marianna

> "Keeping covenants made in baptismal fonts and in temples also provides us with strength to withstand mortality's trials and heartaches."
>
> Dale G. Renlund
>
> "Accessing God's Power through Covenants," Apr. 2023

Doctrine and Covenants 14:7

And, if you keep my commandments and endure to the end you shall have eternal life, which gift is the greatest of all the gifts of God.

Enduring to the End

When you hear "enduring to the end," do you feel excited and hopeful? Or do you feel discouraged and overwhelmed? If I am honest, I used to feel less hope and more hopeless. But as I have aged, I have begun to understand that God doesn't want me to just survive; He wants me to thrive. God wants you to find joy in the journey.

What about expanding what enduring means—to persist, carry on, prevail, live, remain, and experience? That feels more exciting and hopeful. Enduring doesn't have to be white-knuckling it. Yes, we will experience hard times, but God's promises are sure. If we keep showing up and let God prevail in our lives, we will inherit eternal life.

We aren't asked to endure alone. With Christ, all things are possible. So, the next time you grit your teeth as you find yourself clinging to the iron rod, remember those who made it to the tree did so because they consistently persisted, pressing forward in faith. That feels a lot more exciting.

—Ganel-Lyn

> "Because Heavenly Father loves us, He wants us to have the greatest gift He can give the gift of eternal life.'"
>
> Weatherford T. Clayton
>
> "Our Father's Glorious Plan," Apr. 2017

Doctrine and Covenants 14:8

If you shall ask the Father in my name, in faith believing, you shall receive the Holy Ghost . . . that you may stand as a witness of the things which you shall both hear and see.

Tender Mercies

A few weeks ago, my best friend shared with me a terrible secret. She had cancer. My heart stopped and my mind raced as I tried to grasp the horrific news. What should I say to bring her comfort? How could I help her through this difficult trial? If she passed away, how could heaven possibly need her more than we did here on earth?

We talked about the upcoming week and the diagnostic tests that would determine the location and extent of the cancer. She was calm and reassured me that if the Lord needed her elsewhere, she was ready to go.

A few days before testing, she was given a priesthood blessing. She was promised a full, quick recovery if she had faith to be healed and followed the counsel of her doctors. With renewed hope, we were overcome with gratitude when she shared the results of her tests. She explained that a miracle had happened. The potentially deadly cancer had been contained and she would only need routine surgery to completely cure her. No chemo or other treatments would be required.

I am a witness that God deeply cares about each of His children. He knows our needs and stands ready to bless us with infinite wisdom and grace. For reasons known only to Him, not all prayers are answered in the way we hope. But I testify that each prayer is heard and answered by a compassionate, loving Heavenly Father, according to His will. Someday, we will better understand why things happen the way they do. For now, I choose to trust Him.

—Dru

> "The Lord will bless you with miracles *if* you believe in Him, 'doubting nothing.'"
>
> **Russell M. Nelson**
>
> "The Power of Spiritual Momentum," Apr. 2022

Doctrine and Covenants 14:11
Thou art David, and thou art called to assist; which thing if ye do, and are faithful, ye shall be blessed both spiritually and temporally.

Called to Assist

Most of us have heard the story of the Little Red Hen, but I have a suspicion that the real story went differently. Once upon a time, there was a Little Red Hen who found some wheat. "Who will help me harvest this wheat?" she asked. Pig gladly agreed and tried to break the stalk with her teeth, but the Little Red Hen shouted, "You're doing it wrong!" She shooed away Pig and pulled out a sickle. "I'll do it myself."

Then the Little Red Hen said, "Who will help me take the wheat to the mill?" Cat gladly agreed and began carrying the grain up the street, but the Little Red Hen said, "The mill I like is the other way. I'll do it myself!" By the time she got to baking the bread, the Little Red Hen had alienated so many of her friends that no one wanted to help her. Which was fine with her. "I'll do it myself!" she said, and she did.

Being called to assist can be a very difficult task, especially if you are trying to help a metaphorical Little Red Hen. The key is to ask how to help and be meek enough to do what the person you are serving really wants you to do. It's a Christlike skill that takes a humble heart and true charity, but one that will soften and enlarge both the one assisting and the heart of the Little Red Hen herself.

—Christine

> "Compassion is an attribute of Christ. It is born of love for others and knows no bounds."
>
> Ian S. Arden
>
> "Love Thy Neighbor," Oct. 2023

Doctrine and Covenants 15:4

For many times you have desired of me to know that which would be of the most worth unto you.

Many Times

Section 15 is "intimately and impressively personal" (section heading). The Lord tells of what was known only to God and John Whitmer, who later became one of the Eight Witnesses to the Book of Mormon. I love that so much of the Doctrine and Covenants is personal revelation—messages specifically for individuals of the Restoration.

Have you ever prayed repeatedly for something without receiving an answer? When my kids were little, if they really wanted something, they asked and asked and asked, trying to wear me down. I will admit that sometimes it worked and I would change my mind. But ultimately their constant asking gave us a chance to talk more. I always tried to say yes if their requests were good for them, but sometimes I had to explain why my answer was no. Imperfect parents want to give good gifts to their babies. Imagine what a perfect parent, like God, wants to do for His children.

Praying many times isn't about changing the mind of God. It's about bringing our will in line with His. Remember the next time you find yourself praying many times that God wants to talk to you.

—Ganel-Lyn

"Not all of our prayers will be answered as we might wish. Occasionally the answer will be no. We should not be surprised. Loving mortal parents do not say yes to every request of their children."

Russell M. Nelson

"Sweet Power of Prayer," Apr. 2023

Doctrine and Covenants 16:3

And I will tell you that which no man knoweth save me and thee alone.

Best Friends

Have you ever had that one person in your life, that rock you could confide in, a faithful friend who could be trusted to know and safeguard your deepest thoughts and secrets? Someone who understood you, who shared your joys and sorrows, and was always there, knowing what you needed without saying a word? My sweet sister, Leigh, is that person for me. She has always been the one I can trust with the feelings of my heart, who cheers me on as I chase my dreams or try something new, and who laughs with me when life presents crazy surprises.

Jesus is our ultimate confidant and friend. He is the one who knows the things no one else does, who understands our struggles and heartbreaks. He cheers us on and encourages us as we pursue the deepest desires of our hearts. He is there, any hour of the day or night, to comfort us even in our darkest moments.

He knows the demons we are battling, the burdens we carry, and the shame we feel from past mistakes. Just like that trusted friend, He is always by our side, ready to offer relief and His unwavering love and support. Trust Him. He is there for you.

—*Dru*

> "Jesus is my friend. None other has given me so much. He gave His life for me. He opened the way to eternal life. Only a God could do this. I hope that I am deemed worthy of being a friend to Him."
>
> Gordon B. Hinckley
>
> "My Testimony," Apr. 2000

Doctrine and Covenants 16:6

The thing which will be of the most worth unto you will be to declare repentance unto this people.

What Is of Most Worth?

When my husband and I were serving as mission leaders, we had a list of points we would cover with the new missionaries. Some of these points were specific to our mission—don't drink the water and be careful of motorcycles. But most of our counsel was directed toward their missionary purpose and what would be of most worth to them during their eighteen or twenty-four months in Brazil.

This counsel about their missionary purpose would be similar to what missionaries in every mission in the Church would hear as they arrive at their various mission homes. A mission leader's responsibility is to help missionaries understand that their primary purpose is to invite others to come unto Christ through the principles of the gospel. The repetition of this counsel does not belittle it or mean that each missionary is not "special." Instead, the repetition of these concepts illustrates their eternal importance.

When reading sections 15 and 16, you might question why they are so similar. Why did the Lord repeat Himself? His repetition emphasizes that both John and Peter Whitmer Jr. needed to understand what would be of most worth to them as members of His Church—declaring repentance and inviting others to come unto Christ.

—Marianna

"Every one of our Heavenly Father's children . . . deserves to hear the message of the restored gospel of Jesus Christ."

Russell M. Nelson

"Hope of Israel," Worldwide Youth Devotional, June 2018

Doctrine and Covenants 17:8

The gates of hell shall not prevail against you; for my grace is sufficient for you, and you shall be lifted up at the last day.

A Work in Progress

One of my favorite things to do when I am leading a discussion or teaching a class is to ask people to identify something they think of as their weakness. I have heard a lot of people say being patient, being a student, or having faith.

I love doing this activity because 99 percent of the time when a person shares a weakness with the class, others are shocked. The person who says he wants to be more patient is already known for his patience. The one who wants to be a better student is considered one of the smartest people in the class. And the one who says she wants to have more faith is the young woman whom everyone considers their example of discipleship.

Why is it that the thing we see as our weak spot becomes a strength over time? God has promised that His grace is sufficient. When we partner with Christ, hell has no chance. Weaknesses can become strengths as we access and accept His Atonement

—Ganel-Lyn

> "Do we really believe Him? He has also promised to make weak things strong. Are we really willing to submit to that process? Yet if we desire fulness, we cannot hold back part!"
>
> Neal A. Maxwell
> "Consecrate Thy Performance," Apr. 2002

Doctrine and Covenants 18:3–4

Rely upon the things which are written; For in them are all things written concerning the foundation of my church, my gospel, and my rock.

The Answer to Everything

In *The Hitchhiker's Guide to the Galaxy* by Douglas Adams, a supercomputer named Deep Thought spends 7.5 million years calculating the answer to "the meaning of life, the universe, and everything." His answer is 42. He is wrong. The real answer is the scriptures, for the Lord has said they contain "the foundation of [His] Church, [His] gospel, and [His] rock."

When my nonmember friends laughed at me because Joseph Smith's vision seemed weird, I found that all the Old Testament prophets began their ministries with visions of Deity, and my faith increased. When I wondered why the early Saints were so persecuted, I reread about the house of Israel's exodus to the Holy Land, the struggles of the early Christians, and Lehi's family escaping Jerusalem. Creating a society of Christ has always been fraught with challenges but just as many miracles, which turned my focus to those miracles.

Through the scriptures, I've been filled with peace as I have gained a deeper knowledge of temple covenants, found parenting help, and understood how to forgive unjustified offenses. Through written scriptures, we find the words of Jesus Christ, and His words are always the answer.

—Christine

"Whatever questions or problems you have, the answer is always found in the life and teachings of Jesus Christ."

Russell M. Nelson

"The Answer Is Always Jesus Christ," Apr. 2023

Doctrine and Covenants 18:10

Remember the worth of souls is great in the sight of God.

The Least of These

After attending the temple on a hot summer day, I stopped at a local convenience store for a cold drink. As I left my car, I noticed a homeless man, shaking and quietly sobbing as he squatted down and leaned against the side of the building. I approached him and asked if he was okay. He was so weak he could hardly speak. I quickly entered the store and bought bananas, muffins, yogurt, and an icy cold apple juice. When I returned with the food, the man cried and thanked me for my kindness. The local authorities were also contacted, and help was quickly dispatched to assist him.

As I drove away, I silently prayed for my new friend. Just as we go to great lengths to provide for our children, it's important to be watchful of those around us, whether strangers or neighbors, who need love and support. Many hunger and thirst physically and spiritually with needs seen and unseen. Let us pray for new eyes to see every child of God the way our Heavenly Father sees them and willingly lend our hands to lift and serve those around us.

—Dru

> "We are the Lord's hands here upon the earth, with the mandate to serve and to lift His children."
>
> Thomas S. Monson
>
> "Serve the Lord with Love," *Ensign*, Feb. 2014

Doctrine and Covenants 18:15

If . . . you bring, save it be one soul unto me, how great shall be your joy . . . in the kingdom of my Father!

The Worth of My Soul

At the end of their missions, missionaries often worry about their spiritual success. Did they do everything the Lord expected of them on their mission? Too often, the standard for a successful mission becomes how many baptisms they performed during their eighteen months or two years.

The Lord doesn't care about numbers. He cares about becoming converted, making and keeping sacred covenants, and enduring to the end so that each of us will return to the kingdom of our Heavenly Father.

Even though I may cry repentance to all my friends and family during my mortal life, they make their own decisions. But if I am true to my covenants and lovingly help others return to Him, I will save myself. My soul is worth something too.

The Prophet Joseph Smith described this revelation as giving "instructions relative to building up the Church" (section 18 heading). Those instructions have not changed. As we build up the Lord's Church, we are being successful in our missions here on earth and can look forward to joyfully entering into the presence of the Father.

—Marianna

"Always remember the worth of a soul. We do this best by following the Savior's admonition: 'Love one another; as I have loved you.'"

Gary B. Sabin
"Hallmarks of Happiness," Oct. 2023

Doctrine and Covenants 18:35

For it is my voice which speaketh them unto you; for they are given by my Spirit unto you, and by my power you can read them one to another.

God Sounds Like Joy

My son met President Russell M. Nelson and Elder Jeffrey R. Holland while serving a mission in Zimbabwe. Weeks before the prophet and apostle's arrival, the missionaries were eagerly preparing. They studied, prayed, and fasted so that they could receive a greater portion of the Spirit.

The media recorded the long line of missionaries meeting the special Church leaders. Elder Condie shared, "Mom, did you see my face when I met the prophet? I felt joy." He learned that one of the ways the Spirit speaks to him is with the feeling of joy. That new awareness expanded how my son understood the voice of the Spirit. When he was growing up, he had seen me cry often when I was feeling the Spirit. Cameron thought that maybe crying was the primary way to feel a prompting.

Becoming familiar with how the Spirit speaks to you is essential to accessing and receiving the power of God in your life. Do you feel God speaks to you in music, words, or dreams? Consider that God sounds like joy.

—Ganel-Lyn

> "We become acquainted with Him and His voice as we study and feast upon His word in the scriptures, pray to the Father in His name with real intent, and seek for the constant companionship of the Holy Ghost."
>
> David A. Bednar
>
> "If Ye Had Known Me," Oct. 2016

Doctrine and Covenants 19:15
Therefore I command you to repent— repent lest I smite you by the rod of my mouth . . . and your sufferings be sore.

No More Sugar for You!

Since my teenage years, I've battled debilitating arthritis. As an adult, I discovered that shifting to a low-inflammation diet could alleviate most of my symptoms. This included the total avoidance of one of my most-loved, all-time favorite indulgences: sugar. Just as forsaking my much-loved addiction to sugar requires discipline, repentance calls for sincere effort and a willingness to change our ways.

It was not easy at first. I had powerful cravings and setbacks along the way. But just as cutting out sugar leads to feeling better physically, repentance brings peace and spiritual healing. It's like hitting the reset button on our souls. As we let go of what is holding us back, we move toward a much better version of ourselves, a holier way.

And just like staying sugar-free requires ongoing commitment, repentance is a journey, not a one-time fix. It's about making small changes every day, striving to do better, and trusting in the enabling power of the Savior's Atonement to give us strength to overcome our weaknesses and temptations along the way.

—Dru

> "To come unto Christ, we must change anything we can change that may be part of the problem. In short, we must repent."
>
> Jeffrey R. Holland
> "Broken Things to Mend," Apr. 2006

Doctrine and Covenants 19:16–17

I, God, have suffered these things for all, that they might not suffer if they would repent; But if they would not repent they must suffer even as I.

Dirty Dishes

Five of my seven grown children live close to me, and I love nothing more than having big family meals together. The only issue is that after everyone leaves, I'm often too tired to do the dishes and will leave them until the next day.

When I do, the job takes me hours longer. Dried pancake batter, baked cheese on casserole dishes, and other various messes remain stuck when they could have been easily wiped off if I had taken care of them immediately. Cleaning up right away would save me a lot of work and pain.

The same is true of repentance. By repenting daily, little missteps on the covenant path don't turn into debilitating habits, strained relationships can be healed, and we can see more clearly how to improve.

There will still be days we don't want to do the metaphorical dishes, but as we turn to Christ for help, He can give us the strength we need to repent and return to Him.

—Christine

> "Nothing is more liberating, more ennobling, and more crucial to our individual progression than is a regular, daily focus on repentance."
>
> Russell M. Nelson
>
> "We Can Do Better and Be Better" Apr. 2019

Doctrine and Covenants 19:31

Thou shalt declare repentance and faith on the Savior, and remission of sins by baptism, and by fire, yea, even the Holy Ghost.

Conversations and Connections

By the end of 2023, more than 72,000 full-time missionaries were serving around the world. One of those missionaries was my daughter, who was called to serve in two missions: six months at the Mormon Battalion Historic Site as a visitors' center missionary and then twelve months in the Knoxville Tennessee Mission as a proselyting missionary.

At the MTC, she questioned not being a proselyting missionary. Visitors' center missionaries are trained to be friendly while sharing the history of the site. They are not focused on formally teaching the gospel or on baptisms. She wondered if this would be the best use of her time. But after serving in San Diego, Sister Condie realized the blessing it had been to represent the Savior at a historic site. She learned that the best way to share the gospel is through kindness and conversation. While serving, she taught faith, repentance, and baptism in subtle ways by giving tours and making new connections.

Some will be called to put on a badge and knock on doors. Others will be called to stock the shelves at the bishop's storehouse. No matter the location, all are called to build the kingdom with conversations and connections.

—*Ganel-Lyn*

"I promise that as you serve, you will feel the love of the Lord in your life. . . . Your dedicated service to Jesus Christ will inspire and bless your family.

Ronald A. Rasband

"How Great Will Be Your Joy," Oct. 2023

Doctrine and Covenants 19:35
Pay the debt thou hast contracted with the printer. Release thyself from bondage.

Released from Bondage

Martin Harris was told by the Lord to give up part of his land to pay the debt to the printer for the publication of the Book of Mormon. He was counseled to keep that which he needed to care for his family and release himself from the prison of owing money to the printer (and to the Lord). He was also called to be a missionary and preach the restored gospel of Jesus Christ.

He was promised specific blessings if he made this sacrifice and was warned of the consequences if he did not. The Lord promised Martin that if he did this the Lord "will pour out [His] Spirit upon [him], and great shall be [his] blessing—yea, even more than if [he] should obtain treasures of earth and corruptibleness to the extent thereof" (v. 38).

If he did not pay the debt, Martin was warned: "Or canst thou run about longer as a blind guide?" (v. 40). Running while blind never ends well.

Today, a difficult prison to get out of is that of credit card debt. Spending money we don't have can imprison our paychecks, our future, and our families' security. Paying our debts releases us from the worldly and spiritual restrictions indebtedness brings.

—Marianna

"We have earthly debts and heavenly debts. Let us be wise in dealing with each of them."

Joseph B Wirthlin

"Earthly Debts, Heavenly Debts," Apr. 2004

Doctrine and Covenants 20:1

The rise of the Church of Christ in these last days . . . by the will and commandments of God.

Bring Back What Was Lost

Springtime is my favorite season of the year. When the shortened, snow-filled days of winter fade, signs of new life emerge. Days lengthen, blossoms begin to burst from sleepy branches, and gradually, light and warmth transform the world around me.

Imagine a quiet grove of trees, bathed in the soft light of a spring morning. In this tranquil setting, Joseph Smith knelt in prayer, seeking answers to life's deepest questions. In a miraculous moment, God the Father and His Son, Jesus Christ, appeared to him, welcoming the dawn of a new era.

Through heavenly guidance and divine revelation, Joseph began a sacred journey of restoration, translating ancient records and organizing Christ's Church on the earth. Despite facing adversity and persecution, he stood firm, buoyed by his unwavering trust in God's promises.

Today, The Church of Jesus Christ of Latter-day Saints stands as a testament to the ongoing blessings of the Restoration, offering hope, peace, and eternal truths to all who seek them.

—Dru

> "We declare that The Church of Jesus Christ of Latter-day Saints, organized on April 6, 1830, is Christ's New Testament Church restored."
>
> **Russell M. Nelson**
> "Hear Him," Apr. 2020

Doctrine and Covenants 20:11–12

Proving to the world that the holy scriptures are true . . . thereby showing that he is the same God yesterday, today, and forever.

Seeing the Whole Picture

There's a fun game where you show people a picture that represents a small portion of something bigger and they have to guess what the entire object is. The game is difficult because when you see only a small portion of something, you may think the object looks like something else.

For example, the magnified eye of a fly looks like the round plastic bumps on the bottom of a non-slip house slipper. The magnified view of a yellow sponge looks like swiss cheese (though not as tasty).

The Lord sees and knows the whole picture. He knows what really happened yesterday, today, and tomorrow. Through scripture reading and personal revelation, we can understand how to place the small pieces of our life experience into the bigger context of eternity.

Long before His Nativity, Jehovah revealed to prophets the details of His birth, and they wrote them down as scripture. As we look forward to His Second Coming, we can rely on the scriptures to help us see the whole picture and be prepared for what is to come.

—Marianna

> "The pure doctrine of Christ is powerful. It changes the life of everyone who understands it and seeks to implement it in his or her life."
>
> John C. Pingree Jr.
>
> "Eternal Truth," Oct. 2023

Doctrine and Covenants 20:17

We know that there is a God in heaven, who is infinite and eternal, . . . the framer of heaven and earth, and all things which are in them.

Spring Flowers

My favorite season, by far, is autumn. But a close second is spring. The warmer weather and flowers start to push through the frozen ground. I struggle with winter. It sometimes feels like the long nights and cold weather will never end. But the message of spring is one of hope and change.

Change can be hard. So it is comforting that one of the characteristics of God is that He will never change. The Creator of heaven and earth loves you unconditionally. In a world where scientific evidence and headlines change faster than the leaves fall from October trees, what a comfort it is to know the truth.

There is very little that is the same yesterday and today. And even fewer things that are the same forever. When we know more about this unchangeable God, we know more of what matters eternally.

—Ganel-Lyn

> "One of the overarching truths of the Restoration is that God lives and dwells in His heavens . . . and that He is yesterday, today, and forever the same unchangeable God, the fountain of all virtue and truth."
>
> **Keith B. McMullin**
>
> "God Loves and Helps All of His Children," Apr. 2008

Doctrine and Covenants 20:22

He suffered temptations but gave them no heed.

Giving Them No Heed

When I was twelve, I went camping with friends. They stopped at a local store to buy supplies. The outside darkness turned the large front window into a mirror. A stack of unique hats beckoned me, so I tried them on. One made me look like an adventurer, another a posh gardener. There was also a French tam and a fancy cap with a netted veil.

As I lifted my nose, pretending to be a spoiled debutante, I heard laughter outside. Putting my hands against the glass, I saw a small crowd of about twenty people very entertained by my antics. I was mortified and didn't touch the hats again.

When Lehi received his dream of the tree of life, he partook of the fruit, and "it filled [his] soul with exceeding great joy" (1 Nephi 8:12). He wanted his family to join him, so he called for them. It wasn't until after Laman and Lemuel refused that Lehi even noticed the tall and spacious building. Unlike me, once he saw the mocking crowd he "heeded them not" (1 Nephi 8:33).

One of the attributes of Christ is that He heeded not temptations. If our focus is truly on the Savior, we may not even notice those who mock on the other side of the glass.

—Christine

> "I pray that the Holy Ghost will bless and enlighten each of us as we consider together how we can be strengthened to 'heed not' the evil influences and mocking voices of the contemporary world in which we live."
>
> David A. Bednar
>
> "Be We Heeded Them Not," Apr. 2022

Doctrine and Covenants 20:37

All those who humble themselves before God, and desire to be baptized, . . . shall be received by baptism into his church.

Broken

Our family loves horses and has learned about the art of breaking a horse. Training horses takes time, know-how, and an understanding of how horses behave. First, the trainer needs to gain the horse's trust and teach it simple commands. Then, the horse learns to carry a rider and wear tack. Each training session involves working together and communicating until the horse listens and cooperates willingly.

Breaking a horse is like the process of gaining a broken heart and a contrite spirit. Just as breaking a horse involves gentle yet firm guidance, the path to a contrite spirit requires humility and a willingness to be molded by the Master. Just as a trainer patiently works with a horse to build trust and cooperation, individuals on the path of repentance must develop trust in the Savior and align themselves with His will. The breaking of a horse is a gradual process with adjustments, much like the incremental steps taken toward achieving a contrite spirit through sincere repentance and spiritual growth. Ultimately, just as a broken horse becomes a willing and obedient companion, those with contrite hearts find peace and redemption through their humble submission to the Savior's teachings and Atonement.

—Dru

"Humility inclines the heart of the disciple toward repentance and obedience. The Spirit of God is then able to bring truth to that heart, and it will find entry."

Joseph W. Sitati

"Patterns of Discipleship," Oct. 2022

Doctrine and Covenants 21:5
For his word ye shall receive, as if from mine own mouth, in all patience and faith.

Following the Leader

Taking a class of third graders on a field trip can be chaotic and unruly unless you have a strong leader, with a loud but caring voice, who knows where the group is going. Our earthly field trip may seem chaotic, too, unless we find a strong leader who knows where we should go and what we should do.

In section 21, the Lord establishes a hierarchy for the Church and designates unequivocally the leader that Church members must follow. President Harold B. Lee warned, "Your safety and ours depends upon whether or not we follow the ones whom the Lord has placed to preside over his church" ("Let's Keep Our Eye on the President of the Church," CR, October 1970, 152–53).

This was the first formal step toward organizing the leadership of the Church and a precursor to the organization of the First Presidency. The Lord reveals the role of the Saints in His Church: they are to follow His prophet, to labor in His vineyard, and to invite others to come unto Him. Before President Russell M. Nelson was the prophet, he taught that sustaining the prophet is an "oath-like indication" that we recognize his calling, will heed his words, and will follow his lead by preparing for the Second Coming and for eternal salvation.

—Marianna

> "Our sustaining of prophets is a personal commitment that we will do our utmost to uphold their prophetic priorities."
> Russell M. Nelson
> "Sustaining the Prophets," Oct. 2014

Doctrine and Covenants 22:1

All old covenants have I caused to be done away . . . and this is a new and an everlasting covenant, even that which was from the beginning.

Lost Wi-Fi

I love driving up American Fork Canyon. In the summer I see a lot of families camping and swimming in the river. Fall drives are filled with beautiful leaves and cooler temperatures. My Wi-Fi is good until the Timpanogos Cave parking lot. Then cell coverage drops, and I can't make phone calls until leaving the canyon.

Covenants and commandments are about connection with God. It isn't about proving our worth but about a relationship. President Boyd K. Packer said, "A covenant is a sacred promise, as used in the scriptures, a solemn, enduring promise between God and man. The fulness of the gospel itself is defined as the new and everlasting covenant" ("Covenants," Apr. 1987).

Can we have a connection with God without making and keeping covenants? Yes. But just like finding an unexpected Wi-Fi hotspot, making promises with God gives us greater personal access. And we are strengthened by walking the new and everlasting covenant path.

—Ganel-Lyn

"We must remember: it's not the course alone that will exalt us; it's the companion—our Savior. And *this* is the why of covenant relationship."

Emily Belle Freeman
"Walking in Covenant Relationship with Christ," Oct. 2023

Doctrine and Covenants 23:3

Hyrum, . . . thy heart is opened, and thy tongue loosed; and thy calling is to exhortation, and to strengthen the church continually.

Hyrum's Open Heart

Hyrum Smith, Joseph's older brother, believed in the Restoration since the First Vision. When Joseph got the golden plates, Hyrum provided the wooden box. When the Kirtland Temple was announced, Hyrum took a scythe and immediately began clearing the land. Later he recruited many and led a group at Zion's Camp.

Shortly after the Kirtland Safety Society failed, Hyrum comforted the Saints and then accompanied Joseph to find Far West. While there, Hyrum's wife had their sixth child and died shortly after. Joseph encouraged Hyrum to marry Mary Fielding. Though filled with grief, Hyrum did. A few years later when Mary was expecting her first child, Hyrum was taken with his brother and other Church leaders to Liberty Jail.

During the Nauvoo years, Hyrum assisted with building the temple, served as Patriarch, and took Oliver Cowdery's place as first assistant when Cowdery left the Church. He was by Joseph's side when they went to Carthage and remained with his brother until the end.

Hyrum's selfless service to the Church is the reflection of a heart that is ready to hear and is open to love and support. May we each open our hearts and serve as Hyrum did.

—Christine

> "Always remember the price Joseph and Hyrum Smith paid, along with so many other faithful men, women, and children, to establish the Church."
>
> M. Russell Ballard
>
> "Shall We Not Go On in So Great a Cause?," Apr. 2020

Doctrine and Covenants 23:6

You must pray vocally before the world as well as in secret, and in your family, and among your friends, and in all places.

Have a Blessed Day

Let me tell you about my dear friend Candi. She's an incredible example of praying always. Whenever she encounters someone facing challenges, notices someone in need, or senses tension in a room, she doesn't hesitate to offer a heartfelt prayer, seeking divine help and intervention.

Candi's boldness in prayer is truly inspiring. She doesn't hold back when it comes to publicly vocalizing her petitions to the heavens, and she often includes those around her in her prayers, ready or not. Her willingness to openly seek divine help fosters an atmosphere of caring and connection. Her simple faith and willingness to reach out to God in all circumstances serve as a powerful reminder to me of the importance of relying on prayer at all times and in all places.

I love her for her example to me.

—Dru

"Do as the Savior counseled His disciples: 'Watch ye therefore, and pray always' for peace, for comfort, for safety, and for opportunities to serve one another."

M. Russell Ballard

"Watch Ye Therefore, and Pray Always," Oct. 2020

Doctrine and Covenants 24:1

I have lifted thee up out of thine afflictions . . . and thou hast been delivered from the powers of Satan and from darkness!

Lifted Up When You Are Down

Everything was going wrong. I was late for work, I had thrown up because of morning sickness, and I was frustrated with my job. A dark cloud seemed to follow me as I went through my day. When I returned home, I prayed, even though I didn't feel like it. I poured out my concerns and frustrations. Immediately, my mind filled with all the blessings in my life. I had a job. I was pregnant and excited to become a mom. I loved my husband. As blessings continued to flood my mind, the dark cloud lifted. The Lord counseled me to stop looking down and start looking up with gratitude for my blessings. I wrote down the counsel and tried to do it. This counsel would prepare me for future challenges.

After the organization of the Church on April 6, 1830, the persecution of the Saints, especially of Joseph and Emma, increased dramatically. These events were only precursors for future trials. In section 24, the Lord was preparing, strengthening, and instructing the Prophet and the Church as a whole on how to be patient in afflictions, for they would have many in the years to come.

The Lord will lift us up during our dark times. If we follow His counsel, we will be delivered from the powers of darkness. But we must do our part by calling upon God, listening to His counsel, writing down what He tells us, and doing it.

—Marianna

"We should never complain, when we are living worthily, about what happens in our lives."

Richard G. Scott

"Temple Worship: The Source of Strength," Apr. 2009

Doctrine and Covenants 24:13

Require not miracles, except I shall command you, except casting out devils, healing the sick.

Miracles and Mistakes

The parting of the Red Sea, the burning bushes, and the blind receiving their sight are just a few of the mighty miracles featured in the scriptures. Why is it sometimes easier to believe that miracles happened in biblical times but aren't possible today?

One of my favorite verses of scriptures is found in the Book of Mormon when the Savior performs mighty miracles. He asks the crowd gathered at the temple in Bountiful, "Have ye any that are sick among you? Bring them hither. Have ye any that are lame, or blind, or halt, or maimed, or leprous, or that are withered, or that are deaf? . . . Bring them hither and I will heal them, for I have compassion upon you; my bowels are filled with mercy" (3 Nephi 17).

The Restoration of the gospel gives us access to the power of God through His priesthood. Each time we ask for a blessing of healing, partake of the sacrament, and keep our temple covenants we receive the Savior's grace. Miracles and healing are made possible because of the Savior.

—Ganel-Lyn

> "The Savior's healing and redeeming power applies to accidental mistakes, poor decisions, challenges, and trials of every kind—as well as to our sins."
>
> Peter F. Meurs
> "He Could Heal Me!," Apr. 2023

Doctrine and Covenants 25:3

And verily I say unto thee that thou shalt lay aside the things of this world, and seek for things of a better.

Better Things

When our family moved to Nebraska, all my grown children lived at least a day's drive away. Still, I loved our generous home, the friendly ward, and the golf course. I planned to retire there, but the Lord had something better in mind.

About a year later, my son-in-law got a position in Philadelphia, and we went to visit his family. At Hersheypark, we heard about Hershey's non-profit school. My husband felt we should serve there. I was Relief Society president and told him to go ahead and apply, thinking we'd never be accepted.

Within a few weeks, I was proved wrong. It was so hard to leave everything behind to go serve underprivileged kids, but I, too, felt it was right. For nearly two years we loved and cared for four homes of high school girls. On our days off we got to spend time with our four East Coast grandchildren.

When COVID hit, circumstances changed, and we were led to our current home. It is decidedly more humble. Now, most of our married children have settled around us, and I can hug my grandchildren often. To the world, you would think we were much worse off. In reality, we have been blessed abundantly, and we thank the Lord every day for His tender mercies.

—Christine

> "Yes, you are living in the world, but you have very different standards from the world to help you avoid the stain of the world."
>
> **Russell M. Nelson**
>
> Quoted by Neil L. Andersen, "Drawing Closer to the Savior," Oct. 2022

Doctrine and Covenants 25:10
Let your time be devoted to the studying of the scriptures, and to preaching.

Becoming an Elect Lady

I am a big fan of Emma Smith. The more I study her life, the more I am in awe of her charity, patience, faith, and unwavering love for her husband, Joseph. Section 25 was specific counsel for Emma, but it is also counsel for every woman who wants to become an elect lady.

The Lord lists ten specific qualities we must develop as women, and He ends with a blessing and a warning. An elect lady is to be (1) faithful, (2) walk in the paths of virtue, (3) murmur not, (4) comfort others in their afflictions (including husbands), (5) expound scripture and exhort the Church, (6) receive the Holy Ghost and write and learn much, (7) magnify her Church callings, (8) lay aside the things of this world for the things of a better, (9) lift up her heart and rejoice, and (10) continue in meekness and beware of pride. The blessing is that if she will keep the Lord's commandments continually, then she will receive a crown of righteousness. The warning is that if she doesn't do these things, then she cannot go where the Lord dwells.

I desire to become an elect lady like Emma. I hope to meet her in the courts above.

—Marianna

> "Emma was called 'an elect lady.' . . .
> Each of you is an elect lady."
> Gordon B. Hinckley
> "If Thou Art Faithful," Oct. 1984

Doctrine and Covenants 25:12

For my soul delighteth in the song of the heart; yea, the song of the righteous is a prayer unto me.

Then Sings My Soul

As a young child attending church, I sang hymns like "Jesus Loves Me," "Oh, How I Love Jesus," and "How Great Thou Art." These simple melodies filled my heart with tenderness and love for my Savior at an early age.

Isn't it wonderful how sacred music has the unique ability to transcend barriers of age, language, and culture? It invites the Spirit like nothing else can.

Whether listening to a timid toddler sing their first rendition of a Primary song during home evening, basking in the awe-inspiring grandeur of a masterful symphonic orchestra, or hearing the majestic voices of the Tabernacle Choir at Temple Square during general conference, I know that each is a beautiful expression of faith and reverence for God—a prayer unto Him.

—Dru

> "I love to sing the hymns of the Restoration. The combination of inspired lyrics and majestic melodies helps me to learn essential gospel principles and stirs my soul."
>
> David A. Bednar
> "But We Heeded Them Not," Apr. 2022

Doctrine and Covenants 26:1
Let your time be devoted to the studying of the scriptures, and to preaching.

Escape

When life gets too busy and hard to deal with, I tend to want to escape. Usually, that escape is a television show or movie to help me get away from my troubles.

What if I grabbed my scriptures instead of my phone or remote? How different would I feel, and where would my "escape" from my troubles take me? The power of the Word stems from its ability to heal and change us—change our hearts and our minds. The Word encompasses both the scriptures and the words of our latter-day prophets.

Even amid his adversity and afflictions, the Prophet Joseph Smith followed the Lord's counsel to study the scriptures and to preach the gospel. Today we, too, should seek the power of the Word when we are dealing with difficult times.

—Marianna

> "Discipline yourself to have time alone and with your loved ones. Open your heart to God in prayer. Take time to immerse yourself in the scriptures and worship in the temple."
>
> Russell M. Nelson
> "What We Are Learning and Will Never Forget," Apr. 2021

Doctrine and Covenants 27:2

It mattereth not what ye shall eat or . . . drink when ye partake of the sacrament, if it so be that ye do it with an eye single to my glory.

The Chapel Is a Tomb

What matters most on Sunday isn't having our hair perfectly coiffed or dresses that coordinate with ties. What matters most is partaking of the sacrament and worshiping God with an eye single to His glory.

My friend John Fossum shared a beautiful insight about the chapel. When he goes to church on Sundays, he tries to reframe how he sees the chapel. In his mind, the sacrament table and cloth reflect the body of Christ covered in linen. Looking at the chapel as a symbolic tomb can expand our sabbath worship and help us focus on what matters most.

Sister Rebecca L. Craven said, "As we center our lives on Jesus Christ, we will be guided to do what mattereth most. And we will be blessed with spiritual strength, contentment, and with *joy*!" ("Do What Mattereth Most," April 2022).

Try visualizing the chapel with new eyes. Consider the symbolism of the sacrament, the table, the white cloth, and the music. How can you worship God with more glory?

—Ganel-Lyn

> "It makes me ponder that if some things matter not, or matter less, there must be things that matter most. In our efforts to do something or do anything, we might ask ourselves, 'What mattereth most?'"
>
> Rebecca L. Craven
> "Do What Mattereth Most," Apr. 2021

Doctrine and Covenants 27:15–16

Wherefore, lift up your hearts and rejoice, and gird up your loins . . . that ye may be able to stand.

Gird Your Loins

Having our loins gird about with truth seems to be a prerequisite to putting on the armor of God so that we'll "be able to withstand the evil day." In Doctrine and Covenants 106:5, the Lord also says, "Gird up your loins, that you may be the children of light." So, what does this phrase mean?

During biblical times, men wore robes. Girding up their loins was pulling the back of their skirt up between their legs and tying their belt or girdle tight, changing their skirt into pants so they could run or fight. Peter shed further light on this subject when he said, "Gird up the loins of your mind, be sober . . . not fashioning yourselves according to the former lusts in your ignorance" (1 Peter 1:13–14). It is no coincidence that girding involves greater coverage of your private parts, especially in today's society.

We certainly live in an evil day when over a third of all internet downloads are pornography-related and almost half of all families report inappropriate media usage as being a problem in their household. But as we protect ourselves and our children with truth and righteousness, we can "lift up our hearts and rejoice!" And when we put on the whole armor of God, we will be further protected.

—Christine

"As I keep the covenants I have made with God in the house of the Lord, I have symbolically put on Christ, who Himself is an armor of light. He will protect me from evil, give me power and increased capacity, and be my light and guide."

J. Anette Dennis

"Put Ye On the Lord Jesus Christ," Apr. 2024

Doctrine and Covenants 27:15–18

Take upon you my whole armor, that ye may be able to withstand the evil day.

Stand Your Ground

Putting on the armor of God includes filling our minds with truth, our hearts with faith in Jesus Christ, and following the promptings of the Spirit. Years ago, I was invited to fly to another state to speak at a youth fireside. During the fireside, I testified that when we share our knowledge of the gospel and our love of the Savior, many will be touched by the Spirit and want to know more.

When the meeting concluded, I returned to a non-member home where I was staying. As I entered the living room, I was completely caught off guard when I heard a stern voice immediately shout, "Do Mormons believe in Jesus or not!" I was stunned. My heart was pounding through my chest. I stopped, took a deep breath, and quickly pleaded for my Heavenly Father's help. In a quiet, calm voice, I replied, "Yes. Jesus Christ is everything to me."

There is something remarkable about those moments when you feel the Spirit take over. Everything changes and hearts are softened. That night, in a home where the gospel was unfamiliar, I witnessed the power of bearing witness of Christ. It reminded me that no matter where we are, the Spirit can bridge misunderstandings, dispel doubts, and bring peace.

—Dru

"It is time to put on the full armor of God so we can engage in the most important work on earth. As servants of the Lord, we cannot be asleep while this battle rages."

Russell M. Nelson

"We Can Do Better and Be Better," Apr. 2019

Doctrine and Covenants 28:4

And if thou art led at any time by the Comforter to speak or teach, or at all times by the way of commandment unto the church, thou mayest do it.

Did You Write Your Talk?

My favorite part of being a public speaker is the sacred dance I have with the Spirit when I am standing in front of an audience. In preparation, I write a rough outline of thoughts, principles, and stories I feel inspired to share. No matter what is on the paper, when I stand to share, I focus on promptings, not my notes. I try to listen to the Spirit and share what I feel comes to my heart.

After more than three thousand keynote speeches, I have had many sacred experiences speaking all over the world. I love it when God knows that the person sitting in the back row is wrestling with addiction. Or the mom in the front is praying for help for her child. If I cling too tightly to what I thought my talk should be, I give up the opportunity to hear what the Comforter wants me to know and say.

You may not be a keynote speaker, but we can all invite the Spirit to be our guide. In conversations with our teenagers, direction for work, or teaching a Primary class, the Comforter wants to lead us.

—Ganel-Lyn

> "The Spirit does not get our attention by shouting or shaking us with a heavy hand. Rather it whispers. It caresses so gently that if we are preoccupied we may not feel it at all."
>
> Boyd K. Packer
> "The Candle of the Lord," *Ensign*, Jan. 1983

Doctrine and Covenants 28:11

Thou shalt take thy brother, Hiram Page, between him and thee alone, and tell him that those things which he hath written from that stone are not of me.

Between Him and Thee Alone

When we lived in Missouri, one Sunday at church I heard that someone had discovered the grave of Hiram Page up the road. I knew he was one of the Eight Witnesses, but that was all I knew, so I researched more about him.

Hiram Page was married to Catherine Whitmer and was Oliver Cowdery's brother-in-law. Three months after the Church was organized, Hiram found a seer stone and claimed that it gave him revelations concerning the location of Zion. The Whitmer family believed him. Soon after, Joseph received section 28, which instructed Oliver to go to Hiram and denounce the revelations. Oliver did so, and Hiram forsook the stone and continued in the faith for the next eight years.

We can learn a great lesson from Hiram Page making this course correction. Oliver was instructed to take him alone and discuss the issue with love. Sensitive matters of faith are often dealt with too publicly. By having close and honest conversations of faith, we can help others recognize mistakes and bolster faith without injuring both their reputation and their ego so they can continue on the covenant path.

—Christine

> "Truth has the best chance of blessing another when conveyed with Christlike love."
>
> John C. Pingree Jr.
> "Eternal Truth," Oct. 2023

Doctrine and Covenants 28:16

And thou must open thy mouth at all times, declaring my gospel with the sound of rejoicing.

The Unthinkable

Growing up, I was desperately shy. In school, I often found myself sitting quietly in the back of the classroom, too nervous to raise my hand or speak up during discussions. I wanted to make friends and participate in activities, but my fear of rejection and not fitting in held me back.

Shyness continued to hinder my interactions with others throughout junior high and high school. In social settings, I felt like an outcast, unable to join in conversations or approach new people. It wasn't until I had been married for quite some time that I gained confidence and found my voice.

As a Young Women leader, I was asked to share my conversion story with a large crowd at a stake youth conference. At first, I was terrified. But as I prayed for courage and strength, the Lord blessed me in my weakness. In that moment of vulnerability, He calmed my pounding heart and enabled me to share my story and my love of the Savior with confidence. I know He will bless each of us as we humbly try our best to share the good news of the gospel every chance we can.

—Dru

> "True joy rests on our willingness to come closer to Christ and witness for ourselves."
>
> **Bonnie H. Cordon**
> "Never Give Up an Opportunity to Testify of Christ," Apr. 2023

Doctrine and Covenants 29:1–2

Listen to the voice of Jesus Christ . . . who will gather his people even as a hen gathereth her chickens under her wings.

Like a Mother Hen

Every year around Easter time I have an uncontrollable urge to buy baby chicks. Their fluffy little bodies and the anticipation of farm-fresh eggs are simply too irresistible.

I love how protective a hen is of her chicks. When she senses a threat, she lets out a loud cluck to her little ones, who hurry to find safety beneath her protective wings. She selflessly uses her body to shield her chicks from harm, putting herself in harm's way to ensure their safety.

Just as a mother hen protects her chicks, so too does our Savior Jesus Christ offer us refuge and safety from spiritual dangers. He has sacrificed His body as an offering for us. When we heed His call and seek shelter in His loving embrace, we find peace, security, and love.

—Dru

> "It is one of the most powerful paradoxes of the Crucifixion that the arms of the Savior were stretched wide open and then nailed there, unwittingly but accurately portraying that every man, woman, and child in the entire human family is not only welcome but invited into His redeeming, exalting embrace."
>
> **Jeffrey R. Holland**
> "Lifted Up Upon the Cross," Oct. 2022

Doctrine and Covenants 29:13

For a trump shall sound both long and loud . . . and they shall come forth—yea, even the dead which died in me, to receive a crown of righteousness.

The Promise of Temple Covenants

The temple is a refuge from the world. The covenants we make there will enable us to come forth with our Savior during the morning of the First Resurrection. Those who died in Christ will be clothed with robes of righteousness and with crowns upon their heads.

As a little girl, I would pretend to be a princess by putting on a plastic crown with fake jewels made of colored glass. My royal robes were often a cheaply made replica of a Disney princess.

But there is nothing plastic or fake about the crown on my head or the robes of righteousness I will wear if I am found worthy when I rise in the morning of the First Resurrection.

The wonderful part of this promise is that I can help others obtain this same glorious future through vicarious temple work for the dead. Even if my ancestors died without receiving those necessary covenants, I can be their proxy in the temple so that they will receive the same crown and royal robes that I hope to wear.

—Marianna

> "Let us joyfully continue this journey toward our highest spiritual potential and help those around us to do the same through love, service, leadership, and compassion."
>
> **Joy D. Jones**
> "An Especially Noble Calling," Apr. 2020

Doctrine and Covenants 29:34

Wherefore, verily I say unto you that all things unto me are spiritual.

Life Is Like Pizza

One of my grandsons went through a phase of hating cheese and refused to eat it. Ironically, his favorite meal was pizza. It hardly seemed like pizza when he'd pull the cheese off. It was more like saucy bread, but that's how he liked it. Ironically, my daughter decided to go on the keto diet at about the same time. When she went out for pizza, she would only eat the toppings.

Life is a lot like pizza. It has temporal parts similar to the cheese, which include finances, education, physical and social challenges, and housework. Then it has spiritual parts similar to the crust, like scripture reading, parenting, temple and church attendance, prayer, and spiritual promptings. Naturally, some people excel and enjoy the cheesy part, while others find greater joy in the crust.

The Lord said, "All things unto me are spiritual." Temporal challenges can help us rely on the Lord and increase our service to others. As we combine our temporal actions with spiritual motivations, we will find that our relationship with the Savior will grow closer than ever. The key is to learn to enjoy the whole pizza.

—Christine

> "Unfortunately, too often we concentrate so much on our own problems that we lose focus on the solution, our Savior, Jesus Christ."
>
> Milton Camargo
> "Focus on Jesus Christ" Apr. 2023

Doctrine and Covenants 29:37

And they were thrust down, and thus came the devil and his angels.

Satan Is Jealous of You

Guess what? The adversary is jealous of you. You have what he doesn't have. You have a body, a family, and faith. He doesn't have any of those. So, what does he attack? Family, faith, and bodies. President Dallin H. Oaks said, "Unembodied spirits in mortality, Satan and his followers tempt and seek to deceive and captivate the children of God" ("Opposition in All Things," April 2016). Think about that the next time you find yourself wrestling with relationships, conversion, and body image.

God is bigger than the enemy. Satan wants to be anonymous. When we are aware of this and don't fear him, we can overcome his temptations. He is the father of lies. Don't believe him when he lies about your family, your faith, and your body.

—Ganel-Lyn

> "Satan cunningly deceived a third part of Heavenly Father's spirit children into letting him prevail instead of God."
>
> **Ahmad S. Corbitt**
>
> "You Can Gather Israel!," Apr. 2021

Doctrine and Covenants 29:45

For they love darkness rather than light, and their deeds are evil, and they receive their wages of whom they list to obey.

God's Voice Sounds Like . . .

One of my favorite social media posts is a comparison of how God's voice and Satan's voice sound different. God's voice sounds still, leads, restores, enlightens, encourages, comforts, uplifts, calms, and convicts. Satan's voice rushes, pushes, frightens, confuses, discourages, worries, compares, obsesses, and condemns.

It is easy to recognize the voices of friends and those we love. Are we familiar with the voice of God? Do we recognize that the overly critical, shame-based voice comes from the father of darkness? Satan wants to confuse, discourage, and frighten. God wants to lead, comfort, and encourage. Doctrine and Covenants 29:45 teaches us that identifying, clarifying, and obeying the right voice will lead us to more light, not darkness.

—Ganel-Lyn

> "We are here upon the earth to learn how to be happy eternally as we prepare for a glorious resurrection, because man is that he might have joy and we receive our blessings from him whom we list to obey."
>
> Hartman Rector Jr.
> "The Resurrection," Oct. 1990

Doctrine and Covenants 29:46

But behold, I say unto you, that little children . . . cannot sin, for power is not given unto Satan to tempt little children, until they begin to become accountable before me.

Age of Accountability

When I took developmental psychology in college, I was shocked to learn that around the age of eight something magical happens to the human brain—the frontal cortex, the part of the brain responsible for logic and reasoning, starts to come online. Around the age of eight, for the first time, many children begin to look at why they act as they do and believe what they do at a deeper level.

Before this time, most development happens in the limbic or feeling part of the brain. As the frontal cortex becomes stronger, children become less impulsive and more reasonable. This is the age of accountability because our brains are ready to understand and keep our covenants. What are the chances that Joseph Smith would have "guessed" the age of such a significant neurological milestone, and one that wouldn't be discovered for half a century after his death?

This means that although we, as parents, have taught our children when they were young, we cannot stop. After they are baptized, their brains can understand and discuss truth at a deeper level. That's when our conversations and family scripture study became even more meaningful and fun.

—Christine

> "Children are to be taught, by word and example, before and after they have 'arrived unto the years of accountability before God.'"
>
> Joy D. Jones
> "Essential Conversations," Apr. 2021

Doctrine and Covenants 29:5

I am in your midst, and am your advocate with the Father.

Easter

Our Advocate and Our Judge

As part of a criminal law class, I had to observe courtrooms and watch the judge, defendants, and lawyers interact. The relationship between the defendants and their lawyers was different with each case. Some defendants could not afford a lawyer and had a court-appointed lawyer. When the case was brought before the judge, the lawyer would often ask the judge for a continuance or more time to become acquainted with the case. Other defendants, especially those who were wealthy, would have a paid lawyer who knew their case well and would expertly plead for them before the judge.

Each of us has broken eternal laws. We are defendants trying to return to the presence of our Heavenly Father. The Father will hear our case and judge us according to our actions. But our Judge is bound by eternal law, and the law demands eternal justice. The Savior will be our Advocate, without price. His knowledge of our case is perfect. He knows us intimately and is aware of all our sins, our heart's desires, and our willingness to change and follow eternal law. The price He asks from us is to accept Him as our Savior and partake of His Atonement. Our final verdict will be both just and merciful and will determine our eternal destiny. We need not fear that we will be judged unfairly because our Advocate and our Judge love us perfectly.

—Marianna

> "Let us turn them to Jesus, who is their true advocate with the Father."
>
> **Ahmad S. Corbitt**
>
> "Do You Know Why I as a Christian Believe in Christ?," Apr. 2023

Easter

Doctrine and Covenants 76:22

And now, after the many testimonies which have been given of him, this is the testimony, last of all, which we give of him: That he lives!

Women Are Witnesses

James E. Talmage wrote, "The world's greatest champion of woman and womanhood is Jesus the Christ" (*Jesus the Christ*, 3rd ed. [1916], 475). This is such an incredible truth to understand and witness to the world! As women of faith, women who read scriptures, we have a unique opportunity to share our testimony of Christ.

Because of the invention of social media (and the prophet's and apostles' counsel to use it to share the gospel), no one needs to wait for the first Sunday of the month to stand in church and bear testimony to a ward. Women have a unique lens and access to the world. We see it from a woman bearing testimony to a child while driving the carpool to school or from the woman sitting with a grandchild to answer questions they are too afraid to ask anyone other than Grandma. I am in awe of the natural and normal moments we have to testify and witness of Christ.

Women teachers, authors, speakers, and leaders are in the rooms where hearts can be opened and connections with God strengthened. We need to be bold, as were the early witnesses of the Book of Mormon. We need to speak up, post our testimonies online, and teach of Christ every chance we get.

—Ganel-Lyn

"Brothers and sisters, I invite you to seek opportunities to bear your testimony in word and in deed."

Gary E. Stevenson

"Nourishing and Bearing Your Testimony," Oct. 2023

Doctrine and Covenants 110:3–4

His voice was as the sound of the rushing of great waters, even the voice of Jehovah, saying: I am the first and the last.

Easter

The Sound of Rushing Water

In the heart of Texas amid the blare of sirens, traffic, and crowds sits the Fort Worth Water Gardens. As you begin your descent down a twenty-foot stairway, water rushes down every surface around you in an open inverted pyramid. At the bottom, every other sound is gone. The cacophony of the world is canceled by the peaceful sound of rushing water.

When Christ appeared to Joseph Smith during the dedication of the Kirtland Temple, "his voice was as the sound of the rushing of great waters." This sound, known as white noise, is impossible to eliminate using noise-canceling technologies. Because it covers all frequencies, the sound of "the rushing of great water" can override every other sound. Oddly, each person can interpret the sound differently— some recognizing songs amid the sound that others don't hear.

Christ's words truly can become the sound of rushing water to each of us. If we surround ourselves with it, the noise of the world will disappear. When we listen with contrite hearts, many of us will hear songs meant for us alone that will bring peace to our souls. May we listen more carefully and truly hear Him.

—Christine

> "It is one thing to 'hear Him' in a quiet place of contemplation with scriptures wide open. But it is quite another thing to carry our discipleship into this mortal flurry of distractions."
>
> Steven J. Lund
> "Lasting Discipleship," Oct. 2022

Easter

Doctrine and Covenants 18:11

The Lord your Redeemer suffered death in the flesh; wherefore he suffered the pain of all men, that all men might repent and come unto him.

Broken

My ten-year-old daughter, Deborah, was in excruciating pain from playing as her team's goalie during a soccer game at school. (Soccer is a serious business in Brazil, even on the playground.) When the opposing team tried for a goal, Deborah dove for the ball and fell on her arm. Some opposing team members accidentally fell on top of her, snapping a bone in her arm.

Deborah called me in tears to pick her up from school. The problem was, I had driven down to Santos to meet with some sister missionaries. I planned to be back by the time Deborah was normally home from school, but she needed me now and I was an hour away. As I drove to the school, I pleaded with the Lord to take away her pain. I would have gladly taken it on myself if I could have.

Our broken souls from sin will hurt much more than a broken arm. King Benjamin taught his people that the demands of justice will fill the breast of the wicked with pains like an unquenchable fire (see Mosiah 2:38). Our Savior is pleading our cause to take away that pain. He can, He will, and He has taken upon Himself the agonies of our soul. Even though He did not sin, He is willing to take upon Himself ours.

—Marianna

> "Jesus Christ teaches the way back to our eternal home. . . . After all, He is the keystone of it all. He is our Redeemer, our Healer, and our Savior."
>
> Russell M. Nelson
>
> "Come Follow Me," Apr. 2019

The Living Christ

He rose from the grave to "become the firstfruits of them that slept" (1 Corinthians 15:20). As Risen Lord, He visited among those He had loved in life.

Easter

Visitors Welcome

One summer day, there was a knock on my door. I opened it to see my friend Anderson Crankshaw standing on my front porch. It took a minute for my brain to refocus on who I was looking at. Not only had he grown two feet since I had last seen him, but I knew Anderson no longer lived in Utah. His family lived in Washington DC while his parents served as mission leaders. I hugged Anderson like I used to when he was much shorter and younger. Having this unexpected visit from someone I missed and dearly loved was a gift.

I am certain that words can't adequately describe the feelings and thoughts of the Savior's friends and family when they had those visits from the resurrected Jesus. Their brains and hearts were likely trying to sync, just as mine had when I saw Anderson on my porch. How could this even be possible? Hadn't they watched Him die on the cross?

Christ will visit each of us someday. Every knee will bow and every tongue will confess that Jesus is the Christ. Until that glorious day, it is up to each of us to keep going, stay on the covenant path, and maintain our relationship with God. He lives, and He loves you.

—Ganel-Lyn

> "When I stumble, I will keep getting up, relying on the grace and enabling power of Jesus Christ. I will stay in my covenant . . . and work through my questions by study of God's word."
>
> Michelle D. Craig
> "Wholehearted," Apr. 2022

Doctrine and Covenants 30:2

But your mind has been on the things of the earth more than on the things of me . . . and you have not given heed unto my Spirit.

Focused on the Wrong Thing

Once a week I teach a homeschool art class for fun. We have re-created works from the Stone Age, Ancient Egypt, and Sumer. When we studied hieroglyphs, I introduced the idea of a rebus and showed the students the puzzle "hippo birdie two ewes." One of the girls had a birthday that day, so I gave her a little present once the students guessed that the rebus meant "happy birthday to you."

After the class, a sweet five-year-old named Jude informed me her birthday was a week earlier. She looked so sad and forgotten. I promised I'd get her a present the next time we met and wrote a big note on my whiteboard in the kitchen.

The next week was bonkers. The morning of my art class I was rushing around, finishing laundry, vacuuming, and emptying really stinky cat litter. The first two stores I went to were out of sugar cubes to make pyramids. When at last I found them and zipped back home, the kids were arriving. That's when I looked up at the whiteboard and my heart sank.

I imagine Jude's disappointment was equivalent to that of the Holy Spirit or the Savior Himself when we don't remember Him. How blessed we are that we can repent and try again. Just as Jude wore a huge smile when I did remember her gift, the Savior will be full of joy and of forgiveness once we return to Him.

—Christine

"The noise, clamor, and contention prevalent in the world may overpower still, quiet impressions of the Holy Spirit."

Gary E. Stevenson

"Promptings of the Spirit," Oct. 2023

Doctrine and Covenants 31:3

Lift up your heart and rejoice, for the hour of your mission is come; and your tongue shall be loosed, and you shall declare glad tidings of great joy.

Our Time

I vividly remember standing at the bottom of an escalator in the Salt Lake International Airport, eagerly anticipating the arrival of my beloved daughter Amarae, who had served a full-time mission in Jackson, Mississippi. Seeing her again was an absolute joy. Despite missing her every day she was away, I couldn't contain my excitement to hear about her experiences and witness the remarkable growth she had undergone as a devoted disciple of Christ.

We often hear talks from leaders of the Church encouraging young adult men and women to serve full-time missions. But I was totally unprepared for Elder Rasband's recent invitation for senior missionaries to serve. I felt the Spirit overcome me as he spoke. My heart almost pounded out of my chest! I can't wait for the day when my husband and I can go.

Every member of the Church needs to share the gospel message with the world. As representatives of Jesus Christ and with the power of God, missionaries can change lives, including their own. I will be forever grateful for *my* missionaries, Elder Kent Ritchie and Elder Jim Tattersall, who taught me the gospel and invited me to begin my journey on the covenant path many years ago.

—Dru

"Your dedicated service to Jesus Christ will inspire and bless your family, your grandchildren, and great-grandchildren."

Ronald A. Rasband
"How Great Will Be Your Joy," Oct. 2023

Doctrine and Covenants 31:7

Yea, I will open the hearts of the people, and they will receive you.

Prepared

On a rainy, humid day in Mississippi, my missionary daughter and her companion knocked on the door of a woman overwhelmed with sadness and despair. When they told her God loved her, she doubted it, having been taught all her life about an angry and condemning God. After hearing her struggles, the sisters read 3 Nephi 17 with her and asked, "Does that sound like the unmerciful, fearsome Savior you grew up believing in?" The woman replied, "No, completely the opposite. I wish I had heard this sooner."

Prompted by the Spirit, the missionaries asked her to pray and ask God if He loved her. She hesitated, saying she didn't know how, but one sister reassured her, "Just say what's in your heart." The woman prayed, "God . . . I want to know if You are there and if You really love me. In the name of Jesus, amen." They waited, and as they looked up, all were in tears. "How do you feel?" the missionaries asked. The woman replied, "I believe He heard me for the first time. I feel peaceful. For the first time in years, I feel like I'll finally be able to sleep."

When hearts are open and ready, amazing things happen. Lives change, and the promises of eternity are within reach.

—Dru

> "As surely as the Lord has inspired more missionaries to serve, He is also awakening the minds and opening the hearts of more good and honest people to receive His missionaries."
>
> Thomas S. Monson
>
> "It's a Miracle," Apr. 2013

Doctrine and Covenants 32:5

And they shall give heed unto these words and trifle not, and I will bless them.

Unexpected Blessings

Two years before we met, my husband felt very inspired to pursue a girl who had recently put in her mission papers. Greg wrote to her each week while she was serving and didn't date while she was gone. When she got home, he drove out to meet her and was devastated when she rejected him.

Confused, he returned to the singles ward the same week I moved in. We were married six months later. Greg's inspiration kept him available so that we could meet at the right time and marry for time and all eternity.

A similar experience happened to Parley P. Pratt, who was called to preach to the Lamanites. He and his companion hoped the call was in fulfillment of Book of Mormon prophecies. On their way west, Parley took a detour to tell his minister friend, Sidney Rigdon, about the newly restored Church of Christ. Though the two missionaries were expelled from teaching the Lamanites in Missouri, Sidney Rigdon's congregation in Kirtland, Ohio, accepted his message, and 130 new Saints joined the fledgling church, nearly doubling their numbers. When we obey, we are promised blessings. Sometimes, they are very different from what we had expected. But those blessings can lead to glorious outcomes.

—Christine

> "Heavenly Father's prescribed path leads to the best eternal outcomes."
>
> Dale G. Renlund
>
> "Your Divine Nature and Eternal Destiny," Apr. 2022

Doctrine and Covenants 33:17

Wherefore, be faithful, praying always, having your lamps trimmed and burning, and oil with you, that you may be ready at the coming of the Bridegroom.

I Was Lost

The summer of 2023 was full of loss and change. I was a new empty nester and was dealing with the unexpected cancellation of a project I loved. I found myself feeling very lost. I knew my dog, Ruby, needed me to get up each day to feed her. But there were days when I wasn't sure if anyone else would really notice if I even got dressed.

I kept a routine to support my mental health. I would always get up and make my bed. And then what? It was easy to distract myself from the feelings I was having by opening my phone and scrolling. During those first few weeks, I made another important decision. Before I left my room, I would drop to my knees and start my day with prayer.

This simple daily choice made all the difference. Sometimes I was only able to say, "Dear Heavenly Father, I don't know how I feel. I don't know what today will be like. Please help me. Send your Spirit to guide me."

I didn't have a map to guide me through the feelings of insecurity and betrayal, but I knew that if I kept talking to God and asking for His help, I would have enough oil in my lamp to make it through this dark season of my soul.

—Ganel-Lyn

> "How do we begin exercising a little bit of faith every day? . . . When I wake up, instead of looking at my phone, I say a prayer. Even a simple prayer."
>
> **Joaquin E. Costa**
>
> "The Power of Jesus Christ in Our Lives Every Day," Oct. 2023

Doctrine and Covenants 33:8

Open your mouths and they shall be filled, and you shall become even as Nephi of old, who journeyed from Jerusalem in the wilderness.

Open Your Mouths

When missionaries first arrived in the mission home, both my husband and I would warmly welcome them and share a thought and a scripture. I always shared Doctrine and Covenants 33:8–10 and then asked, "Why does the Lord use Nephi as the example of one who opened his mouth? How were sheaves laid upon Nephi's back when his brothers wouldn't even listen to him?"

Nephi's words did not stop with his family. Through the Book of Mormon, Nephi has brought about the conversion of millions of people. He opened his mouth, and generations of people, including people today, have heard his voice. During his lifetime, Nephi had faith that opening his mouth would bring about the conversion of many.

Each of us can have that same faith when we open our mouths to bear testimony of Jesus Christ and His gospel. We do not know where our words will land and who will be touched, but we will be blessed if we thrust in our sickles with all our might, mind, and strength. We will be surprised how much we will reap.

—Marianna

> "Regardless of the outcome, the Lord invites us to open our mouth and share the gospel message with others."
>
> Takashi Wada
> "Feasting on the Words of Christ," Apr. 2019

Doctrine and Covenants 35:13–14

Wherefore, I call upon the weak things of the world, those who are unlearned and despised, to thrash the nations by the power of my Spirit.

Unlearned and Weak

I have often wondered why the Church sends young men to teach the gospel. Most of them have just graduated from high school, they don't have advanced degrees from a university, and they rarely have the wisdom of more advanced years. In these verses, the Lord explains why. He is showing the world that this is His work and His glory. His missionaries are but instruments in His hands.

I have felt unlearned and weak when I have been asked to serve in callings where I have no experience. When that happens, I rely on the Lord's arm, His shield for protection, and His buckler to strengthen my resolve to get the job done. The Lord makes the weak strong (see Ether 12:37).

Joseph Smith was not a learned man. Because his family could not afford the loss of money, time, or manpower of their children, Joseph experienced only three years of formal training. Oliver Cowdery, a learned school teacher, lived with the Smith family for a while to help teach Joseph's younger siblings. But the learned Oliver was not the one called to be the Prophet of the Restoration. The Prophet Joseph Smith may have seemed weak and unlearned to the world, but the Lord caused him to become a man of unsurpassed spiritual learning.

—Marianna

"Everything that is done in the Church is done by ordinary members, the 'weak things of the world.'"

Boyd K. Packer
"The Weak and the Simple of the Church," Oct. 2007

Doctrine and Covenants 37:4

Behold, here is wisdom, and let every man choose for himself until I come. Even so. Amen.

God Doesn't Panic

I love my family and friends. Sometimes I think that worrying will help them overcome their problems. But as Sister Tamara Runia taught, "Worry feels a lot like love, but it's not the same" (Oct. 2023). I have to remember that God doesn't panic. When I see my loved ones through God's lens, I relax more and panic less. I remember what Sister Runia said: "It's the Savior's work to bring our loved ones back. It's His work and His timing. It is our work to provide the hope and a heart they can come home to" (October 2023).

I think it is human nature to try to fix things when we see someone struggling or choosing differently than we want them to. Moms want to do something. Grandmothers and aunties hope that if they just say the right thing then their loved one will make wiser choices. When worry takes over and I become myopically focused on fixing, I remember I can only inspire, not save.

Focus on what you can change. Increase your own faith with more prayer, fasting, temple worship, and scripture study. Listen for what the Spirit prompts you to say or do. Stand still and remember God doesn't panic. There is only One who can save. Your job is to love and be patient.

—Ganel-Lyn

"The God we worship is not bound by time. He sees who our loved ones really are and who we really are. So, He's patient with us, hoping we'll be patient with each other."

Tamara W. Runia
"Seeing God's Family through the Overview Lens," Oct. 2023

Doctrine and Covenants 38:1

Thus saith the Lord your God, even Jesus Christ, . . . the same which knoweth all things, for all things are present before mine eyes.

The Hairy Peanut Butter Jar

When I was young, my mother left out a pair of hair clippers. Though she warned my brother and me not to touch them, how could we resist? Chuck shaved a small circle on the top of my head, and I made a perfect bald flower on top of his.

Hearing Mother coming, we stuffed the loose hair on the floor into an open peanut butter jar and put it in the cupboard. Then we hurried back to our morning television show. Mother's scream upon seeing us still rings in my ears. Though my bald spot was concealed by a small bonnet, Chuck had to have his entire head shaved. Then, we were sent to our rooms for our disobedience.

The whole incident seemed to be over until my mother tried to make peanut butter sandwiches the next week and was surprised by the jar full of hair. We were sent to our rooms a second time. The double punishment seemed so unfair, but Mother explained that trying to hide sin is a serious sin in itself.

In the Garden of Eden, Lucifer's second great lie was that Adam and Eve could hide their transgression from the Lord. Jesus knows everything. We can never hide from Him. When I'm tempted to hide my sins, I remember the extra punishment of the hairy peanut butter jar and simply repent right away.

—Christine

"It is the great deceiver who wants me to hide from God, to turn away from Him, to go at it alone."

Camille N. Johnson

"Jesus Is Relief," Apr. 2023

Doctrine and Covenants 38:27

I say unto you, be one; and if ye are not one ye are not mine.

The Race

In junior high, I was chosen as one of four representatives from our school to participate in a regional track meet. I was assigned to run the third leg of the 4x100 meter sprint relay. My responsibility was to be prepared, focused, and energized as I waited on the track to receive the baton, sprint with cheetah-like speed, and pass it smoothly to the next runner. During practice, our team achieved our best times when we focused on our goal and worked in unison.

Just as in a relay race where each team member must pass the baton seamlessly to the next runner, we must be united with Jesus Christ and pass on the baton of His love and teachings to one another. If we drop the baton or fail to pass it, we risk losing the race. Similarly, if we don't share and exemplify the love of Christ, we risk losing the unity that comes from being His disciples. To stay in the race and remain united, we must hold firm to the baton of His love and pass it on to others with deep determination and unity.

—Dru

> "I say again that it is only in and through our individual loyalty to and love of Jesus Christ that we can hope to be one—one within, one at home, one in the Church, eventually one in Zion, and above all, one with the Father and the Son and the Holy Ghost."
>
> **D. Todd Christofferson**
> "One in Christ," Apr. 2023

Doctrine and Covenants 38:29–30

Ye hear of wars in far countries, and you say that there will soon be wars in far countries. . . . But if ye are prepared ye shall not fear.

Preparing for Hard Times

When I was pregnant, I looked forward with joy and rejoicing to holding my new baby in my arms, but I did not look forward to the pains of childbirth. A few weeks before the baby's birth, the realization of the future pain would hit me, and I would begin to fear the challenge of giving birth. In preparation, I did three things to calm myself. First, I prepared myself physically by reviewing my breathing techniques. Second, I reread in my journal about the births of my previous babies and the joy I felt with each birth. Finally, I sought the Lord's comfort in personal prayer and asked my husband to give me a priesthood blessing. I prepared physically and spiritually for what was to come.

I look forward to the Second Coming of my Savior and to the joy and rejoicing I will feel when He comes again. But I do not look forward to what will happen before His coming. To put my mind at ease, I prepare physically and spiritually by learning how to store food, reading scriptures that give me hope for the future, and seeking the Lord's Spirit and comfort through personal prayers and priesthood blessings so that I am ready for challenging times ahead.

—Marianna

> "The Lord has declared that despite today's unprecedented challenges, those who build their foundations upon Jesus Christ, and have learned how to draw upon His power, need not succumb to the unique anxieties of this era."
>
> Russell M. Nelson
>
> "The Temple and Your Spiritual Foundation," Oct. 2021

Doctrine and Covenants 38:41

And let your preaching be the warning voice, every man to his neighbor, in mildness and in meekness.

Love Helps the Medicine Go Down

I love the movie *Mary Poppins*. One of my favorite songs is about how taking a spoonful of sugar helps the medicine go down. Sugar adds sweetness to the unsavory. And a little more kindness or forgiveness can make the world less scary.

We are called to warn and preach, but verse 41 cautions us to be mild and meek in our missionary efforts. I have learned that the Spirit doesn't beat us over the head. He gently reminds, corrects, and comforts. When we keep the Spirit with us, we can warn our neighbor with a plate of cookies or preach the gospel while riding bikes with a child.

If a little spoonful of sugar helps the medicine go down, imagine what some sweetness can do when talking about the Savior.

—Ganel-Lyn

> "The motivation for raising the warning voice is love—love of God and love of fellowman. To warn is to care. It can be urgent, as when we warn a child not to put his hand in a fire. It must be clear and sometimes firm. On occasion, warning may take the form of reproof 'when moved upon by the Holy Ghost' (Doctrine and Covenants 121:43), but always it is rooted in love."
>
> D. Todd Christofferson
> "The Voice of Warning," Apr. 2017

Doctrine and Covenants 39:6
And this is my gospel—repentance and baptism by water, and then cometh the baptism of fire and the Holy Ghost, even the Comforter, which showeth all things and teacheth the peaceable things of the kingdom.

Endurance

A few years ago, my son-in-law participated in an Ironman triathlon. It consisted of a 2.4-mile swim in the ocean, a 112-mile bike ride, and a 26.2-mile run (a full marathon), completed consecutively in that order. It was a grueling feat that tested the physical and mental capacities of all who dared to participate.

This life is also a test of our strength and endurance. The scriptures define the gospel as faith in Jesus Christ and His Atonement, repentance, baptism, receiving the gift of the Holy Ghost, and enduring to the end. Like a swimmer has confidence in a lifeguard, faith is the act of putting trust in someone else's ability to save when we are weak. Repentance is the Lord's way to make corrections, guiding us back on track when we veer off course. Baptism is our initial plunge into the waters of discipleship, a public display of our commitment to follow Christ. Then comes the gift of the Holy Ghost, whose promptings act as buoys keeping us within the boundaries of safety. Finally, enduring is the consistency of our steady strokes, propelling us forward with the knowledge that with Christ by our side, we will safely reach the shore.

—Dru

> "Attacks against the Church, its doctrine, and our way of life are going to increase. Because of this, we need women who have a bedrock understanding of the doctrine of Christ and who will use that understanding to teach and help raise a sin-resistant generation."
>
> **Russell M. Nelson**
> "A Plea to My Sisters," Oct. 2015

Doctrine and Covenants 39:9

Nevertheless, thou hast seen great sorrow, for thou hast rejected me many times because of pride and the cares of the world.

The Cares of the World

The story of James Covel is a cautionary tale. He was a minister much like Sidney Rigdon and a great debater. He had joined the reformed Methodist movement of which Brigham Young, Wilford Woodruff, and John Taylor were also part. He must have interacted with these pre-prophets as they converted to the gospel and was considering baptism himself. In January 1831 after a general conference of the newly established church, Joseph Smith received a revelation specifically for James. In it, he warned Covel not to be persuaded by "the cares of the world." Afterward, the minister was called to go with the Saints to Ohio.

I imagine James Covel wondered why he wasn't called as a missionary to the eastern states as others were. He had two sons who were preachers, knew many of the contacts in the preaching circuit, and was a respected teacher. Instead, he was supposed to babysit as the Church moved. Unwilling to go out west, James Covel returned to his previous life. We will never know the part he might have played in the Restoration.

In his case, the "cares of the world" were still faith-based, but they weren't what the Lord would have him do. How often do we get callings we don't prefer? It's important to trust in the Lord and be willing to serve wherever we are called.

—Christine

> "The Lord's perspective transcends your mortal wisdom. His response to your prayers may surprise you and will help you to think celestial."
>
> Russell M. Nelson
> "Think Celestial," Oct. 2023

Doctrine and Covenants 41:5

He that receiveth my law and doeth it, the same is my disciple; and he that saith he receiveth it and doeth it not, the same is not my disciple.

Just Do It

My husband likes to watch football, especially BYU football. Over the years, I have gained an appreciation for the game. I am always amazed at the skill of a quarterback to throw a ball so precisely and directly to a receiver. The receiver has the responsibility to catch the ball and then run with it. The quarterback can throw an expert pitch, but if the receiver is being tackled by an opposing player or does not see the ball coming, then the ball is lost and the throw was for naught.

We are blessed with a celestial quarterback who knows all the plays, all the rules of the game, and all the opposition (Satan's team). The ball we have to run with is His law. Our quarterback always throws His law to us perfectly, but it is up to us to receive it and then run with it to our earthly finish line. As a receiver, we have Satan's opposing players who want us to drop His law and not receive it. They will use every tactic to get us to drop it. We can also receive His law but not run with it. When we do that, the opposing team will definitely tackle us to the ground.

In order to stay on the Lord's team, we must receive His law and run with it throughout our life.

—Marianna

> "The kingdom of glory we receive in the Final Judgment is determined by the laws we choose to abide by in our Heavenly Father's loving plan."
>
> **Dallin H. Oaks**
>
> "Divine Love in Father's Plan," Apr. 2022

Doctrine and Covenants 42:14

And the Spirit shall be given unto you by the prayer of faith; and if ye receive not the Spirit ye shall not teach.

Spiritual Kittens

Sometimes when I'm driving somewhere I have been many times, my brain goes on autopilot, and I arrive with no recollection of how I got there. This has been termed highway hypnosis—a person drives in a safe and expected manner but their focus is elsewhere.

Sadly, I've had the same experience with prayers. At times when I'm tired or busy, I pause to bless the food or kneel to start my day and offer a quick, meaningless prayer out of obligation. Then I proceed with what I really want to do. (I'd also add 90 percent of all opening and closing prayers for church meetings to the "prayer-hypnosis" list.)

One day I was driving home with my husband, unfocused on the road, and Greg told me to stop. I did so, afraid I'd almost hit something. He rushed from the car and picked up a little kitten that had been abandoned. I hadn't even seen it.

The Lord has said that "the Spirit shall be given unto you by the prayer of faith." By making those prayers more meaningful, I would allow myself a greater portion of the Spirit and might even see things I'd otherwise miss. How many "spiritual kittens" am I leaving by the side of the road because I'm not asking in faith and opening my mind and heart to see them?

—Christine

"We can be taught by and learn from the Spirit line upon line, receiving what we need, and then when we are ready, we will receive more."

Henry B. Eyring

"Our Constant Companion," Oct. 2023

Doctrine and Covenants 42:45

Thou shalt live together in love, insomuch that thou shalt weep for the loss of them that die, and more especially for those that have not hope of a glorious resurrection.

The Drain Is Clogged

My daughter has long, beautiful, curly hair. Because of how much hair she has, it is really easy for her bathtub drain to get clogged. We have a special tool that reaches down the pipes and grabs whatever is clogging it. Then the water can flow freely.

This is a lot like forgiveness. It doesn't matter how the clog in our hearts got there. Sometimes it develops from others' choices or our own mistakes. No matter the cause of the clog, holding on to the hurt continues to clog the flow of our heart. When we learn how to receive and give forgiveness, we learn to live together in love and unclog the flow of our heart.

We never know when it will be the last chance to have a conversation with someone we love. Don't hold on to the pain for one moment longer than is needed. Ask for forgiveness and then give it. Unclog your heart so you can live better together in love.

—Ganel-Lyn

> "Whether we have caused that pain or been the recipient of the pain, those wounds need to be healed so that life can be as rewarding as God intended it to be."
>
> Jeffrey R. Holland
>
> "The Ministry of Reconciliation," Oct. 2018

Doctrine and Covenants 42:61

If thou shalt ask, thou shalt receive revelation upon revelation, knowledge upon knowledge, that thou mayest know the mysteries and peaceable things . . . which bringeth life eternal.

Just Ask

I do not like to ask for help. It shows that I am weak and can't handle life on my own. I realize that this is my prideful heart talking. If I become humble, acknowledging my inadequacies, challenges, and lack of knowledge, then I am ready to receive help from someone else and from God.

The Lord expects us to humbly acknowledge that we require His help. We only need to ask Him and He will give us the knowledge and help that we seek.

Section 42 was given to the Prophet in Kirtland, Ohio, on February 9, 1831, just ten months after the official organization of the Church. The Saints were already experiencing persecution and were waiting upon the Lord for further instructions. The Lord had previously made the promise that the "law" would be given to the Church in Ohio (see Doctrine and Covenants 38:32). Because the Saints asked, the Lord revealed His law for the Church in this section.

We must continue to ask today. This asking takes humility and the acknowledgment that we need His help to know "the mysteries and peaceable things . . . which bringeth life eternal" (v. 61).

—Marianna

> "Asking seems simple, and yet it is powerful because it reveals our desires and our faith."
>
> Milton Carmago
> "Ask, Seek, and Knock," Oct. 2020

Doctrine and Covenants 42:88

And if thy brother or sister offend thee, though shalt take him or her between him or her and thee alone; and if he or she confess thou shalt be reconciled.

Love at Home

My husband and I tried our best to regularly schedule and hold home evenings when our children were growing up. Every Monday night, we would begin with the same opening hymn, "Love at Home." One evening, one of our children questioned why we always sang the same song. Without missing a beat, my husband responded, "We can't move on to lesson two until we've learned lesson one."

Needless to say, we still sing "Love at Home" when we gather for special home evenings with our children and grandchildren. Maintaining harmonious relationships isn't always easy, even with those most precious to me. When I find myself causing offense or hurt, I want to remember the Lord's counsel to resolve conflicts individually and seek reconciliation quickly. To me, being reconciled means becoming friends again. Nothing is sweeter than the friendships found within my family.

—Dru

> "Through His atoning sacrifice, He can release us from the sin and weight of a warring heart and provide us with the sustenance we need."
>
> **Kristin M. Yee**
>
> "Beauty for Ashes: The Healing Path of Forgiveness," Oct. 2022

Doctrine and Covenants 43:34

Treasure these things up in your hearts, and let the solemnities of eternity rest upon your minds.

Is That the Brooklyn Bridge?

I love visiting New York City. The sites, sounds, and flavors are like nothing else on the planet. On a recent trip there, my husband and I visited the top of a skyscraper, where we could see the whole city skyline from the rooftop. We could see the Empire State Building, the Statue of Liberty, and the Brooklyn Bridge. We had walked across that same bridge the day before, but it looked really different from hundreds of stories up. We could see the design, the structure, and the color.

When things get hard, when life is discouraging, going to the top helps change how we see everything. God's perspective is one of eternity. So often the here and now is hard. But when we look back on the same situation ten days, ten months, or ten years from now, how will it all look or feel?

Pray and ask God for His perspective. Treasure up in your heart what you are shown. You may be surprised by how something looks from the top. With the grace of Christ, we are blessed to not only navigate adversity with poise but help our loved ones move forward as well.

—Ganel-Lyn

> "Poise comes when we see things from an eternal perspective. . . . An eternal view enables Christlike poise. May we seek the blessings of Christlike poise, not only to help ourselves in challenging times but to bless others and help them through the storms in their lives."
>
> Mark A. Bragg
> "Christlike Poise," Apr. 2023

Doctrine and Covenants 44:6

Behold, I say unto you, that ye must visit the poor and the needy and administer to their relief.

Reality Check

Until recently, I felt there were only two things you could do perfectly in the gospel. I mean, you could always be a better teacher, a more patient parent, a more consistent student of the scriptures, a better genealogist, but if you paid your 10 percent tithing and dropped by your home or visiting teaching families each month, you could praise yourself for being perfect in those two things. When visiting teaching was changed to ministering, that number went down to one.

In reality, being a perfect ministering brother or sister was never about a monthly visit. It was about visiting the poor and needy and administering relief. This type of charitable service has been part of the gospel since the time of Christ. In the Bible, James defines pure religion by our willingness to "visit the fatherless and widows in their affliction" (James 1:27). So now, we strive to enlarge our everyday lives to include those assigned to us by our priesthood leaders, and hopefully in the process enlarge our own souls.

I know the prophet is inspired, but I hope tithing never changes. I want to do at least one thing perfectly.

—Christine

> "It is said that those who understand the true spirit of ministering do more than before, while those who do not understand do less. Let's do more."
>
> **Gerrit W. Gong**
> "Ministering," Apr. 2023

Doctrine and Covenants 45:3

Listen to him who is the advocate with the Father, who is pleading your cause before him.

Not Alone

Recently, one of my grandchildren became very ill and had to be rushed to the emergency room. When I learned of the situation, I immediately went to the hospital to offer support. There, I witnessed my daughter stepping into the role of advocate for her child, ensuring her child received necessary care and attention. She effectively communicated the child's symptoms and medical history, asked pertinent questions to fully understand the diagnosis and treatment plan, and arranged follow-up appointments with healthcare providers. Not only did she champion the cause of her child, but she also offered attentive care and emotional comfort to her little one.

Our Savior, Jesus Christ, serves as our advocate. He knows us intimately and stands ready to defend us in our times of need. He is there when we are unable to stand up for ourselves or face challenges on our own. He lovingly offers peace and reassurance when we are discouraged or afraid. In His eyes, we are cherished, supported, and never left to face our struggles on our own.

—Dru

> Christ's advocacy is, at least in part, to remind us that He has paid for our sins and that no one is excluded from the reach of God's mercy.
>
> Dale G. Renlund
> "Choose You This Day," Oct. 2018

Doctrine and Covenants 45:9

I have sent mine everlasting covenant into the world, to be a light to the world and to be a standard for my people.

Standards

Gaithersburg, Maryland, is the headquarters for the National Institute of Standards and Technology. The purpose of this organization is to set national standards for measurement that ensure quality, harmonize documentary standards, and coordinate regulatory practices. These are arbitrary standards set by men. They may be based on scientific principles, but the calibrations and documentary standards are set by scientists.

The Lord has sent His everlasting covenant to be a standard for His people and for the world. These standards are not set by men but by God. These standards are not arbitrary or changeable. They are eternal in nature.

We can rely on these standards to bring light into our lives and to bring us to God. Embracing His standards prepares us to live in harmony with Him throughout eternity.

—*Marianna*

> "We do not lower our standards to fit in or to make someone else feel comfortable. We are disciples of Jesus Christ, and as such we are about elevating others, lifting them to a higher, holier place where they too can reap greater blessings."
>
> Becky Craven
> "Careful versus Casual," Apr. 2019

Doctrine and Covenants 45:32

But my disciples shall stand in holy places, and shall not be moved; but among the wicked, men shall lift up their voices and curse God and die.

One-Bedroom Apartment

Right after we were married, we lived in a small one-bedroom apartment in Phoenix, Arizona. It was nothing fancy. It was filled with hand-me-down furniture and big dreams. One of the kindest compliments we received was when new friends came over and commented on the spirit they felt in that little apartment.

Thirty-three years later, our home has more square footage and nicer furnishings. But our goal has always been to have our home be a holy space. Homes can be sacred places. Young Joseph Smith received knowledge and revelation in his home during a visit to his bedroom from the angel Moroni.

Dedicate your home. Play sacred music. Create an environment that is safe and conducive to feeling the Spirit. No matter the design and quality of the furnishings, make your home a place where Christ can abide and you can walk with Him. Be not moved in this pursuit, no matter how many times you move.

—Ganel-Lyn

> "I promise that individually and collectively we will be blessed to 'stand in holy places, and shall not be moved.' If we abide in Christ, then He will abide in and walk with us."
>
> David A. Bednar
>
> "But We Heeded Them Not," Apr. 2022

Doctrine and Covenant 45:39

And it shall come to pass that he that feareth me shall be looking forth for the great day of the Lord to come, even for the signs of the coming of the Son of Man.

Fearing the Lord

Have you ever met a famous celebrity, a talented musician, or a writer who has changed your way of thinking? When that happens to me, I get completely tongue-tied, my hands get sweaty, and I am a nervous wreck. It's not that I'm afraid of them. In fact, I love them! It's just that all my admiration and gratitude for their gifts ball up in my heart and overwhelm me. I imagine that is only a small part of what is entailed in the proper understanding of the phrase "fearing the Lord."

When Joseph Smith received a revelation detailing the signs of the times, the Lord declared those who have this adoration for Christ will "be looking forth for the great day." We'll look forward to it, grateful for its coming. Although we shouldn't become obsessed with cataloging events nor proclaiming their fulfillment, as we read the scriptures and pray about violent and upsetting current events, many can feel the quiet assurance that the time is far spent. But instead of being filled with fear, we should look forward with joy because our Savior will come again in all His glory and "arise with healing in his wings" (Malachi 4:2).

And when I meet Him, I will be overwhelmed . . . with love.

—Christine

> "But even with the increasing worldly influences around us, we need not fear. The Lord will never desert His covenant people."
>
> Neil L. Andersen
>
> "Drawing Closer to the Savior," Oct. 2022

Doctrine and Covenants 45:56–57
The parable [shall] be fulfilled which I spake concerning the ten virgins. For they that are wise and have received the truth, and have taken the Holy Spirit for their guide, and have not been deceived . . . shall abide the day.

Wise or Foolish

As parents, we yearn for our children to develop a strong testimony of the Savior and embrace His teachings. We want them to be spiritually prepared and equipped with the oil of faith, knowledge, and devotion to the Savior. Just as the wise virgins couldn't share their oil with the foolish ones, we recognize that our children must individually cultivate their testimonies through personal experiences, prayer, and study.

While raising our family, my husband and I have tried to provide our children with opportunities to grow spiritually. We have attended church meetings, worshipped in the temple, taught the gospel, studied the scriptures, and prayed together. Our role is to help each child recognize the importance of spiritual preparedness and guide them on their journey to develop a lasting testimony of Jesus Christ.

Pray for your children, love them, and point the way to Him.

—Dru

> "Make your home a house of prayer, learning, and faith; a house of joyful experiences; a place of belonging; a house of God."
> Dieter F. Uchtdorf
> "Jesus Christ Is the Strength of Parents," Apr. 2023

Doctrine and Covenants 45:67

And the glory of the Lord shall be there, and the terror of the Lord also shall be there, insomuch that the wicked will not come unto it, and it shall be called Zion.

Finding a Safe Place

Steve and I have lived in ten different homes. Before buying each home, we would do research on how safe the community was, how good the schools were, and where the Church was located. Each place became a place of safety for our family.

The early Saints were looking for a place of safety. They had experienced the opposite after they joined the Church. Many of them had left their homes in upstate New York and moved farther west to Kirtland, Ohio, trying to find a safe home for their families. They wanted to find a town where the community would "not be at war one with another" (v. 69). The Lord had given them His law and His standard, and they wanted to live His words.

Section 45 gave them a vision of the millennial future where they will live in "a land of peace, a city of refuge, a place of safety for the saints of the Most High God" (v. 66). In New Jerusalem, Saints will find a safe place because "the wicked will not come unto it" (v. 67).

As Latter-day Saints, we still look forward to living with our families in such a glorious place. But we can be a light to our communities now and be an influence for good where we currently live.

—Marianna

> "Our Savior commanded us to let our light shine like a city on a hill."
>
> Benjamin De Hoyos
>
> "That Our Light May Be a Standard for the Nation," Apr. 2017

Doctrine and Covenants 45:71

It shall come to pass that the righteous shall be gathered out from among all nations, and shall come to Zion, singing with songs of everlasting joy.

I Sound Great in My Car

I am not a great vocalist. I sound great singing in my car, all by myself. My husband and kids are amazing singers. They have been in award-winning choirs and have created beautiful music. People would pay money to hear them perform.

One of the beautiful parts of building Zion is that we are all needed, not just those who can sing. Bring your unique gifts and talents and contribute to the community of Christ. Maybe you are great at baking cakes, fixing cars, or cutting hair. Or, like me, you are brilliant at vacuuming. All of us are needed in God's choir. President Jeffrey R. Holland said, "There is room for those who speak different languages, celebrate diverse cultures, and live in a host of locations. There is room for the single, for the married, for large families, and for the childless. There is room for those who once had questions. . . . There is room for those with differing sexual attractions" (April 2017).

It doesn't matter how well you sing; your unique voice is needed. Zion will be beautiful because it will be diverse. All are invited to gather there.

—Ganel-Lyn

> "We live in a mortal world with many songs we cannot or do not yet sing. . . . I plead with each one of us to stay . . . faithfully in the choir."
>
> Jeffrey R. Holland
> "Songs Sung and Unsung," Apr. 2017

Doctrine and Covenants 46:2

Conduct all meetings as they are directed and guided by the Holy Spirit.

Guided by the Spirit

Recently I was given the opportunity to be observed teaching release-time seminary in hopes of becoming a substitute. I was nervous but well prepared. The hour began with the class president welcoming everyone and asking someone to pray. The area supervisor watched me stand in the corner while this wonderful seminary student fulfilled her calling. Then the supervisor left.

I then opened the class with a game. Each student wrote down their favorite activity, and then we tried to match the person to their preferred pastime. As we all laughed about how many horseback riders and readers there were in the room, the supervisor poked his head in again and left. That was it.

The rest of the lesson went well, and the students were engaged. We spoke of how we could bring Christ more into our daily activities by turning to Him. When I left, the supervisor had nice things to say about the little he had seen.

I thought how much like the Spirit that experience was. At times, promptings or simply a warm confirmation from the Spirit can be fleeting, but they are enough to tell us we are on the right track.

—Christine

> "You can cultivate an attitude and an environment that invites the Spirit . . . but you cannot dictate how or when inspiration comes."
>
> **Gary E. Stevenson**
> "Promptings of the Spirit," Oct. 2023

Doctrine and Covenants 46:11

For all have not every gift given unto them; for there are many gifts, and to every man is given a gift by the Spirit of God.

Unlike Any Other

People are absolutely amazing, each with their own set of talents and abilities that make them unique and wonderful. From the artist who can create breathtaking paintings to the caregiver who offers comfort and support to those in need, the variety of gifts people possess is mindblowing. Some have a natural knack for leadership, while others excel in showing empathy and understanding. Whether it's a talent for music, sports, academics, or craftsmanship, all talents reflect the incredible diversity and creativity of our Creator.

My oldest daughter, Jessica, has many incredible talents, one of which is creating beautiful floral arrangements. Recently, she made and donated two magnificent casket sprays for the funeral of two friends who died tragically. Her offering, crafted with tenderness and love, was a heartfelt tribute in honor of their lives.

Understanding and magnifying our spiritual gifts is essential to fulfilling our divine calling. Each shared talent plays a vital role in advancing God's kingdom on earth. As we cultivate and use our gifts in the service of others, we not only bless those around us but also find greater joy and fulfillment in our own lives.

—Dru

> "My dear sisters, you have special spiritual gifts and propensities. Tonight I urge you, with all the hope of my heart, to pray to understand your spiritual gifts—to cultivate, use, and expand them, even more than you ever have."
>
> Russell M. Nelson
>
> "Sisters' Participation in the Gathering of Israel," Oct. 2018

Doctrine and Covenants 46:13–14

To some it is given by the Holy Ghost to know that Jesus Christ is the Son of God, and that he was crucified for the sins of the world. To others it is given to believe on their words.

The Gift of Testimony and Belief

On Saturday evening, a companionship of sister missionaries decided to talk to everyone they met on the street. They were not having much success until they randomly stopped a young man close to their apartment and started teaching him the first discussion on the street.

They bore their testimonies of the truthfulness of the gospel of Jesus Christ and then invited the young man to attend church the next day. He came and told the sisters that it was the first time he felt good at church. The sisters continued teaching him, bearing their testimonies that Christ lives and His gospel is restored on the earth today. The man was baptized soon after.

A similar story happens to missionaries all around the world. They have the gift of testimony, and their investigators have the gift of belief in their words. There is a symbiotic relationship between those who know through the Holy Ghost that the Church is true and those who believe because of their testimonies. This brings a closeness and a divine relationship between the Saints, forming a wonderful community in Christ.

—Marianna

> "In a similar way that the Solimões and Negro Rivers flow together to make the great Amazon River, the children of God come together in the restored Church of Jesus Christ from different social backgrounds, traditions, and cultures, forming this wonderful community of Saints in Christ."
>
> Ulisses Soares
> "One in Christ," Oct. 2018

Doctrine and Covenants 46:15

To some it is given by the Holy Ghost to know the differences of administration, . . . according as the Lord will, suiting his mercies according to the conditions of the children of men.

Love Languages

My top two love languages are words of affirmation and acts of service. Each of us has different ways of giving and receiving love. God can speak all languages. Someone who speaks Mandarin or Japanese will hear the voice of the Spirit in their own language. Don't be surprised when you wonder if what you are hearing is from God or your own thoughts. It will sound familiar.

The Lord individualizes His messages to us and our spiritual gifts. Through Christ, we can receive all that God wants to give us. Don't be surprised when promptings sound like your thoughts and spiritual gifts feel like normal, everyday talents. Don't underestimate how much your Heavenly Father wants to talk to you and bless you. He knows your love language. His tender mercies will show up in the normal and common places in extraordinary and miraculous ways.

—Ganel-Lyn

> "I believe I have come to better understand that the Lord's tender mercies are the very personal and individualized blessings, strength, protection, assurances, guidance, loving-kindnesses, . . . and spiritual gifts which we receive from and because of and through the Lord Jesus Christ."
>
> **David A. Bednar**
>
> "The Tender Mercies of the Lord," Apr. 2005

Doctrine and Covenants 46:19–20

And again, to some it is given to have faith to be healed; And to others it is given to have faith to heal.

Taproots of Faith

I have pulled my fair share of weeds both physically and metaphorically. One thing I've found is that the roots of a plant have little to do with what shows above ground. In our current yard, the thistles that shoot up to three feet tall in a few weeks often take little effort to pull because their roots are shallow. In contrast, there is a plant called burdock that has low leaves and doesn't flower the first year because it is growing an incredibly deep taproot that is almost impossible to remove once it's been established.

Growing faith can be similar to growing burdock. As we pray for healing, we may feel inspired to reach out to others while our wound is still sore. Although we have all heard of miraculous healing experiences and they do happen, more often the process of receiving gifts of the Spirit takes some time and effort. Like the non-flowering burdock plant, we may still feel the sting of our injury for a season and be surprised it is taking so long. But if we turn to the Lord with our pain and do as the Spirit prompts, our taproot of faith will grow deeper and deeper.

We may not even notice when our faith finally flowers, but we are promised we will be healed, sometimes as we heal another.

—Christine

> "While assisting others to repent and helping them to feel the compassion, mercy, and love of the Savior, I realized that He could heal me."
>
> Peter F. Meurs
>
> "He Could Heal Me!" Apr. 2023

Doctrine and Covenants 46:32

And ye must give thanks unto God in the Spirit for whatsoever blessing ye are blessed with.

Unexpected Blessings

On a scorching day in Arizona, my husband sought relief from the heat by waterskiing with friends at Saguaro Lake. As they were preparing to leave, he discovered his wallet was missing from the pocket of his bathing suit. Feeling a little embarrassed, he reluctantly shared the news with me when he returned home, accepting the fact we would probably never recover it. A few hours later, we received an unexpected phone call from a Latino man speaking broken English. He informed us that he had found the wallet floating on the lake's surface and invited us to his home to retrieve it.

When we entered the man's modest cinder block house, we were met with a warm and friendly smile. We inspected the wallet and found all its contents intact. A sense of relief washed over us. As a token of our gratitude, my husband offered the man the cash in his wallet and thanked him for his honesty and kindness.

Blessings come in unexpected ways. As we heed the promptings of the Spirit and have eyes to see, each of us can be a blessing to those around us.

—Dru

> "Let me recommend that periodically you and I offer a prayer in which we only give thanks and express gratitude. Ask for nothing; simply let our souls rejoice and strive to communicate appreciation with all the energy of our hearts."
>
> David A. Bednar
>
> "Pray Always," Oct. 2008

Doctrine and Covenants 48:13–14
And inasmuch as ye have lands ye shall impart to the eastern brethren . . . for it must needs be necessary that they have places to live for the present time.

Sharing

I once took my two-year-old grandson to a dinosaur museum. At the final exhibit, the children pretend they are archaeologists and use digging tools to find dinosaur bones hidden in the sand. Often, there are not enough digging tools to go around. Some of the children are very respectful of other children's space and wait for their turn, others grab the tools away from a littler child's hands, and others are more aggressive and throw sand at other children or scream until the tool is given to them. What happens in the sand pit is a wonderful analogy of how adults share.

In section 48, the Saints are asked to save their money to prepare for Zion, even though the whereabouts of Zion has not been revealed yet. The Saints are asked to start gathering and live the law of consecration by sharing their lands with other Saints, especially those who left their homes back east.

How would you feel giving up your land and home to others because the Lord commanded it? What kind of a sharer would you be—respectful to others' needs or aggressive in keeping your possessions for yourself and your family?

—Marianna

> "Sacrifice and consecration are two heavenly laws that we covenant to obey in the holy temple."
> Dieter F. Uchtdorf
> "Our Heartfelt All," Oct. 2020

Doctrine and Covenants 49:6

[The Son of Man] has taken his power on the right hand of his glory, and now reigneth in the heavens, and will reign till he descends on the earth to put all enemies under his feet.

Say His Name

When I speak to teens, I talk to them about the power of saying the name of Christ. Whether you are walking down a crowded hallway at school or sitting in the middle of a test, you are never really alone. If stress is starting to suffocate your soul, say His name. Repeating the name of Jesus, even silently, gives us power to overcome any enemy.

The Savior of the World also created the world. He is our everything and can help us "put all enemies" behind us. Try it the next time your stress is skyrocketing. You are never alone. Just say His name. It really works because He really reigns in the heavens. All enemies will be overcome through the Atonement of Christ, including depression and discouragement.

—Ganel-Lyn

> "The Most Innocent suffered the most when some of His subjects did unto Him 'as they listed.' Bearer of the only salvational name, yet the Lord of the Universe lived modestly as a person 'of no reputation.'"
>
> Neal A. Maxwell
>
> "Apply the Atoning Blood of Christ," Oct. 1997

Doctrine and Covenants 49:15–16

Marriage is ordained of God unto man. . . . And they twain shall be one flesh, and all this that the earth might answer the end of its creation.

The Best Prize of All

When my family goes to the arcade, I like to find the game that gives me the most tickets. I always feel like the arcade experience is only half the fun. If I can leave with a cool prize, that's even better. Our time on earth is a little like playing at an arcade. Many enjoyable pastimes bring no long-term reward. But there is one game that gives the very best prizes of all, and that is marriage. The joy I've received from being sealed to my sweet husband is immeasurable. Add my children and grandchildren to the mix, and the prize is beyond amazing.

Today, Satan tries to hide that fact by making other options seem more enticing, and many have lost their way. According to recent census data, 53.6 percent of adults are not married, the highest number on record, and 25 percent of those over forty have never married. Although some faithful people may not receive this blessing in their mortal life through no fault of their own, all the faithful should strive for marriage. A covenant union brings the greatest opportunities for joy in this life.

—Christine

> "God's plan . . . requires that exaltation can be attained only through faithfulness to the covenants of eternal marriage between a man and a woman in the holy temple, which marriage will ultimately be available to all the faithful."
>
> Dallin H. Oaks
> "Kingdoms of Glory," Oct. 2023

Doctrine and Covenants 49:25

Zion shall flourish upon the hills and rejoice upon the mountains, and shall be assembled together unto the place which I have appointed.

Sisters in Zion

One of my favorite memories takes me back to a cool summer night at our ward Young Women camp. It was our last night together, and we sat around a campfire, sharing stories, love, and our faith in the Savior. Singing "As Sisters in Zion" made us feel incredibly close and like we were all part of something truly extraordinary.

Even now, years later, whenever I sing that hymn with my sisters in the gospel, I feel that same bond. We are all in this together as daughters of God and followers of Jesus Christ. If we stick by each other and keep our faith strong, we can handle whatever comes our way. Our unity and belief in Christ help us through the tough times and let us celebrate the good ones. As we look forward to the future, we can work together to lift and build His kingdom and anticipate the day when He will return, just as He promised.

—Dru

> "You will be an essential force in the gathering of Israel and in the creation of a Zion people who will dwell in peace in the New Jerusalem."
>
> Henry B. Eyring
> "Sisters in Zion," Oct. 2020

Doctrine and Covenants 49:26–28

Ask and ye shall receive; knock and it shall be opened unto you. Behold, I will go before you and be your rearward; and I will be in your midst, and you shall not be confounded.

Ask and Knock

Because we have a large family, I need to reserve multiple rooms when we stay at a hotel. One Christmas, we decided to stay at Disney World. I had tried to get rooms that were close together, but I made the reservation too late so we stayed in rooms far from each other. My children were so excited to arrive at Disney World that as soon as they grabbed their room keys, they ran off to their rooms without finding out their parents' room number. Later, they realized they did not know where Mom and Dad were staying.

My children knocked on the doors of quite a few unsuspecting hotel guests, trying to find us. But Steve and I were waiting in the lobby. As soon as my children saw us, they immediately asked us what our room number was. They needed to ask, then knock to come and visit us in our room. We also need to make sure we are knocking on the right door when we approach the Lord.

In the scriptures, the Lord always puts asking first and then knocking. When we pray, we are asking Him for direction and help to return to Him. Knocking is an action that illustrates that one really wants to have the door opened and go inside. Knocking on the Lord's door is acting on His instructions and being spiritually prepared to enter into His presence.

—Marianna

> "To knock is to act in faith. When we actively follow Him, the Lord opens the way before us."
>
> Milton Camargo
>
> "Ask, Seek, and Knock," Oct. 2020

Doctrine and Covenants 50:24

That which is of God is light; and he that receiveth light, and continueth in God, receiveth more light; and that light groweth brighter and brighter until the perfect day.

Namaste

I am a certified yoga instructor. While going through my two-hundred-hour certification, I learned how to be Christ-focused during my practice. One of my favorite parts of yoga is the individuality of this type of movement. At the end of a yoga class, the instructor will say *namaste*, which means "the light inside of me bows to the light in you."

Each of God's children and creations carries a portion of the light of Christ inside them. That light can grow brighter and brighter. When we protect and recognize that light, in ourselves and in others, it can increase. Elder Timothy J. Dyches said, "When your desires and actions are centered on the covenant path, the Holy Ghost, as a light within you, will reveal and testify of truth, warn of danger, comfort and cleanse, and provide peace to your soul" (April 2021).

But light can also be dimmed by sin, trauma, heartbreak, and pain. When we find the light starting to feel dimmer, remember that God's love for you is eternal. Turn to Him. With His Atonement, you will receive greater light from His grace.

—Ganel-Lyn

> "As we intensify our faith in Christ, we receive light in intensifying measure until it dispels all darkness that might gather around us."
>
> Timothy J. Dyches
> "Light Cleaveth unto Light," Apr. 2021

Doctrine and Covenant 50:40

Behold, ye are little children and ye cannot bear all things now; ye must grow in grace and in the knowledge of truth.

Ye Must Grow

All living things carry certain characteristics. They must receive nourishment, grow, and reproduce. When an organism or cell stops functioning and growing, it is considered neither living nor non-living until it undergoes decomposition. Then it is considered truly dead.

When it comes to our spiritual lives, the Lord has said that we must grow in grace and in the knowledge of truth. Growing in grace happens when we seek forgiveness for our sins and feel the Savior's grace in our hearts. Then we can share that grace more easily with others. As we seek truth and test it in new situations in our lives, we grow in the knowledge of truth. If neither of these functions are happening, we can become stagnant in the gospel, and our testimonies can begin to decay and ultimately die.

Most cells and other organisms only reproduce when they are healthy and strong. If our testimonies are growing, then we are able to share them openly and spread the truth to others. May we each grow, share, and live!

—Christine

> "[Jesus Christ] loves me and can make all the difference in my life. As I repent, His grace will transform me."
>
> D. Todd Christofferson
>
> "The Doctrine of Belonging," Oct. 2022

Doctrine and Covenants 50:45–46

And the day cometh that you shall hear my voice and see me, and know that I am. Watch, therefore, that ye may be ready.

When We See Him

In 3 Nephi 11, the people experienced a miraculous event when they saw and heard the resurrected Savior. Just as they felt His wounds and heard His voice, we await a similar fate. This anticipation fills us with hope, knowing that one day we will see Him face to face. Just like those who beheld Him in ancient America, we will be filled with awe and gratitude as we witness His majesty and glory.

One of my dear friends passed away when she was in her mid-twenties, leaving behind her devoted husband and three beautiful young children. She had appeared to be healthy and vibrant up until a few weeks before she died of cancer. This experience was a wake-up call and reminded me of how fragile life is.

We don't know when it will happen, but we will have the privilege of being in the Savior's presence again someday. It may occur during the Second Coming, or it may happen tomorrow. Because of this uncertainty, one thing is certain—now is the time to prepare to meet God.

—Dru

> "Now is the time to prepare. Then, when death comes, we can move toward the celestial glory that Heavenly Father has prepared for His faithful children."
>
> **Russell M. Nelson**
> "Now Is the Time to Prepare," Apr. 2005

Doctrine and Covenants 51:9

And let every man deal honestly, and be alike among this people, and receive alike, that ye may be one, even as I have commanded you.

Be Alike

The young women in the stake were given a very specific list of what they should take to the stake high-adventure activity. Each girl still showed her personality and individuality through what she took on the hike. Some girls took extra stuff, such as snacks. When they placed everything in their packs, the girls who had taken extra found out that their packs were too heavy. Most of them had to give some of their stuff away in order to finish the hike.

In May of 1831, the Saints, immigrating from the eastern states to Ohio arrived with very little, if any, resources. Bishop Edward Partridge had to make arrangements for their settlement. He had the job of distributing food and clothes, trying to care for their needs and their wants. Bishop Partridge needed the extra resources possessed by the current Saint in Kirtland, Ohio. These Saints gave what they had to support these desperate immigrants.

The Lord cares about both our wants and our needs. But He expects us to give our surplus to those who are less fortunate so that we can be alike (not necessarily the same). By doing this, we become one as the Lord has commanded us to do.

—*Marianna*

> "In our acquisitive society the desire to get and to have seems almost insatiable at times. We want and we take with no thought of others' needs. We often desire more than anyone needs or deserves."
>
> **Ruth E. Brasher**
> "That We May Become," BYU devotional, July 12, 1983

Doctrine and Covenants 51:19

And whoso is found a faithful, a just, and a wise steward shall enter into the joy of his Lord, and shall inherit eternal life.

Joy Is More than Happy

I wrote a book called *I Can Choose Joy with God*. It was a compilation of stories of heartbreak and hope. I learned so much about what joy really means after reading those stories. Joy is so much more than happiness. It is deeper, more complex, and more long-lasting. Joy comes after working through adversity. It is the other side of the hardship coin.

We are sometimes asked to steward over heaviness and hurt. But we aren't asked to do it alone. Because of Christ, we can someday enter the joy of the Lord and inherit all that God has to give us. If you are living through a difficult stewardship, remain faithful. Seek wisdom and strength, which only come through the redeeming power of the Savior's grace.

Your season of joy is coming. It will be deeper, longer-lasting, and more hopeful than you can imagine. Your miracle of joy may be in this life or in the next, but God's promises are sure. The faithful shall inherit eternal life.

—Ganel-Lyn

> "Those who have overcome the world will themselves then be overcome by the generosity of the Father, as the Father shares 'all that [the] Father hath' (D&C 84:38)."
>
> Neal A. Maxwell
> "For I Will Lead You Along," Apr. 1988

Doctrine and Covenants 52:14

I will give unto you a pattern in all things, that ye may not be deceived; for Satan is abroad in the land, and he goeth forth deceiving the nations.

The Divine Pattern

As those who love to sew, do crafts, or cook with complex recipes know, a good pattern can help improve outcomes in any area of our lives. So when the Lord presents a divine pattern for not being deceived, it would be a good idea to follow it. In Doctrine and Covenants 52:15–18, the Lord presents three qualifiers that allow us to know who to trust. Look at the voices you rely on and ask these questions:

1. Do they pray with a contrite spirit *and* obey God's ordinances?
2. Do they speak with a contrite spirit, with language meek and edifying, *and* obey God's ordinances?
3. When they "tremble" under God's power, do they turn to God, become strong, and bring forth good fruit?

Then the Lord says that if they are overcome and do not bring forth fruits, you will know they are not of God. As we look at the people who give us advice, we must take their personal choices into account and only follow those who follow God.

Too often we listen to smooth and intelligent voices from people who do not obey God's covenants. Though their words may be brilliant and entertaining, according to this pattern, they can deceive us. Let's focus on righteous voices by turning to the Lord when we feel overwhelmed.

—Christine

> "There is no end to the adversary's deceptions. Please be prepared. Never take counsel from those who do not believe. Seek guidance from voices you can trust."
>
> **Russell M. Nelson**
> "Think Celestial!," Oct. 2023

Doctrine and Covenants 52:40

And remember in all things the poor and the needy, the sick and the afflicted, for he that doeth not these things, the same is not my disciple.

What Can I Give?

I have tender memories of watching my mother reach into her purse to offer a donation years ago. She had been widowed for the third time and had worked twelve-hour shifts at a factory job most of her life to make ends meet. Having no money to spare, she struggled to pay for necessities and never indulged in anything else. But when there was a need, she didn't think twice. With trust in the Lord and faith in knowing He would take care of our family, she always opened her heart and wallet whenever she was asked and did what she could.

Her beautiful example has guided my actions as I have had opportunities to give and serve throughout my life. When I see a need, I try to think of my mom and help however I can. We've all been given so much, and it's our privilege to give back freely to others.

—Dru

> "When we love and serve the Lord and love and serve our neighbors, we will naturally feel more happiness that comes to us in no better way."
>
> Jeffrey R. Holland
>
> "Are We Not All Beggars?," Oct. 2014

Doctrine and Covenants 53:7

And again, I would that ye should learn that he only is saved who endureth unto the end.

Enduring to the End

All of us have had experiences where we just needed to hold on tight until the trial was over. It could have been a long sickness, six months of morning sickness, a difficult job, or a half-marathon race. Each of these experiences helps us understand the concept of enduring to the end, even when it's hard. But enduring to the end is more than just gritting your teeth until the trial's over. Instead, it is changing to the end, becoming better to the end, and working hard to the end. We need to see endurance as a positive quality rather than a struggle.

Algernon Sidney Gilbert had asked the Prophet for a revelation to direct his life. The Lord gave Sidney the revelation, which is now section 53, and warned Sidney that he must endure to the end in order to be saved. And he did. Before being baptized, he was a partner in the Newel K. Whitney store. After becoming a member, he never wavered from his testimony, even when faced with severe persecution. He moved to Independence, Missouri, where he was persecuted and imprisoned for his beliefs. Finally, he was driven from his home in Jackson County to Clay County. After all of these trials, he died of cholera in a refugee camp in Clay County. Sidney is a great example of staying strong in the Lord and enduring to the end.

—Marianna

> "Enduring to the end means *changing* to the end. I now understand that I am not starting over with each failed attempt, but that with each try, I am continuing my process of change."
>
> Becky Craven
> "Keep the Change," Oct. 2020

Doctrine and Covenants 54:6

But blessed are they who have kept the covenant and observed the commandment, for they shall obtain mercy.

New Young Women Theme

I was in Young Women in the eighties when the first theme was introduced. I grew up repeating the theme every Sunday in class. Saying it out loud helped me remember what matters most and eventually make decisions that have eternal consequences.

I rejoiced in 2019 when the original beloved theme was revised. One of the powerful changes made was the addition of this sentence: "I will strengthen my home and family, and keep sacred covenants, and receive the ordinances and blessings of the holy temple."

One of the other changes was the shift from *we* to *I*. Our individual relationship with God is what making and keeping covenants is really all about. Covenants are about connection, not just about checking off boxes of obedience.

When you keep covenants, covenants will keep you. I look back on a lifetime of making and keeping covenants, and it is hard to articulate how receiving sacred ordinances strengthens and enables me.

—Ganel-Lyn

> "I testify that as we choose to make covenants with Heavenly Father and access the power of the Savior to keep them, we will be blessed with more happiness in this life than we can now imagine and a glorious eternal life to come."
>
> Jean B. Bingham
>
> "Covenants with God Strengthen, Protect, and Prepare Us for Eternal Glory," Apr. 2022

Doctrine and Covenants 57:2–3
Wherefore, this is the land of promise, and the place for the city of Zion. . . . Behold, the place which is now called Independence is the center place; and a spot for the temple is lying westward.

Promises Yet to Be Fulfilled

When I was expecting my fifth child, a brilliant young sister was struggling with infertility. My husband gave her a blessing that promised as she stayed faithful, she would be called a mother. A year later we moved, but she had not yet been able to carry a child.

Some years later, our paths crossed again. I found out her husband had been arrested, and they had divorced. She was still hopeful of the blessing and assumed that gift would come with a new husband. Oddly, many years later we chanced upon each other again. This sweet sister told me that although she never remarried, her blessing had come true. She had a niece in an unstable environment whom she had adopted, and now that child did indeed call her Mother.

Like this dear friend, the early Saints were working and praying for something they wanted very much—the establishment of Zion. In section 57 they are told the center spot of Zion will be in Independence. We don't know how this promise will be fulfilled, but the temple was built westward. Sometimes we need to remember the Lord's ways are not our ways, and stay faithful as we see miracles unfold. And then at last His words will come to pass in ways we never imagined.

—Christine

> "May we marvel at the great promises that the Father has in His hands and that He has prepared for those who are faithful."
>
> Ulisses Soares
>
> "In Awe of Christ and His Gospel," Apr. 2022

Doctrine and Covenants 58:3–5

Ye cannot behold with your natural eyes, for the present time, the design of your God concerning those things which shall come hereafter, and the glory which shall follow after much tribulation.

Once in a Lifetime

In 2017, millions of eyes gathered in anticipation of a rare celestial dance. Each person patiently looked upward with wonder. It was the first time in ninety-nine years that such a spectacle graced the entire span of the United States.

During this total solar eclipse, the moon positioned itself between the earth and the sun, momentarily dimming the sun's brilliant light. It was unbelievable. Everyone who saw it was amazed. It was the chance of a lifetime.

In 1 Corinthians 2:9, we read: "Eye hath not seen, nor ear heard, neither have entered into the heart of man, the things which God hath prepared for them that love him." In our current state, we cannot begin to imagine what it will be like to be crowned with glory and to see and receive all that Heavenly Father has in store for those who love Him. Certainly it, too, will be an opportunity of a lifetime.

—Dru

> "May we ever believe, trust, and align our lives so that we will understand our true eternal worth and potential."
>
> Dieter F. Uchtdorf
>
> "You Matter to Him," Oct. 2011

Doctrine and Covenants 58:21

Let no man break the laws of the land, for he that keepeth the laws of God hath no need to break the laws of the land.

Don't Break the Law

Late for an early-morning meeting, I sat at a red light, frustrated that no one was on the street, yet I could not move. Then I thought, "Well, I could move. No one would know. The purpose of the law is to stop car accidents, and there were no cars around to crash into."

Then I remembered a talk in general conference way back in 1987 by Elder Adney Y. Komatsu. He had been in a very similar situation. He, too, was in a hurry and no one was on the street. He thought about running through the red light, but he would know he was breaking the traffic laws and the Lord would know too. He concluded his story: "We must always be examples to the world as members of the Lord's kingdom and keep the laws of the land and the laws of God" ("Looking to the Savior," Apr. 1987).

Because of Elder Komatsu's talk, I waited until the light turned green, realizing that I, as a Latter-day Saint, have a responsibility to never break the laws of the land whether or not people are watching me. I also need to follow the law, even when I am frustrated with it and don't agree with it.

—Marianna

> "The laws of man often move outside the boundaries set by the laws of God. For those desiring to please God, faith, patience, and diligence are surely needed."
>
> Neil L. Andersen
> "The Eye of Faith," Apr. 2019

Doctrine and Covenants 58:27

Men should be anxiously engaged in a good cause, and do many things of their own free will, and bring to pass much righteousness.

Lunchtime Kindness

When my daughter graduated high school, I found out something that I didn't know about during the entire four years she was in high school. Brooklyn and her friends sat with the exceptional and neurodivergent students at her school during lunch. They were kids who are often called "special needs." One day, when meeting one of these extraordinary students, Brooklyn ran up to her and said hello. I asked about her. "Oh, that's my friend I eat with every day at school," Brooklyn replied.

I tried to praise Brooklyn for her kindness, and she quickly corrected me. She said it was them that should be thanked. They made her life better, not the other way around.

My high school experience was really different from my daughter's. I am sad to say that the special-needs students weren't always included. I don't remember anyone doing mean or harmful things to them. But sometimes not doing the kind thing is unkind. These were missed opportunities. Being anxiously engaged in a good cause brings about much righteousness.

—Ganel-Lyn

> "We should also strive to become like Him. We then approach others with compassion and try to alleviate unfairness where we find it; we can try to make things right within our sphere of influence."
>
> Dale G. Renlund
>
> "Infuriating Unfairness," Apr. 2021

Doctrine and Covenants 59:10

For verily this is a day appointed unto you to rest from your labors, and to pay thy devotions unto the Most High God.

I Will Give You Rest

Life can feel overwhelming at times. From juggling family duties and work commitments to managing household chores, grocery shopping, and chauffeuring kids to various activities all over town, it's easy to feel exhausted. How do we manage it all?

Each Sabbath day, when I turn my thoughts from worldly cares and focus on what matters most, I find physical and spiritual peace. By renewing my covenant relationship with God through taking the sacrament, I feel strengthened by His mercy and grace. I am cleansed, and begin my journey anew, ready to face another week with faith and thanksgiving.

If we allow it, each Sunday can be a time to let go of our worries and give our cares to the Lord. We can replace thoughts of worldly concerns with remembrances of our covenants, and refocus our sights on our Savior, Jesus Christ. As we honor this sacred day, we are gently reminded of what really matters, and we can choose to realign our will with His.

—Dru

> "The Sabbath is God's time, a *sacred time* specifically set apart for worshipping Him and for receiving and remembering His great and precious promises."
>
> **David A. Bednar**
> "Exceeding Great and Precious Promises" Oct. 2017

Doctrine and Covenants 59:15

Do these things with thanksgiving, with cheerful hearts and countenances, not with much laughter, for this is sin, but with a glad heart and a cheerful countenance.

A Cheerful Countenance

I met Jane many years ago when I needed her peace and smile. As a young mom with four preschoolers, I was overwhelmed, had little sleep, and was married to the bishop. Jane helped me see the joy in my life. She did not have children, even though she wanted them. She was alone, even though she would have liked to be married. Jane taught me to have a glad, cheerful heart and to be thankful, no matter my circumstance.

Section 59 was written in August 1831 when the Prophet was in Jackson County, Missouri. This section is a vision of what Zion will look like but also what the people who live in Zion shall be like. In verses 5–9, the Lord sets out seven "thou shalts" for the Saints of Zion to obey and become. The Prophet's vision of Zion laid out commandments to be followed with a grateful, cheerful heart. The Zion standard is not just obedience but living the Lord's commandments with thankful, happy hearts and countenances.

Even though her life had not turned out the way she wanted, Jane's smile warmed everyone's heart. Jane lived the Lord's standard and taught me how to be more Zion-like.

—Marianna

> "When the focus of our lives is on Jesus Christ and His gospel, we can feel joy regardless of what is happening—or not happening—in our lives."
>
> **Russell M. Nelson**
> "Joy and Spiritual Survival," Oct. 2016

Doctrine and Covenants 59:23

He who doeth the works of righteousness shall receive his reward, even peace in this world, and eternal life in the world to come.

Reap Peace

As Latter-day Saints, we believe in the law of the harvest—you reap what you sow, right? Well, mostly.

In Minnesota, I was serving as an early-morning seminary teacher and then would taxi most of the class to school in my fifteen-passenger van. My husband was serving as branch president and coordinating re-activation efforts that were working. We'd seen our branch over double in size when quite suddenly my husband was let go from his position at work. We were shocked the Lord wasn't blessing us for our efforts. Instead, we had to move to Missouri with little warning. Later, we realized what a blessing that would be.

Similarly, Joseph Smith's family planted crops that failed multiple years in a row, causing them to move to Palmyra, New York, four years before the First Vision. They had put in the effort, but due to volcanic eruptions and strange weather systems, instead of being blessed with abundance they were blessed in a very different way.

In our own lives as we work and reach to do as the Lord directs, it's important to remember that the reward of righteousness is "peace in this life, and eternal life in the world to come." Let's remember to reap that peace and enjoy it, and not be overwhelmed when our worldly crop may not be doing so well.

—Christine

> "I love the Lord Jesus Christ and testify that His gospel is the only enduring solution for peace. His is a gospel of peace."
>
> Russell M. Nelson
>
> "Preaching the Gospel of Peace," Apr. 2022

Doctrine and Covenants 60:2

But with some I am not well pleased, for they will not open their mouths, but they hide the talent which I have given unto them, because of the fear of man.

Frozen

When my girls were little, they couldn't contain their excitement about joining a cheer camp hosted by our local high school. For a whole week, they practiced alongside the high school cheerleaders, mastering cheers and dances, culminating in a performance at the stadium and being cheered on by family and friends.

My adorable granddaughter Emma, full of spunk and energy, had the same opportunity. When her mom mentioned the community's cheer camp, Emma jumped at the chance. With enthusiasm she learned her routines, proudly showcasing her newfound skills at home. When the big day arrived, we smiled and screamed from the stands as we anticipated her grand performance. We watched as she took her place near the fifty-yard line and then . . . nothing. Absolutely nothing. Nerves got the best of her. Standing on the football field, she froze, leaving us all in shock and disbelief.

Aren't we like Emma sometimes? We're blessed with talents and abilities, yet fear holds us back from sharing them. Let's gather our courage, grab those metaphorical pom-poms, and get out there to glorify God with the gifts He's given us.

—Dru

"We are the Lord's hands here upon the earth, with the mandate to serve and to lift His children."

Thomas S. Monson

"Serve the Lord with Love," Feb. 2014

Doctrine and Covenants 60:5

Let there be a craft made, or bought, as seemeth you good, it mattereth not unto me.

It Mattereth Not unto Me

Sometimes the greatest test the Lord gives us is letting us make a decision on our own. That is what happened to the Prophet Joseph Smith and the elders who were returning back East after being with the Saints in Independence, Missouri. They wanted direction as to what means of transportation they should use for the journey. Should they buy a boat? Should they build one? The Lord's answer was "it mattereth not."

Our life is a journey, and sometimes we don't know which way to go or how to get from one place to another. The Lord may not always tell us the answer, and the test may be for us to figure it out on our own. Elder Uchtdorf described our mortal experience as "an open-ended, choose-your-own adventure story." He pointed out that we have the commandments, latter-day prophets, covenants, and the gift of the Holy Ghost to guide and direct us. But God will not tell us everything. Elder Uchtdorf concluded: "Beyond that, don't despair if you make some decisions that are less than perfect. That is how you learn. That's part of the adventure" ("The Adventure of Mortality," Worldwide YA devotional, January 14, 2018).

—Marianna

> "Men and women may be tested, exercise their agency, find joy, and learn and progress so that they may one day return to the presence of their Creator and inherit eternal life."
>
> **Gerald Causse**
> "Our Earthly Stewardship," Oct. 2022

Doctrine and Covenants 61:18

And now I give unto you a commandment that what I say unto one I say unto all.

Star Wars Reminds Me Of . . .

My kids make fun of me a little bit. I can't watch a movie without finding an analogy or metaphor to apply to life or the gospel. Especially sci-fi movies. The Star Wars series has some great applications and crossover imagery. Maybe it is the teacher in me, but I love finding ways to illustrate complex issues using simple word pictures.

God uses parables to teach us principles. He says that when He gives a commandment to one, it is given to all of us. Maybe that's because He also loves finding ways to teach the complex with concise and clear words.

So, the next time you are reading the scriptures, you have full permission to find the analogy that applies specifically to your life. When God is talking to someone in the scriptures, He is really talking directly to you.

—Ganel-Lyn

> "All doctrine in scripture can benefit us, even though it be given to a specific individual, for God has repeatedly said, 'What I say unto one I say unto all.'"
>
> Richard G. Scott
> "He Lives," Oct. 1999

Doctrine and Covenants 61:36

Be of good cheer, little children, for I am in your midst, and I have not forsaken you.

Acting Like Children

One summer my sixteen-year-old daughter was driving home from a family reunion and got in a fight with her older brother over the radio. The argument grew surprisingly heated, and my attempts to intervene from the back seat proved useless. No one was behaving well, not even me. Finally, I shouted, "Nobody in this car can say another word!"

A heavy silence settled over us. A few minutes later I felt the car drifting to the right. My daughter had fallen asleep behind the wheel. We were in the Rocky Mountains with a severe dropoff on both sides of the road. As she awoke in a panic, she floored the gas instead of hitting the brake and whipped the steering wheel toward the cliff's edge.

At that moment a semi-truck passed us. She bounced off its side, slowed, and pulled over. If the truck had not been there, our family would have been seriously injured or killed. Although the semi didn't have a dent, on one side of our car the mirror, wheel wells, and trim were scraped clean. When we got out, our petty attitudes had completely changed. We prayed together and thanked the Lord for protecting us. Even though we were acting like little children, He was in our midst.

—Christine

> "My plea to our youth, and to you parents . . . is to begin your search for happiness by embracing the bounty we already received from the giver of every good gift."
>
> **Jeffrey R. Holland**
>
> "Fear Not: Believe Only!," Apr. 2022

Doctrine and Covenants 61:38

Pray always that you enter not into temptation, that you may abide the day of his coming.

He's There

Women lead vastly different lives. Some are single, still in school, or working hard. Others are busy moms, juggling the chaos of raising kids. Some have faced tough times, like divorce or losing a partner, and are raising kids alone. Others are growing older and navigating poor health and loneliness. And let's not forget those who are caretakers of aging parents, showing them love and support when they need it most.

There have been times when I've felt alone in my struggles, watching others who seemed to have it all together. In those moments, I've learned to turn to my Heavenly Father, who understands what I'm going through and offers His unwavering support. I am His daughter. He knows and cares about me. He sends angels, mortal and immortal, to lift my burdens. He is there. His love for me will never change. He stands ready to help; I only need to ask.

—Dru

> "I promise you that you will one day stand aside and look at your difficult times, and you will realize that He was always there beside you."
>
> Thomas S. Monson
> "We Never Walk Alone," Oct. 2013

Doctrine and Covenants 62:1

Even Jesus Christ . . . who knoweth the weakness of man and how to succor them who are tempted.

Weaknesses

Satan knows the weaknesses of man. In C. S. Lewis' book *The Screwtape Letters*, the experienced devil, Screwtape, is teaching his nephew, Wormwood, how to tempt and deceive mortal men and women. Screwtape advises Wormwood that the road to hell is a gradual slope rather than a steep one. Satan's way is not full of sudden turns but is a gentle and soft decline, until a person is bound by the sins he or she has committed.

But the Savior also knows our weaknesses. The Lord told Moroni: "And if men come unto me I will show unto them their weakness. I give unto men weakness that they may be humble; and my grace is sufficient for all men that humble themselves before me; for if they humble themselves before me, and have faith in me, then will I make weak things become strong unto them" (Ether 12:27).

If we allow Satan to bind us to our natural-man tendencies, then we become bound to those weaknesses and our determination to change will be defeated. If our natural-man tendencies humble us and we look to the Lord for succor or strength, then these weaknesses will not defeat us. Instead, through repentance, these weak tendencies will depart from our souls and we will become strong in the Lord.

—Marianna

"In other words, as we first change our fallen natures, our weakness, then we will be able to change our behaviors, our weaknesses."

Kevin S. Hamilton

"Then Will I Make Weak Things Become Strong," Apr. 2022

Doctrine and Covenants 62:3

Ye are blessed, for the testimony which ye have borne is recorded in heaven for the angels to look upon; and they rejoice over you, and your sins are forgiven.

Emails Are Testimonies

Social media sometimes gets a bad rap. While my children were serving full-time missions, they sent home weekly emails. I would post their messages, with pictures, on my Facebook page. I loved sharing my kids' experiences with my diverse friend list. People from all walks of life messaged and commented about how my missionaries' letters touched their hearts, answered their prayers, or helped them in some other way.

Bearing testimony is now possible on many platforms and in many places. Your testimony, when borne, is recorded in heaven. And your sins are forgiven. That is some big motivation to open your mouth the next time you are nervous to step up to the podium in a fast and testimony meeting.

I told my kids many times that their full-time missionary work made a difference in a lot of people's lives. Especially in those weekly testimony emails.

—Ganel-Lyn

> "Please understand that there are remarkable blessings in sharing the gospel of Jesus Christ. The scriptures speak of joy and peace, forgiveness of sins, protection from temptations, and sustaining power from God."
>
> Quentin L. Cook
> "Safely Gathered Home," Apr. 2023

Doctrine and Covenants 63:1

Hearken, O ye people . . . listen, you that call yourself the people of the Lord.

Who Am I Really?

Years ago I was driving a teenager home from early-morning seminary. The class had enjoyed a great gospel discussion, and I asked what he thought of it. He turned to me seriously and said, "It doesn't matter. It's not me. None of this is me." I asked him what that meant. Who was he?

He told me that he felt he was walking around with a mask on, pretending to be something he wasn't. He wanted to be a rock star covered with tattoos. That's how he saw himself. When I asked why he felt that way, he said, "Rock stars are cool, and I'm cool. None of this is."

What we want to become is the foundation of our personal identity. But understanding why we feel that way and the purpose of our lives is equally critical. This boy had no interest exploring why this had become his ambition.

As I dropped him off at his home, I thought about what I wanted to be and why. What do I call myself when no one is looking? Although I often fall short, underneath it all I have a true desire to be one of God's people. To me those are the coolest people of all. Some are even rock stars!

—Christine

> "The more you understand your true identity and purpose, soul deep, the more it will influence everything in your life."
>
> Michelle D Craig
>
> "Eyes to See," Oct. 2020

Doctrine and Covenants 63:9–10

Faith cometh not by signs, but signs follow those that believe. Yea, signs come by faith, not by the will of men, not as they please, but by the will of God.

First Things First

I love raising baby chicks and enjoying the fresh eggs hens provide. Laying eggs is hard work. You can hear the poor things saying buck-buck-buck just as a hen lays an egg or is preparing to lay one. Can you imagine if a hen woke up one morning and said, "I want an egg!" without doing any work herself?

Faith is like that sometimes. We have to have faith before we see the magic happen. When we faithfully follow the guidance or commandments we have been given, blessings come our way. Think of Moses and the brass serpent. By looking upon it, healing was found. And what about tithing? It's a principle of trust—a small offering leading to an overflow of heavenly blessings. If we want miracles to happen in our lives, we have to heed the counsel President Russell M. Nelson gave us: "The Lord will bless *you* with miracles *if* you believe in Him, 'doubting nothing.' Do the spiritual work to seek miracles. Prayerfully ask God to help you exercise that kind of faith" ("The Power of Spiritual Momentum," Apr. 2022).

—Dru

> "Every book of scripture demonstrates how willing the Lord is to intervene in the lives of those who believe in Him."
>
> **Russell M. Nelson**
> "The Power of Spiritual Momentum," Apr. 2022

Doctrine and Covenants 63:15–16

Let such beware and repent speedily, lest judgment shall come upon them as a snare. . . . He that looketh on a woman to lust after her, or if any shall commit adultery in their hearts, they shall not have the Spirit.

The Snare of Pornography

A snare is a trap for catching birds and small animals. Usually, there is a noose made of wire or rope that is hidden so that the unsuspecting prey will walk into the noose unaware. Then, the noose is pulled and the animal is bound, unable to escape. The purpose of a snare is to destroy through deception.

Recently, I wanted to add Instagram on my phone so I could follow my children and grandchildren. The home page of the app finally came up on my phone. There was a picture of a naked woman. I screamed. I was so shocked. I did not ask for this picture. I did not want this picture on my phone, yet it was thrown into my face without me looking for it.

The snare of pornography is a noose that binds. Pornography is not hidden anymore. It is thrown at you, whether you want to see it or not. To be safe from the snare, we cannot enter into platforms or apps where the possibility of seeing such things is highly probable. When we do, we need to immediately get rid of them, rather than follow them into the noose that binds.

—Marianna

"If we are not careful with our thoughts, words, and actions, we may end up being entangled by the cunning tricks of the enemy, destroying our relationships with the people around us and our loved ones."

Ulisses Soares

"Followers of the Prince of Peace," Apr. 2023

Doctrine and Covenants 63:23

But unto him that keepeth my commandments I will give the mysteries of my kingdom, and the same shall be in him a well of living water, springing up unto everlasting life.

Reverse Osmosis Water

I am kind of a water snob. In our last two homes, we have had a special water system installed called a reverse osmosis system. It removes all the impurities in the water. No matter what is in the water line, the water is made safe to drink. Reverse osmosis water tastes amazing. Once you taste it, you won't want anything else.

Christ is called by many names, one of which is the Living Water. Because of Him, all the impurities and flaws of mortality can be removed. Once you experience this kind of love, you won't want anything else. Jesus's grace is everlasting and gives life like a spring of living water.

That sounds simple. But remember, we need to make the choice to receive His love.

—Ganel-Lyn

> "If some of you are looking to fill what some call 'a bucket list,' this is it: fill your bucket with oil in the form of the living water of Jesus Christ, which is a representation of His life and teachings."
>
> Ronald A. Rasband
>
> "Hosanna to the Most High God," Apr. 2023

Doctrine and Covenants 63:25, 27

I, the Lord, hold [Zion] in mine own hands. . . . Wherefore, I the Lord will that you should purchase the lands, that you may have advantage of the world.

Advantage of the World

A few years ago the *Wall Street Journal* came out with an article about the Church's finances. Since then, The Church of Jesus Christ of Latter-Day Saints has been revealed to be one of the most prosperous Christian churches in the world and one of the largest private landowners in the United States.

Surprisingly, in response to these facts, I've heard some members express concern. One friend was very upset by a large land purchase the Church had made, wondering why we aren't given tithing refunds instead.

We pulled out our scriptures and read section 63 of the Doctrine and Covenants. Zion is in the Lord's hands, and He will inspire our leaders to use the Lord's resources so that His restored Church will have every "advantage of the world." As we see temples available to members everywhere and watch humanitarian aid make a difference in the lives of the most vulnerable, I am grateful to know that the Lord's kingdom on earth is prospering to our advantage as we head into perilous economic times.

—Christine

> "The added abundance of the Lord conveyed through your generous tithes has strengthened the reserves of the Church, providing opportunities to advance the Lord's work beyond anything we have yet experienced."
>
> **Neil L. Andersen**
> "Tithing: Opening the Windows of Heaven," Oct. 2023

Doctrine and Covenants 63:34
And the saints also shall hardly escape; nevertheless, I, the Lord, am with them, and will come down in heaven from the presence of my Father and consume the wicked with unquenchable fire.

Cougar Attack

Living near the base of a mountain, we often encounter wild animals like black bears, skunks, and other critters. One summer, a cougar roamed the valley, leaving a trail of dead animals in its tracks, including a goat head we found in our backyard. At dusk several days later, I took our two white labrador retrievers for a walk. Suddenly, I heard a loud growl directly behind me. My dogs bolted for home and so did I! A car approached from the opposite direction. Desperate to escape, I jumped onto the hood in a final attempt to save my life.

Perched on the car, I surveyed the scene. One of my labs had a small baby raccoon in its mouth, and the growls were coming from its frantic mother trying to retrieve her baby. The terror of fleeing from a vicious animal subsided and was replaced by a wave of relief as I realized what had happened.

Looking back, I am grateful for the Lord's protection in both real and imaginary dangers. In moments of fear and uncertainty, He is there for us, to provide comfort and assurance. When destruction seems imminent, He is there to fight our battles and bring us safely home.

—Dru

> "The Lord has pledged that He will "fight [our] battles, and [our] children's battles, and our children's children's [battles] . . . to the third and fourth generation!"
>
> Russell M. Nelson
> "Let God Prevail," Oct. 2020

Doctrine and Covenants 63:59

I am over all, and in all, and through all, and search all things, and the day cometh that all things shall be subject unto me.

All Things

Our family loves hiking in southern Utah. Recently, Steve and I hiked the Overlook Trail. The hike begins with a set of rock stairs. The rocks are gray and not spectacular. Along the way, there are glimpses of beauty, but again, nothing spectacular. At the end of the trail, the final view is magnificent. As I viewed miles of colored rock formations, glimpses of green, and a brilliant blue sky, I was awed by its beauty and inspired by the majesty of God's creations.

I feel the same way when I hold a newborn baby or work in my garden and view the blossoms on my peach tree and the final delicious fruit that I harvest. When I walk in the mornings and watch the sun come up over the mountain peaks, I feel a swelling in my breast and I know that God is real. All things bear testimony that there is a grand design and a celestial hand in Earth's creations and heavenly stars. Philosophers, writers, and poets have declared these thoughts much more beautifully than I have. Our Lord and Savior has said it best: "I am over all, and in all, and through all." Sometimes, like the hike, I may need to work to find beauty. But all things bear testimony. I look forward to the day when the Lord returns and transforms the telestial beauty of our earth to its paradisiacal glory.

—Marianna

> "And a brief gaze and reflection upon the wonders of the heavens arrayed with numberless stars and galaxies prompt the soul of the believing heart to proclaim, 'My God, how great thou art!'"
>
> Joseph W. Sitati
>
> "Patterns of Discipleship," Oct. 2022

Doctrine and Covenants 64:2

For verily I say unto you, I will that ye should overcome the world; wherefore I will have compassion upon you.

Flying

Last winter, my husband and I decided to get out of town and go to a place where we could warm up and renew our mental health. It was a glorious week of sand and sun. As we landed in Salt Lake City, we flew into one of the most massive winter storms of the year. Descending over the clouds, we had no idea what cold and ice was waiting for us below. Once we were on the ground, the airport had to be shut down because of how treacherous the weather was. Flying had protected us from the frigid winter temperatures.

President Nelson taught that the Savior can protect us from the "present precarious world." He said, "Because the Savior, through His infinite Atonement, redeemed each of us from weakness, mistakes, and sin, and because He experienced every pain, worry, and burden you have ever had, then as you truly repent and seek His help, you can rise above this present precarious world" (Russell M. Nelson, Oct. 2022).

Yoking ourselves with Christ acts as an airplane for life. Because of Him we can rise above hurt and heartache. Unlike a trip out of town, we can't escape the adversity of mortality. But through a covenantal relationship with God, we are empowered and equipped to endure.

—Ganel-Lyn

> "Because Jesus Christ overcame this fallen world, and because He atoned for each of us, you too can overcome this sin-saturated, self-centered, and often exhausting world."
>
> Russell M. Nelson
> "Overcome the World and Find Rest," Oct. 2022

Doctrine and Covenants 64:9

For he that forgiveth not his brother his trespasses standeth condemned before the Lord; for there remaineth in him the greater sin.

The Greater Sin

Forgiveness has always been difficult for me. It takes a lot to hurt my feelings, but once you do, my righteous indignation feels superglued to my heart. My mind struggles, and I ask, How can simply being upset by someone who is intentionally hurting me be the greater sin?

It is because sin always injures in a way that separates us from the Spirit. Often those who hurt us are not even aware of the havoc they have caused, or they simply don't care. Yet we can carry that concealed wound for years. A wound that can darken all the joy around us.

I love that in this scripture, the Lord doesn't only give us a commandment, but a way to live it better. He says, "Ye ought to say in your hearts—let God judge between me and thee" (Doctrine and Covenants 64:11). I never considered that not forgiving someone meant I was judging them and punishing them, which is the Lord's responsibility, not mine. Understanding that, I'll work harder to improve my self-talk and hand judgment over to the Lord so I can be healed.

—Christine

> "As disciples of Jesus Christ, we are asked to trust Heavenly Father and our Savior and not attempt to replace Them. Jesus Christ knows everyone's imperfections perfectly and will judge them perfectly."
>
> Gary B. Sabin
> "Hallmarks of Happiness," Oct. 2023

Doctrine and Covenants 64:33

Be not weary in well-doing, for ye are laying the foundation of a great work. And out of small things proceedeth that which is great.

Saturday Morning Blues

It was one of those days when all the kids woke up on the wrong side of the bed, bickering over the smallest things. Early in the afternoon, my husband announced that our family had been asked to clean the church building. My children acted as if he had asked them to trek a thousand miles across the plains. Nevertheless, we finally got everyone into the car and headed to the chapel to start the task.

To our amazement, once we began working, everyone started getting along and even began to tease and have fun with each other. As we finished up and drove home, we couldn't help but notice the stark contrast from the tense ride to the church earlier. This experience reminded us that serving others is the key to finding joy. When we focus on serving instead of dwelling on our own needs, happiness will follow.

—Dru

> "When we love and serve the Lord and love and serve our neighbors, we will naturally feel more happiness that comes to us in no better way."
>
> M. Russell Ballard
> "The True, Pure, and Simple Gospel of Jesus Christ," Apr. 2019

Doctrine and Covenants 64:34

Behold, the Lord requireth the heart and a willing mind; and the willing and obedient shall eat the good of the land of Zion in these last days.

Willing and Obedient

The behavioral scientist Dr. John B. Watson experimented with classical conditioning on a young child, Albert. Originally, Albert loved to play with anything white, cuddly, and fuzzy. Dr. Watson would cause a loud noise to sound every time Albert played with something white and fuzzy. This frightened Albert. Over time, after experiencing this fear over and over again, the toddler developed fear anytime he even saw something white and fuzzy. Through this unethical experiment, Dr. Watson illustrated that humans can be conditioned to feel fear or enjoyment.

Similarly, the Lord could condition us to always do what is right. If every time we chose the right we were immediately blessed, then we would become conditioned to doing it. Our agency would be compromised because we would not be doing it willingly, but rather we would be conditioned to be obedient.

The early Saints were not immediately blessed for their obedience to the Lord. They experienced hardship and persecution. But their willing obedience to God, in spite of these hardships, illustrated that they were prepared for the future latter-day Zion.

—Marianna

> "Some misunderstand the promises of God to mean that obedience to Him yields specific outcomes on a fixed schedule. . . . If life doesn't fall out precisely this way or according to an expected timetable, they may feel betrayed by God. But things are not so mechanical in the divine economy."
>
> D. Todd Christofferson
>
> "Our Relationship with God," Apr. 2022

Doctrine and Covenants 66:2

Blessed are you for receiving mine everlasting covenant, even the fulness of my gospel, . . . that they might have life and be made partakers of the glories which are to be revealed in the last days.

What I Wished For

It was June 1, 1991. Rob and I were being sealed in the Portland Oregon Temple (in Lake Oswego). The sealer never said my name correctly, but it was nonetheless a beautiful ceremony. We had big plans for how life would go. It didn't go the way we thought it would. Now, thirty-three years later, I can look back and see how making and keeping our covenants has made all the difference.

Some marriages end, no matter how hard the people involved try to stay on the covenant path. What I wished for back in Portland was a life of loving and learning. That has happened, although sometimes that loving and learning hurts.

But as we make and keep covenants, we stay in a relationship with God, even when other relationships struggle or end. Trust in God. He knows your name. You just need to choose to receive what He has to offer.

—Ganel-Lyn

> "Consider a marriage covenant. The wedding date is important, but equally important is the relationship forged through the life lived together afterward.
> The same is true with a covenant relationship with God. . . . He invites each of us to come as we are . . . and to 'press forward' . . . trusting that His promised blessings will come."
>
> **Emily Belle Freeman**
> "Walking in Covenant Relationship with Christ," Oct. 2023

Doctrine and Covenants 66:3

You are clean, but not all; repent, therefore, of those things which are not pleasing in my sight, saith the Lord, for the Lord will show them unto you.

Clean but Not All

One day while attending the temple, I was walking out of the dressing room in my whites when someone pointed to a huge ink spot near my pocket. A pen in the bottom of my bag had leaked. Though the rest of the dress was perfect and lovely, the large spot made me feel inappropriate for temple service. I ran to the bathroom and scrubbed the fabric with hand soap, praying it would do the trick.

Section 66 of the Doctrine and Covenants was given to William McLellin, a recent convert from Paris. His call to repentance reflects many of us trying to walk the covenant path. We are mostly clean, although there is often a weakness that we try to hide from others or even ourselves. But we know it's there. Speaking of those spots or weaknesses, the Lord promises that as we draw near unto Him, He "will show them unto [us]."

Like the spot on my dress, which I normally would have ignored or hidden, being in the temple changed things. I tried frantically to clean it up. Shockingly, the spot came out completely. It seemed a miracle to remind me of the promise of repentance. I believe the combination of my focused scrubbing and pointed prayer made all the difference and still does.

—Christine

> "When we choose to repent, we choose to change! We allow the Savior to transform us into the best version of ourselves."
>
> Russell M. Nelson
>
> "We Can Do Better and Be Better," Apr. 2019

Doctrine and Covenants 66:8

He that is faithful shall be made strong in every place; and I, the Lord, will go with you.

Bloomers on the Calf

For a few years, my sister and I worked in the office of a coaxial cable company. It may sound boring, but things got wild at our annual company party. Someone came up with a competition called Bloomers on the Calf. The goal? One person had to wrangle a calf (weighing seventy-five to one hundred pounds) and twist its neck until it toppled over, while the other person slapped a pair of bloomers on it. And you won't believe it—the prize was a whopping two hundred dollars!

My sister and I looked at each other and thought, Why not? We'd never tackled a calf before, let alone put bloomers on one, but we could do this thing! So, there we were, me wrestling the calf and my sister trying to wrangle those bloomers on. It was like a scene out of an old comedy movie. But guess what? We won! Can you believe it?

To this day I still laugh thinking about our crazy idea and how we came out on top. Just as we conquered the rodeo challenge, if we are faithful to the Lord and determined to follow Him, He will make us strong with the ability to come out victorious as we face our challenges in life.

—Dru

> "Our greatest weaknesses can become our greatest strengths. We can be changed and "become new creatures." Weak things literally can 'become strong unto [us].'"
>
> Kevin S. Hamilton
>
> "Then Will I Make Weak Things Become Strong," Apr. 2022

Doctrine and Covenants 68:28

And they shall also teach their children to pray, and to walk uprightly before the Lord.

Too Hard to Resist

One evening, while my grandson was visiting for dinner, his mom reminded him, "Don't eat your chocolate pie until you finish your dinner." Despite her words, a few minutes later, she discovered chocolate smeared all over his hands and face. When she asked if he had eaten the pie, he shamefully dropped his head and replied, "No."

Teaching our children to walk uprightly before the Lord means instilling in them the importance of doing what is right in the eyes of God. There's another aspect to walking uprightly that comes to mind—it's about standing tall physically. When we walk uprightly before God, not only are we living in a way that pleases our Heavenly Father, but we're also carrying ourselves with confidence and dignity.

By teaching our children to walk uprightly before the Lord, we are empowering them to navigate life with a strong moral compass and a sense of self-assurance. Walking upright becomes a symbol of their steadfast commitment to living a life of purpose and righteousness, and it enables them to walk confidently on their journey of faith, knowing that they are pleasing to God.

—Dru

> "The health of any society, the happiness of its people, their prosperity, and their peace all find common roots in the teaching of children in the home."
>
> L. Tom Perry
>
> "Mothers Teaching Children in the Home," May 2010

Doctrine and Covenants 67:8

Neither can any natural man abide the presence of God, neither after the carnal mind.

The Natural Mind

In November 1831, a special conference was held with members of the Church in Hiram, Ohio. The conference centered on the publication of the revelations received by the Prophet Joseph Smith from the Lord. Some of the leaders of the Church thought the language of the revelations reflected Joseph's lack of education, even though the Lord assured them that the revelations contained righteousness "from the Father of lights" (v. 9). The Lord gave the doubters a challenge to see if they could write a revelation like the ones the Prophet Joseph had written. The Lord warned, "But if ye cannot make one like unto it, ye are under condemnation if ye do not bear record that they are true" (Doctrine and Covenants 67:8). And they could not.

Sometimes we may think that we can do a calling better than someone else. We may question their leadership abilities, their organizational abilities, and even their spirituality. But when we do that, it is our natural minds at work. Our natural minds may think: "I have a degree in business. I have been trained to lead meetings. This priesthood leader does not have the skills that I do." We don't understand the Lord's needs for that calling. He is in charge of His work, and our natural, carnal minds cannot understand or abide the presence of God.

—Marianna

"So the primary battle is between our divine and spiritual nature and the carnal natural man. . . . We can receive spiritual help through the influence of the Holy Ghost that can 'teach you all things.'"

M. Russell Ballard

"Giving Our Spirits Control over Our Bodies," Oct. 2019

Doctrine and Covenants 68:1

[Orson Hyde] was called by his ordination to proclaim the everlasting gospel, the Spirit of the living God, from people to people, and from land to land.

Feather River California Temple

I grew up in the best small Northern California town, about sixty miles north of Sacramento. It is diverse culturally and religiously. When a temple was announced there, the joy the locals felt was overwhelming. I was excited to invite some of my friends from junior high and high school who are not of our faith to the open house. Sitting in the celestial room and sharing my testimony with people I have known most of my life was a true gift.

We are all called to proclaim the gospel. It doesn't always include a black name badge. As we humbly share our beliefs, hearts are opened. Having a temple in my hometown is a miracle. That day in the Feather River Temple, I was reminded that conversion comes in different forms and ultimately from connection and communication. We don't have to force our faith on our friends. We just need to have real intent and be kind. And then trust God's timetable.

—Ganel-Lyn

> "When we humbly share our testimony of the Lord through our words and actions, the Holy Ghost confirms to those with real intent, open hearts, and willing minds that Jesus is indeed the Christ."
>
> Adilson de Paula Parrella
> "Bearing Witness of Jesus Christ in Word and Actions," Oct. 2023

Doctrine and Covenants 68:6

Wherefore, be of good cheer, and do not fear, for I the Lord am with you, and will stand by you.

Good Advice for Life

A recent John Hopkins study showed that our attitudes affect our health. Those with a positive attitude were 13 percent less likely to have a heart attack or stroke than those who weren't, even among those with a history of heart disease.

The study used four criteria for rating how positive a person was. The first was how cheerful they are. A related study showed that when a person smiles, even if it's a fake smile, it reduces their heart rate and blood pressure. We can see why the Lord says to "be of good cheer."

The next criteria was anxiety levels, which is the next advice in the above scripture—do not fear. The author of the novel *Dune* said, "Fear is the mind-killer." Rarely do we make our best decisions based on fear.

The last two criteria for positivity are being physically active and generally satisfied with your overall life. If the Lord is with us, then He'll keep us plenty busy, and we can feel peace when we look at what we've accomplished.

Yup, this one scripture covers it all. It's very similar to Alma's advice to his sons: "Look to God and live" (Alma 37:47).

—*Christine*

"Obedience paves the way for a joyful life today and a grand, eternal reward tomorrow."
Russell M. Nelson,
"Think Celestial," Oct. 2023

Doctrine and Covenants 69:8
Preaching and expounding, writing, copying, selecting, and obtaining all things which shall be for the good of the church, and for the rising generations that shall grow up on the land of Zion.

Finding Our Roots

Roots Tech has become an incredible opportunity for people to find out about their ancestors. With over three million people attending in person and online, the event has become a worldwide phenomenon that strives to help people find and keep records. The stories of our ancestors are important to collect, write, and publish, but our own stories and records are also important to document so that our posterity will know and understand who we are.

From the beginning of the organization of the Church, the Lord taught the Saints the importance of record keeping. John Whitmer was called as the first Church historian. He was to gather information by traveling "from place to place, and from church to church" (v. 7). His list of responsibilities included a charge from the Lord to preach, teach, write, copy, select, and collect "all things which shall be for the good of the church" (v. 8) with an eye on the needs of future generations.

As Church members, we are blessed to study the lives of previous generations and gain strength through them. We should also be keepers of our own personal story and records.

—Marianna

> "Connect the roots and branches in your living family tree. . . . We each have a story. Come discover yours."
>
> **Gerrit W. Gong**
> "We Each Have a Story," Apr. 2022

Doctrine and Covenants 70:9

Behold, this is what the Lord requires of every man in his stewardship, even as I, the Lord, have appointed . . . unto any man.

Free Car

One of my favorite memories was when our family gave away a car. We didn't have a lot. We had planned on selling this car, but then a whole neighborhood was devastated by a landslide. One family lost everything they owned, including all of their cars. After shoveling mud from homes, we drove home and got the keys to give the car to this deserving family.

Fast forward a decade, and our son was learning to drive. His Young Men leader secretly worked on a car to give to Cameron. Our boy was overwhelmed with gratitude when he drove that little red car for the first time. Instead of selling his car to go on a mission, he decided to give his car away. And so it went.

President Spencer W. Kimball taught, "We are stewards over our bodies, minds, families, and properties. . . . A faithful steward is one who exercises righteous dominion, cares for his own, and looks to the poor and needy" ("Welfare Services: The Gospel in Action," *Ensign*, Nov. 1977, 78). Nothing we have is really ours. Our stuff, relationships, and time are all stewardships. We need to share what we have as if it's God's. Because it is.

—Ganel-Lyn

> "Review individually and as families the stewardships for which we have responsibility and accountability . . . knowing we are ultimately accountable to God."
>
> Quentin L. Cook
>
> "Stewardship—a Sacred Trust," Oct. 2009

Doctrine and Covenants 70:14

In your temporal things you shall be equal, and this not grudgingly, otherwise the abundance of the manifestations of the Spirit shall be withheld.

The Law of Consecration Now

As a young mother, I was called in the middle of the night to watch my ministering sister's children while she took her disabled son to the hospital. This was not the first time she had to make such a trip, and the cost in dollars, time, and emotional stability were taking their toll.

As she was preparing to leave, she turned to me and said, "We are at the bottom of the barrel with everything. What will happen when we are asked to live the law of consecration?"

"You'll get whatever you need!" I laughed, but then I turned to her and said, "You're giving over a hundred percent to raising this family righteously and taking care of your son. You are already giving all your resources to the building of the kingdom."

As she left, I felt strongly she was living the law of consecration now. If we are truly doing our best and using our resources to build the kingdom of God as the Spirit directs, we are living that covenant, even if our resources are kept in our own bank accounts. Like my friend, we can and should live the law of consecration now.

—Christine

"We can partner with the Savior to help provide temporal and spiritual relief for those in need—and in the process find our own relief in Jesus Christ."

Camille N. Johnson

"Jesus Christ Is Relief," Apr. 2023

Doctrine and Covenants 71:6
For unto him that receiveth it shall be given more abundantly, even power.

Enough Is Enough

One summer, our garden decided to bless us with an overabundance of zucchinis. It seemed like every time we turned around, another one had sprouted overnight, leaving us with more zucchini than we knew what to do with. We tried everything from grilling to baking, but they just kept coming. Eventually, we found ourselves with such a massive supply that we didn't know where to store them anymore.

In a moment of desperation, we remembered the scripture in Malachi 3:10, which says, "Prove me now herewith . . . if I will not open you the windows of heaven, and pour you out a blessing, that there shall not be room enough to receive it." With that in mind, we decided to embrace the squashy overload and get creative. We started leaving baskets of these delicious delights on our neighbors' doorsteps, accompanied by a note that said, "May your summer be as bountiful as our harvest!" Needless to say, our neighbors were both amused and grateful for the unexpected gifts, and we had a good laugh about our zucchini adventures that summer. We learned a valuable lesson that when God blesses us abundantly, we can find happiness by sharing the overflowing harvest of His goodness with those around us.

—Dru

> "We as a people must recognize that we have been blessed abundantly with the resources of this world; yet we know that whatever we have is the Lord's and that he has blessed us with these things to see how we will use them."
>
> Franklin D Richards
> "The Law of Abundance," Apr. 1971

Doctrine and Covenants 71:9–10

There is no weapon that is formed against you shall prosper; And if any man lift his voice against you he shall be confounded in mine own due time.

In Mine Own Due Time

Waiting is tough. I like to plan what my life will be like and what is going to happen when. The problem is that it never happens the way I planned. Usually, my plans take a lot longer to happen than I had hoped. The older I get, the more I realize that the Lord is in charge, not me, when it comes to timing.

For the first decade of our married life, we were very poor. We lived without furniture and very little in the way of material goods, spending all of our money on our rapidly growing family. One day when I was feeling sorry for myself, I wrote a list of everything I would like to have someday—a home with enough bedrooms for all my children, a nice dining room set, a grandfather clock, a spiral staircase. Writing these things down was a fun activity, but I did not know when or if I would ever be able to afford them.

A decade later, I was unpacking boxes in our new home. I was sitting on my spiral staircase with the grandfather clock in the hallway. I found that piece of paper where I had written down my list. In the Lord's timing, I had been blessed with all those things I had wanted.

—Marianna

"Remember to be patient and trust in the Lord's timing. Guidance is given by an omniscient Lord when He 'deliberately chooses to school us.'"

Quentin L. Cook

"The Blessings of Continuing Revelation and Personal Revelation," Apr. 2020

Doctrine and Covenants 72:4

For he who is faithful and wise in time is accounted worthy to inherit the mansions prepared for him of my Father.

Cleaning Bathrooms

My mom, Lou Ree, is a master dishwasher and bathroom cleaner. Mom could gold medal in this if she competed in it as an event at the Olympics. Her heart is so good. Lou Ree is filled with charity and has been known to clean bathrooms for many neighbors and ward members in need. When she is visiting her adult children, Mom is the first to stand up and help with dishes. She is quick to help, and no one has to ask her. Lou Ree has never had a ton of wealth, but what she has, she gives.

I think about the countless people she has helped during her lifetime. Some of her service is known only by Heavenly Father. A record is kept of how faithful and wise she has been in using her time on earth. And I believe that all she has given will come back to her.

I can't wait to see the mansion that is being prepared for my sweet mother because of her charitable nature. Those who have lived humbly on earth and have always shared what they have been given with others can trust that God is preparing mansions for them in the eternities.

—Ganel-Lyn

> "Without charity, we are nothing and we cannot inherit the place the Lord has prepared for us in the mansions of our Heavenly Father."
>
> Ulisses Soares
>
> "Followers of the Prince of Peace," Apr. 2023

Doctrine and Covenants 73:3.4

It is expedient to translate again. . . . Continue the work of translation until it be finished.

The Lord's Purpose Fulfilled

When I was on my mission in England, I loved asking those interested in learning about the restored gospel of Christ to bring me their scriptures. Although most people didn't attend church, at that time the majority of them had a King James Version of the Bible. I loved reading the great prophecies of the Restoration from their own scriptures. It made accepting the Book of Mormon easier because we shared so much truth, as we had identical Bibles.

I was surprised to later find out that Joseph Smith had intended to publish the Book of Mormon and the Joseph Smith Translation of the Bible in a single volume. At his death, Emma kept the marked Bible that Joseph had used for the translation, and the Church did not have access to it, although portions were included in JS–Matthew and most of section 76 of the Doctrine and Covenants.

In 1979, the Community of Christ (formerly the RLDS Church) granted permission to include excerpts of the Joseph Smith translation in the footnotes of our current scriptures. I am grateful that we still share the same Bible with many other Christians but have access to those revelatory inclusions as well. Sometimes, I'm amazed how the Lord can make everything work out so well in His own due time.

—Christine

> "All is known by the Lord, and in time, we will see His sacred purposes fulfilled."
>
> Neil L Andersen
>
> "Tithing: Opening the Windows of Heaven," Oct. 2023

Doctrine and Covenants 74:7

But little children are holy, being sanctified through the atonement of Jesus Christ.

Jesus Loves Me

Like so many precious children, my granddaughter has a tender heart full of love for her family, friends, and Jesus. Each fast Sunday, she tries her best to share her testimony in her ward, offering a heartfelt witness of what He means to her. Recently, she chose to begin her journey on the covenant path by being baptized. As part of the baptismal program, she sang a children's song, "Gethsemane" by Melanie Hoffman. My heart was full of love for her and my Savior. The words of the song were a gentle reminder that Jesus demonstrated His great love for us by willingly going to Gethsemane, offering us the gift of eternal life.

> The hardest thing that ever was done,
> The greatest pain that ever was known,
> The biggest battle that ever was won—
> This was done by Jesus! The fight was won by Jesus!
> Gethsemane. Jesus loves me,
> So He gave His gift to me in Gethsemane.

Children are priceless gifts of God. They are Christlike examples in countless ways. Through their innocence and sincerity, they teach us profound truths about faith and the simplicity of love.

—Dru

> "These precious children of God come to us with believing hearts. . . . They are often the first to love and the first to forgive."
>
> Jean A. Stevens
>
> "Become as a Little Child," Apr. 2011

Doctrine and Covenants 75:3

Behold, I say unto you that it is my will that you should go forth and not tarry, neither be idle but labor with your might.

Saturday Chores

Saturday chores are always difficult to do. It doesn't matter how old you are. Because every week is tough, all you want to do is sleep in Saturday morning and junk out. The last thing anyone wants to do is chores.

In order to get my family to work on Saturdays, I tried to think of ways to make it fun. I put chores and fun activities in a jar and each person had to pick five. I also planned a fun outing as soon as everyone had done their jobs. These activities improved our Saturdays greatly.

Missionary work can feel like Saturday chores. It's something we know that we are supposed to do. But we want to tarry and be idle and definitely not labor with all our might.

Yet, as members of the Church, we have a responsibility to spread the good news to those who have not heard it. How can we make missionary work fun? Some ideas may include using social media to spread the word, inviting people to a ward activity, or giving the gift of the Book of Mormon to your friends with your testimony in it. Be creative and have fun spreading the good news!

—Marianna

> "He bids us labor in the vineyard with our might this 'last time,' and He labors with us. It would probably be more accurate to say He permits us to labor with Him."
>
> D. Todd Christofferson
>
> "Preparing for the Lord's Return," Apr. 2019

Doctrine and Covenants 75:16

And he who is faithful shall overcome all things, and shall be lifted up at the last day.

Carry-On Luggage

I love traveling. But when it comes to packing, I have some anxiety. I tend to pack more than everyone else in my family and put all the extras in my carry-on luggage. Books, my computer, medicine, and journals help me feel at home when I am away from home. My suitcases have wheels, which make it easier to walk through the terminals. But wheels don't help me lift my carry-on and store it in the overhead compartments.

After I shattered my left wrist, it became much more difficult to lift my luggage. I tend to be a bit overly independent and don't always remember to ask for help. When I am traveling with my husband, Rob, he is great at noticing and offering to step in and help. He can safely and easily lift my carry-on and place it into the overhead compartments. What is hard for me is effortless for him—no matter how many books I pack.

That's the way it is with God. What is difficult and heavy for us is totally possible for Him. That includes us, even the heaviest of us. If we remain faithful, ask for help, and rely on Christ's Atonement, we can rest in the assurance that we will be lifted up at the last day.

—Ganel-Lyn

> "Exercising faith in our Savior, Jesus Christ, helps us overcome discouragement no matter what obstacles we encounter."
>
> Carl B. Cook
>
> "Just Keep Going—with Faith," Apr. 2023

Doctrine and Covenants 76:10

For by my Spirit will I enlighten them, and by my power will I make known unto them the secrets of my will.

Enlightenment

Recently, I have worked as a grader at a local college. One of the real challenges I've faced is that some students use ChatGPT exclusively instead of doing their own work, but it is very difficult to tell the truth. Discerning between what is real and what is illusion has never been more difficult. As our access to information increases, so does the likelihood that what we are reading is actually misinformation. Life has never been so confusing.

In section 76, the Lord promises the faithful that His Spirit will enlighten us. According to the Merriam-Webster dictionary, enlightenment is being "freed from ignorance and misinformation." Of course, the Spirit may not enlighten us on every matter, but we are promised that by His power we will know "the secrets of [His] will." And as long as I know what to do, I can move forward with faith.

With my grading, I realized I could simply go to the source and see how closely it matches. We all need to base our beliefs on the source of truth, which is the Spirit, for He testifies of Jesus Christ.

—Christine

> "But in the coming days, it will not be possible to survive spiritually without the guiding, directing, comforting, and constant influence of the Holy Ghost."
>
> Russell M. Nelson
>
> "Revelation for the Church, Revelation for Our Lives," Apr. 2018

Doctrine and Covenants 76:20

And we beheld the glory of the Son, on the right hand of the Father, and received of his fulness.

This Is the Christ

Elder James E. Faust penned the words to one of the most beautiful songs I have ever heard, "This Is the Christ." As I think about the lyrics of this song, I feel a profound sense of reverence and gratitude wash over me. The description of hearing the Savior's voice and witnessing His presence fills me with humility, reminding me of the sacredness of His atoning sacrifice. I stand in awe of the Savior's love and mercy.

As I read about Christ's agony in Gethsemane and the drops of blood He shed for me, I am overcome with emotion. The thought of His unspeakable suffering and selfless sacrifice brings tears to my eyes, yet it also fills me with an overwhelming sense of love and gratitude.

In moments like these, I am reminded of my relationship with the Savior and His infinite love for me. I feel a deep connection to Him. Through these words of this inspired song, I am reminded of the sacred privilege we have to know and worship the holy Son of God, our Savior and Redeemer.

—Dru

> "I witness that the day will come when every knee will bow and every tongue confess that Jesus is the Christ."
>
> Neil L. Andersen
>
> "We Talk of Christ," Oct. 2020

Doctrine and Covenants 76:29–30

Wherefore, he maketh war with the saints of God, and encompasseth them round about. And we saw a vision of the sufferings of those with whom he made war and overcame.

We Shall Overcome

I was a young teenager during the Civil Rights Movement. I was living in New Jersey when Martin Luther King Jr. gave his famous "We Shall Overcome" speech in 1965 at Temple Israel of Hollywood. He said, "We shall overcome. We shall overcome. Deep in my heart I do believe we shall overcome. And I believe it because somehow the arc of the moral universe is long, but it bends towards justice." This became the mantra of the followers of Dr. King and a message of hope for all the downtrodden in America.

The Saints were also downtrodden and persecuted for their beliefs. Neighbors and community leaders made war with the Saints and encompassed them, ousting them from their homes.

But the hope of the Saints was that the Lord would overcome their enemies. The arc of the moral universe does bend toward justice, even though that arc may be long. The Saints experienced that too. When we feel downtrodden or depressed, we can have the same hope that through the help of the Lord, we can overcome.

—*Marianna*

"[Satan] knows of your divine heritage and seeks to limit your earthly and heavenly potential by using the three Ds: deception, distraction, and discouragement."

Peter M. Johnson

"Power to Overcome the Adversary," Oct. 2019

Doctrine and Covenants 76:53

And who overcome by faith, and are sealed by the Holy Spirit of promise, which the Father sheds forth upon all those who are just and true.

Faith Fruit Snacks

Wouldn't it be great if when we feel low on faith, we could just eat a few "faith fruit snacks" and whoop—immediately our faith grows? Of course, it isn't like that.

Faith is not knowing; it is hoping, believing, trusting, and trying. I love the example of the woman with the issue of blood and her decision to try one more thing after investing all her time and money for thirteen long years. After she touches the hem of the Savior's robe, He tells her that her healing came because of her faith. I am sure she wondered, What faith?

Over those many years of being sick, her efforts hadn't led to the healing she was seeking. But during the years of disappointment, her faith was growing strong and leading to the miracle with Jesus.

Mortality is about walking by faith and with our agency, putting ourselves in a place to ultimately receive the Holy Spirit of Promise and other spiritual gifts of God. Faith can be messy, but it's not fruit snacks.

—Ganel-Lyn

> "We are to 'walk by faith, not by sight' (2 Cor. 5:7). Life is so designed that we are to 'overcome by faith,' not by intellectual acuity or wealth or political prowess."
>
> Neal A. Maxwell
>
> "Lest Ye Be Wearied and Faint in Your Minds," Apr. 1991

Doctrine and Covenants 76:86–88

These are they who receive not of his fulness in the eternal world, but of the Holy Spirit through the ministration of the terrestrial; and the terrestrial through the ministration of the celestial.

Ministers Forever

Recently I came across this quote by Sister Jean B. Bingham: "And what better way to prepare to meet Him than to strive to become *like* Him through lovingly ministering to one another!"

President Joseph F. Smith taught that the faithful who have passed away in this dispensation continue to preach the gospel to those in darkness in the spirit world. He said that the good sisters chosen to serve in the House of God for both the living and the dead would be empowered to preach the gospel and minister to women in the spirit world, similar to the elders and prophets' roles for men (*Gospel Doctrine*, 460–461).

Over the years, many who have ministered to me or with me have become my closest friends. Their selfless Christlike service has created bonds of compassion and unity. As we love and minister to those within our influence, we express our love for Jesus through faithful service to Him. This service, whether in this life or the next, deepens our connections and strengthens our faith.

—Dru

"We see faithful women who understand the power inherent in their callings and in their endowment and other temple ordinances. . . . These are spiritually strong women who lead, teach, and minister fearlessly in their callings with the power and authority of God!"

Russell M. Nelson

"Ministering with the Power and Authority of God," Apr. 2018

Doctrine and Covenants 76:114–116

Great and marvelous are the works of the Lord, and the mysteries of his kingdom which he showed unto us.

Unlocking Secrets

Young adult fiction often has a teenage protagonist who needs to solve a mystery surrounding his or her baffling bloodline or a family secret. It often turns into a quest for solving a mystery that has stumped mankind for ages. The main characters of these stories are usually given a clue, sometimes an amulet or an item passed to them by a curious-looking stranger. They are told that they must find the answer through a series of strange quests. Often, the youths have help along the way, but they are told to keep their quest a secret or evil people will get in their way and try to stop them.

Unlocking the mysteries of the Lord's kingdom is not like a blockbuster movie or a young adult novel. Instead, the only way that we can see and understand these mysteries is through the power of the Holy Spirit, a gift given to us at baptism. But, we must receive this gift in order to use it. We receive it by following the Lord's commandments, always remembering Him, and taking His name upon us. The temple is also a place where we gain an understanding of the mysteries of God. It is through our faith in the Savior that we unlock the mysteries of His kingdom.

—Marianna

> "Allowing God to prevail in our lives begins with faith that He is willing to guide us. . . . It is our faith that unlocks the power of God in our lives."
>
> **Russell M. Nelson**
>
> "Christ Is Risen: Faith in Him Will Move Mountains," Apr. 2021

Doctrine and Covenants 76:70–71, 81

These are they whose bodies are celestial, whose glory is that of the sun, even the glory of God . . . they who are of the terrestrial, whose glory differs . . . even as that of the moon differs from the sun. . . . We saw the glory of the telestial, which glory is . . . even as the glory of the stars.

A Sun or a Star

Most scientists today consider our sun an ordinary star. Other stars have been found that are up to one hundred times larger. But our sun has a huge effect on our planet because it is near us. Our sun literally holds our solar system together with its gravitational force. It provides the heat and light necessary for the earth to support life. Without the sun, our planet would be dead.

In contrast, the moon holds no light at all. It merely reflects the sun's light as though it were its own. How appropriate these symbols are in explaining the concept of degrees of glory.

Some people only want a pale reflection of truth. They want the feel of the sun without the work, and they enjoy the glory of the moon. Others get distracted by faraway ideas and try to make those their suns. In so doing, they simply get lost.

Let us remember what brings life eternal. When we stay close to the *Son* through our choices and actions, His influence changes who we are. That is how we become like the Son.

—Christine

"True joy rests on our willingness to come closer to Christ and witness for ourselves."

Bonnie Cordon

"Never Give up an Opportunity to Testify of Christ," Apr. 2023

Doctrine and Covenants 76:92–93

And thus we saw the glory of the celestial . . . where God, even the Father reigns . . . before whose throne all things bow in humble reverence.

Reverence Is a Waterfall

Have you ever watched a waterfall and stood in awe of its beauty? My grandparents had a cabin up behind Sundance (a ski resort near Provo, Utah), and we would walk to Stewart Falls. In the spring the waterfall was especially full, billowing water off the cliff face with such power that the spray would soak you. But it wasn't the beauty that had you spellbound. It was the power. Those falls were lethal and exuded strength that continued without ceasing in a way that's hard to comprehend. The feeling of respecting that power is reverence.

The Primary children sing a song that says, "Reverence is more than just quietly sitting, it's thinking of Father above." But it's more than simply thinking about Him. It's seeing His power. It's realizing that He has more power than the greatest waterfall, than all the oceans. He has power over life and death and is willing to grant us that power as we reverence Him and seek to understand His commands and live by our covenants.

Reverence is what you feel in the presence of a real king, even the King of Kings.

—Christine

> "Let us always speak with warm and reverent gratitude for God's work and glory and the merits, mercy, and grace of Jesus Christ and His atoning sacrifice."
>
> Gerrit W. Gong
>
> "Love Is Spoken Here," Oct. 2020

Doctrine and Covenants 77:3

That which is spiritual being in the likeness of that which is temporal; and that which is temporal in the likeness of that which is spiritual; the spirit of man in the likeness of his person.

Bonnie's Funeral

When I was nine years old, my baby sister, Bonnie, died. She was born with a heart defect and spent a year at home with her family. Then she returned to the hospital for another heart surgery—and she never came home again.

Her funeral included an open-casket viewing. I remember staring at Bonnie's little lifeless body, just wishing her to open her eyes. I knew she was my little baby sister. She looked like her but at the same time did not look like her. That was one of my earliest testimonies of the connection between the spirit and the body. Bonnie's personality and light were not from her beautiful blue eyes but from her beautiful spirit.

In the Prophet Joseph's observations about the Revelation of St. John, we learn that the spirit looks like the body but that the spirit is where the personality and life come from.

—Ganel-Lyn

> "The spirit provides the body with animation and personality. In this life and in the next, spirit and body, when joined together, become a living soul of supernal worth."
>
> Russell M. Nelson
> "Thanks Be to God," April 2012

Doctrine and Covenants 77:11

What are we to understand by sealing the one hundred and forty-four thousand, out of all the tribes of Israel?

Who Are the 144,000?

When we lived in Missouri, our stake president held a stake priesthood meeting. My oldest son had just been ordained a deacon and was thrilled he could go with my husband. When they came home, they both had pins on their lapels that said 12^2 M. I scratched my head and asked them what it meant.

"It stands for the 144,000," my son explained.

I raised my eyebrows. "Really?"

He looked serious. "It's all about quorums. A complete quorum in God's kingdom consists of twelve even if there are more. So when all twelve tribes are complete, it is 12 times 12, or 144."

"Yes," I said, trying to follow. "What about the thousand?"

"That just means it's of God. Like one day is a thousand to the Lord, you know."

I nodded. "So, why are you wearing that pin?"

That's when he smiled. "Because I'm a worthy priesthood holder and part of a quorum, so I'm one of them!"

—Christine

"I bless you with the courage to repent daily and learn how to exercise full priesthood power."

Russell M. Nelson

"We Can Do Better and Be Better," Apr. 2019

Doctrine and Covenants 78:17

Ye are little children, and ye have not as yet understood how great blessings the Father hath in his own hands and prepared for you.

Buzz Lightyear

When my youngest son was almost three, he was obsessed with Buzz Lightyear from *Toy Story*. As his birthday approached, he excitedly wondered about the presents he might receive at his party. He had no idea that among his gifts was a Buzz Lightyear costume with wings and a talking action figure. We couldn't wait to see his little face light up when he finally got to unwrap his gifts on his special day. Although we thought he would love his gifts, we were surprised that he wore his new outfit every single day for the next two years . . . until he literally couldn't fit into it anymore!

The Lord compares His blessings to the anticipation of a child waiting for a gift. Just like the child eagerly awaiting a present without fully understanding its value, we may not always comprehend the full extent of the blessings God has in store for us. However, with faith and trust, we can eagerly anticipate the wonderful blessings He has prepared, knowing that they will bring us joy and happiness beyond measure when we finally receive them.

—Dru

"Those who come unto Christ, repent of their sins, and live in faith will reside forever in peace. Think of the worth of this eternal gift. Surrounded by those we love, we will know the meaning of ultimate joy as we progress in knowledge and in happiness."

Dieter F. Uchtdorf

"The Infinite Power of Hope," Oct. 2008

Doctrine and Covenants 78:19

And he who receiveth all things with thankfulness shall be made glorious.

Receiving with Thankfulness

Have you ever received a gift with great anticipation only to feel let down? The initial gratitude in your heart for the gift was replaced by disappointment.

I was expecting a baby. My father had a tradition of buying my mother a new robe, slippers, and nightgown with every new baby. He would buy her something to make her feel beautiful while she was recovering and living in her pajamas. I had mentioned this to my husband, hoping he would continue the tradition. After the baby was born, my husband handed me a package. I knew what it was. In my mind, I had a vision of a pink soft satin robe—something that would make me feel like a princess. When I opened it, I discovered the robe was made of a heavy, rough material and was a dark blue. I initially looked at the robe and tried to force a smile. I knew my husband had worked hard to find something for me, and I appreciated his effort. But right then, I was not thankful for the gift.

This baby was born in the middle of winter, and we lived in a cold and drafty apartment. After coming home from the hospital, I put the robe on. The bulky material kept me warm and comfortable. I became thankful for that robe. I had been wrong in not receiving it with thankfulness.

—Marianna

> "Failure to appreciate our blessings can result in a sense of dissatisfaction, which can rob us of the joy and happiness that gratitude engenders."
>
> Gary B. Sabin
> "Hallmarks of Happiness," Oct. 2023

Doctrine and Covenants 79:1

From place to place, and from city to city, . . . proclaiming glad tidings of great joy, even the everlasting gospel.

All the Good Stuff Is the Hard Stuff

I have taught my children that all the good stuff in life is also the hard stuff. Missions, marriage, and parenting are some of the most important stewardships of life. And they stretch us. As each of my kids has gone out to serve as full-time missionaries, I have reminded them that when they hit the hard times, God will be by their side.

Section 79 of the Doctrine and Covenants is about a mission call for Jared Carter. The record shows that he was able to baptize and bring some souls to the covenant path. But the success of a mission isn't dependent on the number of baptisms. It is measured by the willingness of the missionary to make the offering.

Whether it is a service mission, a mission at a historic site, or a mission in a far-off land, all efforts to help gather Israel are important. A mission is about proclaiming the gospel of Christ, wherever you are called and no matter how hard it may be.

—Ganel-Lyn

> "We were born at this time for . . . the gathering of Israel. When we serve as full-time missionaries, we will be challenged. . . . He understands what a difficult mission is. With His help, we can do hard things. He will be by our side."
>
> Marcos A. Aidukaitis
> "Lift Up Your Heart and Rejoice," Apr. 2022

Doctrine and Covenants 80:1

Go ye, go ye into the world and preach the gospel to every creature that cometh under the sound of your voice.

Am I Noisy Enough?

Okay, I'll admit it. I'm sort of noisy. It all comes from moving a lot growing up. I hated being surrounded by strangers, so my strategy was to start talking, trying to make those strangers my friends. Then I'd be comfortable.

Now, it happens in the grocery store. At the hairdresser. At the post office. If you are standing next to me, I'll probably leave knowing your life history. I can't help it.

But what if my small-talk was gospel focused? We are told to share the gospel with everyone under the sound of our voice. It doesn't have to be something brash or annoying. It could be reminding someone of the beauty of the temple, sharing my latest scriptural insight and asking for theirs, or rehearsing the highlights of a clever talk at church.

During some periods of my life I've found this easy, but with recent events, I haven't thought about it in a while. In fact, it is easy never to see other people at all when we shop online and work remotely. We have electronic voices with social media where we can be heard. And, maybe part of the assignment is to put our voice in places people can hear.

Challenge accepted, I've got something to pick up at the store.

—Christine

> "In whatever ways seem natural and normal to you, share with people why Jesus Christ and His Church are important to you."
>
> Dieter F. Uchtdorf
>
> "Missionary Work: Sharing What Is in Your Heart," Apr. 2019

Doctrine and Covenants 80:4
Therefore, declare the things which ye have heard, and verily believe, and know to be true.

Like a Lighthouse

As a young adult, I listened to the song "Like a Lighthouse" written by Michael Webb:

> Like a lighthouse standing bold against the gray,
> shining through the night to warn of dangers in our way.
> Like a lighthouse built on solid stone,
> shedding light on weary seamen,
> who have drifted far from home.

Like a beacon of light shining in the darkness, the gospel of Jesus Christ illuminates the path for those who are lost or struggling. Just as a lighthouse guides ships safely to shore, the teachings of Christ offer hope, direction, and salvation to all who heed them. As disciples of Christ, we have the opportunity to be like lighthouses, sharing the light of His love and truth with others. By reaching out with kindness and sharing our testimonies, we can help guide others through life's storms and lead them safely to Jesus Christ.

—Dru

"Each of us came to earth having been given the Light of Christ. As we follow the example of the Savior and live as He lived and as He taught, that light will burn within us and will light the way for others."

Thomas S. Monson
"Be an Example and a Light," Oct. 2015

Doctrine and Covenants 81:5

Succor the weak, lift up the hands which hang down, and strengthen the feeble knees.

Feeble Knees

After giving birth to twelve children, my knees and hips are definitely not as strong as before. (I like to blame it on children rather than old age.) It is difficult for me to bend down and pick up things from the ground or to get up after scrubbing floors. My feeble knees even make it difficult for me to bend down and get up when I kneel to pray. But I am not feeble in my desires to pray to God.

Section 81 was given to the Prophet when he was trying to organize the First Presidency. The first man he called to be his counselor, Jesse Gause, definitely had feeble knees and was excommunicated not long after he was called. Frederick G. Williams was to take his place, and the Lord warned Brother Williams that he should act "in prayer always, vocally and in thy heart, in public and in private" (v. 3). He was not to have feeble knees.

His other commission was to strengthen the feeble knees of others and to lighten the burdens of the struggling Saints. We, too, have the same commission. As a ministering sister, we have the opportunity to strengthen other sisters through charity and prayer.

—Marianna

> "What is relief? It is the removal or lightening of something painful, troubling, or burdensome, or the strength to endure it. . . . Brothers and sisters, Jesus Christ is relief."
>
> Camille N. Johnson
>
> "Jesus Christ Is Relief," Apr. 2023

Doctrine and Covenants 82:3

For of him unto whom much is given much is required; and he who sins against the greater light shall receive the greater condemnation.

Stretching Studios

Did you know there are places you can go to have someone stretch you? Stretching studios are spreading around the country. The idea is that if you regularly stretch, injuries are limited and strength is increased. The basic principle is that if you keep pushing your body, you will be able to do more.

Our mortality is like a lifelong stretching studio. As women of faith, we are expected to pray and patiently practice principles of faith toward eternal glory. Sometimes it looks like the rest of the world is always on vacation. No tithing paying, covenant making, or callings to serve in. But what happens when little is required? Little is given.

I love that these new stretching studios have people who support and help you move your body. We have that same thing in life, if we look for helpers along the way. You aren't alone in this.

—Ganel-Lyn

> "With these privileges comes great responsibility, for 'unto whom much is given much is required' and at times the demands of discipleship are heavy."
>
> Sheri L. Dew
> "We Are Women of God," Oct. 1999

Doctrine and Covenants 82:7

Go your way and sin no more; for unto that soul who sinneth shall the former sins return, saith the Lord.

The Former Sins Return

This scripture used to seem so unfair to me! One slipup and God puts you back to square one? In reality, the Lord isn't condemning us. He is warning us about the way our mortal minds and bodies work.

Years ago I visited the wife of the most faithful elders quorum president I'd ever met. She had stopped attending the ward because she smoked. I was so impressed by her strong testimony. She told me she quit smoking when she was baptized and enjoyed serving in the temple and the Church for years. Then her father grew ill, and her family came to sit in vigil. When he passed, she was sitting by her sister who was smoking, and she picked up her sister's cigarette without thinking.

Once she did, all the years of not smoking were gone, and she felt she couldn't quit again. I invited her to come to church anyway. She did and soon found the power to quit again, right before her husband was called as bishop.

Relapse is real, but even if our sins return, the Savior will help us to heal and return to Him if we keep trying.

—Christine

> "I plead with you to come unto Him so that He can heal you! He will heal you from sin as you repent. He will heal you from sadness and fear. He will heal you from the wounds of this world."
>
> **Russell M. Nelson**
>
> "The Answer Is Always Jesus Christ," Apr. 2023

Doctrine and Covenants 82:10

I, the Lord, am bound when ye do what I say; but when ye do not what I say, ye have no promise.

Promises Kept

When I was about eight years old, on a hot summer day in Tennessee, I went with Granddaddy to a nearby field to pick tomatoes. He promised that if I worked hard, I could enjoy an ice-cold bottle of Coca-Cola when we returned home. This wasn't just any soda bottle; the broken fridge on his porch nearly froze the sodas, leaving bits of floating ice at the top. As I worked hard, all I could think about was the reward waiting for me when we were done. That day, Granddaddy kept his word.

I often think about how important it is to keep our promises and commitments. Keeping our word shows that we have integrity and honor our agreements. Staying true to our promises, whether to God or others, helps us build trust, grow closer to each other, and connect in powerful ways.

Looking at the life of Jesus Christ, we see the best example of keeping promises and commitments. He always did what He said He would do and fulfilled every promise He made. His life teaches us the importance of being faithful and true to our word, just like He was.

—Dru

> "Our Savior, Jesus Christ, is our great Exemplar when it comes to making and keeping promises and covenants. . . . He has honored every one of His promises."
>
> Ronald A. Rasband
> "Standing by Our Promises and Covenants," Oct. 2019

Doctrine and Covenants 82:14

Zion must arise and put on her beautiful garments.

Put on Beautiful Garments

When I was a young mom, I would rise in the morning and throw on clothes that I thought were easiest to put on—usually sweats and a T-shirt. I found myself constantly feeling ugly and frumpy. I complained about it to my husband, who said, "Well, why don't you put on different clothes that make you feel better about yourself."

I thought about it. My excuse for putting on ugly clothes was that they were somehow faster to put on. But that was not the case; it takes just as long to put on ugly clothes as it does to put on something nice. Time was not the problem; it was my frame of mind. My husband was right. I started wearing dresses and cuter clothes, rather than sweatpants and T-shirts. I began to feel much better about myself. I realized that putting on nicer clothes is worth the effort.

Going to the temple allows us the opportunity to put on beautiful garments that represent our commitment to our covenants with the Lord. They make us look beautiful but also help us feel beautiful.

—Marianna

> "In preparation for my first trip to the temple, my mother and experienced Relief Society sisters helped me select the items I would need, including beautiful ceremonial clothing."
>
> Jean B. Bingham
>
> "Covenants with God Strengthen, Protect, and Prepare Us for Eternal Glory," Apr. 2022

Doctrine and Covenants 82:19

Every man seeking the interest of his neighbor, and doing all things with an eye single to the glory of God.

My True Motives

As Joseph Smith taught the early Church what it meant to build Zion, he suggested that as Saints we should seek the interest of our neighbor and do all things with an eye single to the glory of God. These should be our true motives, and both are based on love. That caused me to pause and consider my own motives.

When women I admire come to my house to visit, I run around beforehand like a crazy woman putting everything in place so they won't judge me as a terrible homemaker. More often than not, fear is my strongest motivator. It's exhausting.

In contrast, if I have a grandchild coming over, I often spend time focused on preparing a nice treat or fun activity to do together. Love is my strongest motivator. My time with those children feeds me, and I can't wait to see them again.

Love creates long-term change that feeds us rather than exhausts us. If we are struggling with enjoying our time in serving others and the Lord, we should look at what is driving us. Let the fear go and increase the love.

—Christine

> "May we each learn to speak and hear His love here, in our hearts and homes, and in our gospel callings, activities, ministering, and service."
>
> Gerrit W. Gong
> "Love Is Spoken Here," Oct. 2023

Doctrine and Covenants 83:6

And the storehouse shall be kept by the consecrations of the church: and widows and orphans shall be provided for, as also the poor.

Alone But Not Forgotten

When I was six years old, my father passed away, leaving my mother widowed for the second time. She faced the daunting task of caring for four young children alone. It must have been overwhelming for her, having to work long hours to meet the needs of her family by providing food, shelter, and protection. Having witnessed the difficulties of her widowhood, my heart goes out to those who find themselves without a spouse. I especially have tender feelings for children left without parents to care for them.

The term "widow" held deep meaning for the Savior Himself. He warned His disciples about the hypocrisy of those who appeared righteous but exploited widows.

May we all heed His timeless words encouraging us to show kindness and give generously of our means to provide for those in need: "Inasmuch as ye have done it unto one of the least of these . . . ye have done it unto me" (Matthew 25:40).

—Dru

> "The grieving widow, the fatherless child, and the lonely of heart everywhere will be gladdened, comforted, and sustained through our service."
>
> Thomas S. Monson
>
> "The Fatherless and the Widows—Beloved of God," Oct. 1994

Doctrine and Covenants 84:5

This generation shall not pass away until an house shall be built unto the Lord, and a cloud shall rest upon it, which cloud shall be even the glory of the Lord, which shall fill the house.

A Cloud and a Rainbow

The Lord often causes natural earthly manifestations to occur as an illustration of His love and glory. When the children of Israel fled the Egyptian Pharaoh, the Lord sent them a cloud to hide them from their enemies during the day and a pillar of fire to scare the evil soldiers away and bring the Israelites light and warmth at night (see Exodus 13).

My mother's funeral was held on a cloudy, misty day. Our family felt like nature was crying with us. But after the funeral, a beautiful, vivid rainbow pierced the sky and brought joy into our hearts. I will always be grateful for the manifestation of God's love for my family.

The Kirtland Saints were sacrificing so much to build the first temple in this dispensation. They were promised that after it was built, a cloud representing the glory of the Lord would fill His house. The Saints shouted with joy when they saw this fulfilled.

—Marianna

> "How much of life do we miss by waiting to see the rainbow before thanking God that there is rain?"
>
> Dieter F. Uchtdorf
>
> "Grateful in Any Circumstances," Apr. 2014

Doctrine and Covenants 84:33

For whoso is faithful unto . . . the magnifying their calling, are sanctified by the Spirit unto the renewing of their bodies.

The Crayon Monitor

An elementary school teacher gave each student in her class a job. There was a chalkboard monitor, a door monitor, a flag monitor, a paper monitor, and a trash monitor. The teacher had to stretch to find something for everyone, but she did.

Then a new little girl moved in. She asked the teacher what her job could be. The teacher said, "I don't have any jobs left." The little girl smiled. "What if I'm the crayon monitor? When we color, I'll collect all the broken crayons." It seemed like a silly job, but the teacher agreed.

The next day the little girl brought a big glittery box with her. When students left out their crayons or broke them, she would put the crayons in the box. She even brought extra crayons in cool colors and lent them out to people, and she complimented their pictures. Pretty soon during coloring time, everyone would ask for her advice or to borrow her special crayons.

When it was time to switch jobs, what job do you think all those children wanted to be? The crayon monitor because that little girl truly magnified her calling. Let's do the same.

—Christine

> "Keep an eternal perspective. Magnify your callings."
>
> Russell M. Nelson
>
> "A New Normal," Oct. 2020

Doctrine and Covenants 84:34

They become the sons of Moses and of Aaron and the seed of Abraham, and the church and kingdom, and the elect of God.

Elections versus Elected

Winning elections is based on the public agreeing with a politician's vision for their city, community, and country. The person running for election commits to doing certain things for his or her constituents. As a voter, you can vote for the person you agree with the most. Your vote allows you to make your voice and feelings heard.

I once ran a losing campaign for public office. I felt compelled to because of an issue I was worried about in the city. I put up signs, spoke in a debate, and tried to meet and talk with the people in my community. After my experience, I have a greater appreciation for the amount of work and effort it takes to get elected.

Becoming the elect of God is not an election. We do not need to debate the reasons we should be elected. Becoming the elect of God is up to God and no one else. It is not a vote. Instead, we must receive His priesthood, His servants, and Him in order to be elected of Him.

—Marianna

> "We are not elected or selected from applications. Without any specific professional preparation, we are called and ordained to bear testimony of the name of Jesus Christ throughout the world until our final breath."
>
> **Neil L. Andersen**
> "Following Jesus: Being a Peacemaker," Apr. 2022

Doctrine and Covenants 84:46
And the Spirit giveth light to every man that cometh into the world; and the Spirit enlighteneth every man through the world, that hearkeneth to the voice of the Spirit.

Turn on the Light

I have always been a little afraid of the dark. Many times, I have had to venture out into our pasture after sundown to feed livestock, turn off water hoses, or retrieve items from the shed. Each time, my heart would race, and I would feel relieved once I completed my task and hurried back inside. When I remembered to bring a flashlight, it provided comfort and reassurance, dispelling any fear of danger lurking in the shadows.

In John 8:12, Jesus declared, "I am the light of the world: he that followeth me shall not walk in darkness, but shall have the light of life." This scripture teaches that we must take action to receive His light. We must follow Him, and then His light will guide us. With Him by our side, we can walk confidently and not be afraid.

—Dru

> "The very moment you begin to seek your Heavenly Father, in that moment, the hope of His light will begin to awaken, enliven, and ennoble your soul."
>
> Dieter F. Uchtdorf
> "The Hope of God's Light," Apr. 2013

Doctrine and Covenants 84:85
Neither take ye thought beforehand what ye shall say; but treasure up in your minds continually the words of life, and it shall be given you in the very hour that portion that shall be meted unto every man.

Edge Pieces

When I put together a puzzle, I always start with the edge pieces. It helps me make sense of the big picture and find direction. Recently, I have been working on a puzzle where the edge pieces aren't coming together so easily. My son suggested that we work on the middle parts first. We sorted them by color and pattern. And then we tried to see what matched.

I feel like this is the pattern of faith and teaching. If we take time to read scriptures and treasure up conference messages, we will have the puzzle pieces. We may not know beforehand what to do or say, or what matches to make, but eventually we will. If we keep showing up, it will be given to us when we need the answers and the strength. Conversion is not a one-time decision or event. It is about daily choices of feeding our faith. That is what is meant by staying in our conversion.

When you are missing a piece of the puzzle, don't stop trying to move forward in faith on the sometimes bumpy, twisty path.

—Ganel-Lyn

> "Take more time to pray, to ponder, and to meditate on spiritual matters. You will have knowledge of truth poured out upon you and grow in your power to nurture others in your family."
>
> Henry B. Eyring
> "Women and Gospel Learning in the Home," Oct. 2018

Doctrine and Covenants 84:88

I will go before your face. I will be on your right hand and on your left, and my Spirit shall be in your hearts, and my angels round about to bear you up.

Angels Will Bear You Up

One year my children really wanted to go to a haunted corn maze at night. It was supposed to be terrifying and fun for those who think terrifying is fun. I was still recovering from an illness but agreed to go. As we started across the uneven ground between the eight-foot stalks of corn, I was struggling to keep my balance. It didn't help that ghouls dressed in black jumped out with chainsaws or shined flashlights in our eyes, blinding us to the potholes ahead.

At last, one of my sons noticed and took my arm. My husband took the other, and my youngest son walked in front of me to warn me about what was coming. Suddenly, the treacherous journey became a joy. Couched in the buffer of my protectors, I'd laugh at the actors attempting to scare me.

Those trying to do the Lord's will are given that same promise. The Lord will help them and send angels to bear them up. But like my sons and husband, we can choose to be those angels, reaching out to those struggling to stay on the covenant path and turning what might be scary into joy.

—Christine

> "I promise that if we are willing to serve, the Lord will give us opportunities to be ministering angels. He knows who needs angelic help, and He will put them in our path."
>
> Carlos A. Godoy
> "I Believe in Angels," Oct. 2020

Doctrine and Covenants 84:98

Until all shall know me . . . and shall be filled with the knowledge of the Lord, and shall see eye to eye.

Seeing Eye to Eye

In our bedroom my husband has a nice recliner that sits up against a big window facing the woods. He likes to sit and watch the wildlife go by. He'll say, "Hey, look at those deer!" or "That hawk sure hopes we let the chickens out."

One day I was lying in bed and Greg said, "Look at that moose! It's amazing."

I sat up and looked at the same window from across the room. "I can't see a moose."

"Yes, you can," said my husband. "It's right there. I know you can see it."

From where I was sitting there was no moose. But when I stood up and looked out the window next to him, I saw the moose in the garden eating our corn. "Nice," I said, not meaning it.

Often people do not see eye to eye because they have different perspectives. When the Lord comes and we are filled with His knowledge, we will all see eye to eye whether we enjoy it or not. That perspective is, as President Nelson said, "Think[ing] celestial."

—Christine

> "The Lord's perspective transcends your mortal wisdom. His response to your prayers may surprise you and help you think celestial."
>
> Russell M. Nelson
> "Think Celestial!," Oct. 2023

Doctrine and Covenants 84:106

And if any man among you be strong in the Spirit, let him take with him him that is weak, that he may be edified in all meekness, that he may become strong also.

Together Strong

In Luke 22, we are taught, "And when thou art converted, strengthen thy brother." This scripture underscores the importance of sharing our faith and supporting others in their spiritual journey. Conversion isn't just about personal growth; it prompts us to reach out and uplift those around us. As we deepen our commitment to follow Christ, our focus naturally turns outward, and we desire to extend a helping hand to others.

Building and reinforcing the faith of those around us requires empathy and patience. Over the years, family and friends have come to me with questions or doubts about various doctrines or teachings of the Church. In these moments, I strive to offer a nonjudgmental ear and listen to understand their perspective. Creating a safe space where they feel unconditionally loved allows each person to share openly from their hearts. When I am prayerful, seeking blessings from my Father in Heaven, He guides me to find words that strengthen faith and foster mutual understanding as I share my testimony. This is His work, and He will help us.

—Dru

> "Conversion is an offering of self, of love, and of loyalty we give to God in gratitude for the gift of testimony."
>
> David A. Bednar
>
> "Converted unto the Lord," Oct. 2012

Doctrine and Covenants 84:109

Let every man stand in his own office, and labor in his own calling; and let not the head say unto the feet it hath no need of the feet; for without the feet how shall the body be able to stand.

Hugs and Snacks

As newlyweds, my husband and I were called to serve as nursery leaders in our ward. We had just moved into our first apartment and didn't know anyone in the area. I remember feeling isolated from the other members and as if our efforts to care for ten toddlers made no difference at all.

When I became a parent myself, I wanted my children to have a positive experience when they started attending Primary. I quickly realized that these early experiences would influence their attitudes toward going to church for years to come. I was thrilled when they were greeted by kind, loving teachers who welcomed them with open arms and yummy treats.

Every calling in the Church matters and is important. Wherever we serve, let's do our best and allow others to witness God's love for them through our actions.

—Dru

> "Your obligation is as serious in your sphere of responsibility as is my obligation in my sphere. No calling in this church is small or of little consequence."
>
> **Gordon B. Hinckley**
>
> "This Is the Work of the Master," Apr. 1995

Doctrine and Covenants 85:6

Yea, thus saith the still small voice, which whispered through and pierceth all things, and often times it maketh my bones to quake while it maketh manifest.

The Power of His Voice

My daughter is a vocal coach. She helps people improve their singing and speaking in large public settings, especially when performing on stage. She has her students practice a variety of exercises to learn how to control their breathing and to focus the air coming out of their mouths. It is not necessarily volume that allows you to be heard. A loud noise is often not understandable, especially in a large, open space. But a penetrating sound, even a whisper, will enable people in a large auditorium to hear your voice.

The Spirit has complete control of His focus and breath. You can feel and hear the still, small voice of the Spirit because your heart will burn and your bones will shake. The Nephites described His voice this way: "It being a small voice it did pierce them that did hear to the center, insomuch that there was no part of their frame that it did not cause to quake; yea, it did pierce them to the very soul, and did cause their hearts to burn" (3 Nephi 11:3). We need to practice hearing Him and listening for His voice, even in a loud and noisy world.

The power of His voice will change us forever, if we willingly listen, hearken, and heed what He says to us.

—Marianna

> "In a world with so many competing voices, our Heavenly Father has made it possible for us to hear and follow His."
>
> Russell M. Nelson
>
> "Hearing His Voice," Apr. 2019

Doctrine and Covenants 85:8

Who was called of God and appointed, that putteth forth his hand to steady the ark of God shall fall by the shaft of death.

God's Not Stressed

Steadying the ark refers to the ancient event when the ark of the covenant was being moved. As the ark was in transit, it started to fall. Uzzah tried to stop the ark from falling by steadying it (see Samuel 6:1–11). Uzzah was struck dead when he responded in stress. Even though he meant well, Uzzah's response was too casual for something that represented the presence of God and His throne.

I often respond to the wobbly stewardships of life with stress instead of with trust in the sacred. Sometimes I have to remember that God is not stressed. He sees the beginning from the end. And I remind myself that if something hasn't worked out, it isn't yet the end. So, before you overreact to a child or coworker with an overreaching hand, ask God to show you how to wisely handle the situation.

—Ganel-Lyn

"I think there is no occasion for any person in this Church to fear for the destiny of the kingdom. We do not need to steady the ark."

Bruce R. McConkie

"Valiance to the Truth," Oct. 1947

Doctrine and Covenants 86:6
Pluck not up the tares while the blade is yet tender... lest you destroy the wheat also.

What Is a Weed?

According to the *Britannica* dictionary, a weed is a wild plant that grows quickly where it is not wanted and covers or kills more desirable plants. In the past, I've always considered the parable of the wheat and the tares (or weeds) to be about people. From reading section 86, I have discovered that an alternate interpretation could be that they are ideas. Wheat is truth, the building blocks for the bread of life. The tares are lies disguised as truth.

One way we can tell the difference is to look at how the idea was "sown" into our hearts. Concepts that are scripture-based or have come through inspiration are wheat. Tares are sown by those who desire the destruction of the Church or the praise of the world. It's important that we help those struggling and that we ask questions ourselves and search out the answers. There should be small tares among our wheat because that is how we learn both truth and empathy, but beware to not let those tares crowd out or kill the good wheat.

My mother used to say, "The grass is always greener where you water it." Let's take care to water those good seeds in our hearts and minds that have been planted by the Lord.

—Christine

> "I witness that fidelity to the covenants and ordinances of the Savior's restored gospel enables us to *press* on in the work of the Lord, to *hold* fast to Him as the Word of God, and to *heed* not the allurements of the adversary."
>
> David A. Bednar
>
> "But We Heeded Them Not," Apr. 2022

Doctrine and Covenants 86:11

Blessed are ye if ye continue in my goodness, a light unto the Gentiles, and through this priesthood, a savior unto my people Israel.

The Power to Save

My best friend was taking a lifeguard certification course and asked me to join her. I was not a good swimmer, but I liked spending time with my friend. The scariest part of the course was saving a drowning person. The woman who taught the class was very strong. She would be our drowning victim, and she loved trying to drown her rescuers. Our final test for the course was saving her and swimming her back one lap to the other end of the pool.

When it was my turn, she did everything she could to try to stop me. I needed to become stronger than her if I was going to save her and myself from drowning.

When I go to the temple, I can do the temple work by proxy for those who have died. I can save them from drowning, but I must first save myself and be strong enough to endure to the end so that I do not drown myself as well. Attending the temple saves us both from drowning.

I can become a savior of men (see Doctrine and Covenants 103:10) if I continue in His goodness, follow in His light, and do the temple work for others.

—Marianna

> "The gospel of Jesus Christ is a gospel of transformation. It takes us as men and women of the earth and refines us into men and women for the eternities."
>
> **Joseph B. Wirthlin**
> "The Great Commandment," Oct. 2007

Doctrine and Covenants 87:6
[By] sword and by bloodshed the inhabitants of the earth shall mourn; and with famine, and plague, and earthquake, and the thunder of heaven, and the fierce and vivid lightning also, shall the inhabitants of the earth be made to feel the wrath.

It Is Going to Get Harder

Elder Neal A. Maxwell wrote, "Yes, Armageddon lies ahead. But so does Adam-ondi-Ahman!" ("O, Divine Redeemer," October 1981). I love this reminder. The scriptures are clear about what is coming. A few of the top hits of an online search of the last days include war, bloodshed, and famine. But we have been promised that as intense as life will get in the last days, so will the miracles and good works of God increase.

As life gets harder and headlines become even more heartbreaking, are we becoming myopic about the bad? We must also seek the signs of Adam-ondi-Ahman. When Jesus comes again, all will kneel and proclaim that He truly is the Savior of the World. I don't know about you, but sometimes it feels easier to be afraid than it is to be hopeful.

Each night before bed, I write at least one sentence in my journal: "The miracle I saw today was ____." Instead of going to sleep fearful, I try to focus on the heavenly help I received that day. Yes, it is going to get harder, but it will also get more heavenly.

—Ganel-Lyn

> "Prophecies of the last days scared me and caused me to pray that the Second Coming would not come in my lifetime. . . . Now I pray for the opposite. . . . When Christ returns to reign, all of His creations will 'lie down safely.'"
>
> Allen D. Haynie
> "A Living Prophet for the Latter Days," Apr. 2023

Doctrine and Covenants 87:8

Wherefore, stand ye in holy places, and be not moved, until the day of the Lord come.

The Holy Place

The ancient temple at Jerusalem had an outer courtyard that all the faithful heads of households could enter to give sacrifice. The temple itself was very sacred, and the average covenant man could never enter. One had to be specially ordained and served only two days out of the year. First, he would enter the holy place where the menorah was lit and cleaned daily and the twelve large loaves of shewbread and wine were replaced weekly. At the end of that room was the veil, which covered the Holy of Holies, a place only the high priest entered once a year on the Day of Atonement to pray for the Saints.

I believe the Lord's admonition to stand in holy places is a reference to the holy place in His first temple. Not only is it a symbol that we should live within our temple covenants, but we should daily light and clean our candles that shine Christ's light in our homes through repentance, prayer, and study. Then weekly we should partake of the sacrament to turn our hearts to Him and remind us of our covenants.

How blessed we are to live in a time when all the faithful can enter the temple. But it is up to us to help keep the holy places sacred.

—Christine

> "If you hope to feel the Spirit, be in a place where the Spirit can easily dwell."
>
> Gary E. Stevenson
>
> "Promptings of the Spirit," Oct. 2023

Doctrine and Covenants 88:3–4

I now send upon you another Comforter. . . . This Comforter is the promise which I give unto you of eternal life, even the glory of the celestial kingdom.

Becoming a Pickle

While studying at Brigham Young University, I faced a challenging statistics class. The professor cautioned that many students struggled to earn above a C- and often had to retake the course. Instead of feeling discouraged, I saw it as an opportunity to prove him wrong. Driven by my determination to succeed, I sought guidance from a friend who served as the Department Chair of Statistics. His advice? "Become a pickle." I asked for clarification. He explained that just as an ordinary cucumber becomes a pickle when immersed in salt brine for an extended time, immersing myself in the language, processes, and logic of statistical calculations would eventually lead to understanding and success. I took his advice to heart. I diligently attended classes and labs, completed every homework assignment, and ultimately earned an A- in the course.

This experience taught me an important lesson: just like learning statistics takes time and effort, gaining eternal life is a process. By putting our trust in Jesus, staying on the covenant path, and faithfully enduring to the end, we can receive the greatest of all the gifts of God, even eternal life.

—Dru

> "Purifying and sealing by the Holy Spirit of Promise constitute the culminating steps in the process of being born again."
>
> David A. Bednar
>
> "Ye Must Be Born Again," Apr. 2007

Doctrine and Covenants 88:22

For he who is not able to abide the law of a celestial kingdom cannot abide a celestial glory.

Abide with Me

One of the definitions for the verb *abide* is "to accept or to act in accordance with a rule, law, or directive," and the second is "to tolerate" (*Webster's Dictionary*). The Lord invites us to abide by His law (or accept and act in accordance with it) so that we can abide (or tolerate) His presence. Tolerating His law is not abiding by His law. The Lord teaches us that "all kingdoms have a law given" (v. 36). If we do not abide celestial laws, then we cannot tolerate the light and knowledge given to celestial beings.

How can we know if we are abiding a celestial law? Parley P. Pratt gave us a standard to measure a celestial person: "In the presence of such persons one feels to enjoy the light of their countenances, as the genial rays of a sunbeam. Their very atmosphere diffuses a thrill, a warm glow of pure gladness and sympathy, to the heart and nerves of others who have kindred feelings, or sympathy of spirit" (*Key to Theology*, 100). What do people feel when they are in your presence? Do they feel the warmth of celestial light? Do they feel the Savior's love?

His invitation is "Abide with Me." And we can do so now.

—Marianna

> "Christ is everything to us and we are to 'abide' in Him permanently, unyieldingly, steadfastly, forever."
>
> **Jeffrey R. Holland**
> "Abide in Me," Apr. 2004

Doctrine and Covenants 88:63

Draw near unto me and I will draw near unto you; seek me diligently and ye shall find me; ask, and ye shall receive; knock, and it shall be opened unto you.

Diving Lessons

My dad taught me how to dive. When I was a little girl, he threw his keys to the bottom of my grandparents' pool and told me to make my hands like an arrow, arch them toward the keys, and dive. I swam and reached, grabbing the keys and heading back up to the surface of the water. Again and again we practiced my form, reach, dive, and recovery. Over time, I learned what I needed to do to dive and get the keys back to my dad.

Our prophet, President Russell M. Nelson, taught, "When you reach up for the Lord's power in your life with the same intensity that a drowning person has when grasping and gasping for air, power from Jesus Christ will be yours" ("Drawing the Power of Jesus Christ into Our Lives," Apr. 2017).

Trusting that my father was watching, I knew he would make sure I was safe. He knew that if I had something to find it would make it easier to stay diligent in the process. So it is with God. As we find ways to draw near to Him, ask, knock, and receive, our Heavenly Father will open up the way of greater power and knowledge.

—Ganel-Lyn

"Take a few more steps on the covenant path, even if it's too dark to see very far. The lights will come back on."

Sharon Eubank

"Christ: The Light That Shines in Darkness," Apr. 2019

Doctrine and Covenants 88:68

Sanctify yourselves that your minds become single to God, and the days will come that you shall see him; for he will unveil his face unto you.

How to Become Sanctified

When I was studying C. S. Lewis, I came across a concept in *Mere Christianity* that left me baffled. He said that many of us think we have overcome temptation, but in reality we just get older and less passionate. Lewis believed if our older spirits were in our younger bodies and met the same temptation today, we would probably fall again.

Gratefully, that is not what the restored gospel of Jesus Christ teaches. After baptism we are offered a precious gift that can truly change us from the inside out and make us a new creature. The Holy Ghost has been given the title of the sanctifier. He has the power to purify our hearts when we are worthy and invite Him in.

We become sanctified as our goals focus on keeping that connection strong, on listening to the words of Christ He brings to our minds and hearts. We desire to attend the temple more to feel a greater portion of the Spirit. When that becomes truly important to us, everything else we do centers on it.

With that, we are changed, day by day and line upon line. The best part is the promise of sanctification. Those who are sanctified will see Jesus's face individually, for He will unveil it unto them "in his own time and in his own way" (Doctrine and Covenants 88:68).

I think of that day and wonder what His expression will be. I wonder what He'll say. How I hope to hear, "Well done."

—Christine

"I am sanctified with His Spirit, endowed with His power, and set apart to build His kingdom."

Emily Belle Freeman

"Walking in Covenant Relationship with Christ," Oct. 2023

Doctrine and Covenants 88:118
And as all have not faith, seek ye diligently and teach one another words of wisdom; yea, seek ye out of the best books words of wisdom; seek learning, even by study and also by faith.

#YouChoose

Fasting, whether from food or other distractions, is never easy. Reflecting on the invitation from President Nelson to fast from social media for ten days in 2018, I must admit it was much more difficult than I thought it would be. After participating, I realized the extent to which social media had become an integral part of my daily life, woven into my routine far deeper than I had realized until I was asked to abstain from it.

In reality, the majority of learning seems to come from online sources in our world today. When we want to try a new recipe, find the best deal on a new pair of shoes, or navigate to an unknown address, we rely on technology. The internet has introduced an explosion of knowledge, with a constant stream of information bombarding us through a variety of platforms. It can be incredibly useful, but we can get swept away in the digital tide if we aren't careful. If we choose to be good stewards of our time and focus on those things that are uplifting and fill us with light, we can master these tools for good.

—Dru

> "If most of the information you get comes from social or other media, your ability to hear the whisperings of the Spirit will be diminished."
>
> Russell M. Nelson
> "Make Time for the Lord," Oct. 2021

Doctrine and Covenants 88:119

Organize yourself; prepare every needful thing; and establish a house, even a house of prayer, a house of fasting, a house of faith, a house of learning, a house of glory, a house of order, a house of God.

A House of Order

My parents moved a lot, but with each home, my mother added her touch and flair. She loved color and had an unmistakable style. When she died, each of her children took some of the furniture, pictures, and accessories from her home to grace theirs. When I visit my siblings' homes, I can see pieces of my mother's home as part of their own.

In order for our homes to become a home patterned after our Heavenly Father's, we need to have memorable pieces of His house as part of our own, such as scriptures, pictures of temples and the Savior, Church manuals, hymnbooks, and a temple recommend.

We must also have people living in our home who are acting like the Savior. We need to regularly pray, fast, study, learn, and praise God in our homes. As we do these things, our home will become a house where God would feel comfortable to enter.

—Marianna

"From the Lord's perspective, establishing the finest homes has everything to do with the personal qualities of the people who live there."

L. Whitney Clayton

"The Finest Homes," Apr. 2020

Doctrine and Covenants 88:125

And above all things, clothe yourselves with the bond of charity, as with a mantle, which is the bond of perfectness and peace.

The Son-in-Law Coat

Right after my husband and I were married, my stepfather, Jim, gave my husband, Rob, his utilitarian-style brown coat. We were at my parents' California home for a visit, and the morning fog had created a blanket of chill across the city. On our way out of town, Rob tried to return the jacket, but my dad insisted that he keep it. Eventually Jim bought another coat exactly like the one he had given away. And then he gave that one away to my new brother-in-law. After that, it was named the "son-in-law coat."

We still have the son-in-law coat hanging in our closet, thirty years later. It is a daily reminder that when we clothe ourselves in charity, we are bonded to one another.

Of all the Christlike characteristics, charity is the answer to war, discord, and conflict. It is a gift we can confidently ask for and receive. But once received, we are asked to share it with others. It is like a coat that is given away and then replaced and given away again. Everyone who puts it on is made warm in God's peace.

—Ganel-Lyn

> "Charity is not only related to something we donate to someone, but it's an attribute of the Savior and can become part of our character."
>
> **Ulisses Soares**
> "Followers of the Prince of Peace," Apr. 2023

Doctrine and Covenants 89:3

Given for a principle with a promise, adapted to the capacity of the weak, and the weakest of all saints, who are or can be called saints.

I Can Do It!

My mother used to love to tell the story of my second sister who as a preschooler decided the slide at their local park was too high for her, only she didn't make that decision until after she had climbed up to the very top. All she had to do was sit down, and my mother would catch her at the bottom of the slide.

Despite my mother's pleading, little Julia cried, "I can't do it! I'm going to fall."

"You won't fall," my mother said. "Sit down, and I'll catch you."

"No!" said the child. "I'm going to fall!" And with that she jumped off the top of the slide to prove she was right and got quite scraped up in the gravel below.

Much like that stubborn child, sometimes we feel like some aspects of the gospel are too hard. At the beginning of the revelation on the Word of Wisdom, the Lord states that even the weakest of all Saints can do this, if we simply stay on the covenant path. Too often, we jump off to our own peril. Whatever your challenge, hold on. For if you do, in the end the Lord will catch you.

—Christine

"We can be blessed to move forward along the covenant path, no matter how rocky it becomes, and eventually receive eternal life!"

Carl B. Cook

"Just Keep Going—With Faith," Apr. 2023

Doctrine and Covenants 89:10–11

All wholesome herbs God hath ordained for the constitution, nature, and use of man—every herb in the season thereof and every fruit in the season thereof.

Broccoli or Bust

In a kitchen not too far away from my own, a passionate parent encountered a perplexing problem precisely at dusk. She positioned a plate piled plentifully with peas, potatoes, parsnips, and peppers in front of her posterity, prescribing they polish off every portion before parting from their parents' presence.

With wide eyes and unbelief, determination, and apprehension, all of the children began the battle of wills with their forks in hand. Time seemed to stretch into hours as they struggled to choke down each bite. Among cries, tears, clenched faces, and fists, the mom finally relinquished her request and allowed the children to depart.

The Lord has counseled that every herb and fruit in its season is for our use and has been provided for our good. As parents, our efforts to encourage our children to eat them eventually paid off. Despite their initial resistance, most of my kids eventually grew to appreciate healthy foods and overcome their childhood struggles. Now, as adults, they look back on those dinner table tug-of-wars with laughter. Although some still don't like eating veggies, they will eat them from time to time, at least when their mom's around.

—Dru

> "Obedience to God's commandments doesn't always feel very joyful. . . . We grit our teeth and force ourselves to comply so that we can move on to more desirable activities."
>
> Dieter F. Uchtdorf
>
> "Living the Gospel Joyful," Oct. 2014

Doctrine and Covenants 89:20–21

And shall run and not be weary, and shall walk and not faint. And I, the Lord, give unto them a promise, that the destroying angel shall pass by them.

Only One Cinnamon Roll, Please

I love a good cinnamon roll. But whenever I eat more than one, I feel gross. My physical overindulgence affects my spirit, too.

Have you noticed how a spiritual problem can cause a physical illness? In Zeezrom's story in the Book of Mormon, he was so troubled in his mind that he became physically ill. He thought he was the cause of Alma's and Amulek's deaths and "this great sin, and his many other sins, did harrow up his mind until it did become exceedingly sore, having no deliverance; therefore he began to be scorched with a burning heat" (Alma 15:3). His sins had made him physically ill.

In section 89, the Lord teaches the "weakest of all saints" (v. 3) that there is an intimate link between body, mind, and spirit. Following the Lord's law of health for our bodies not only helps us to run and walk but also helps us obtain wisdom and knowledge. And the most important promise is that the destroying angel will pass us by. Our current prophet lives these promises. He knows how important it is to take care of his body so he can be the Lord's servant.

—Marianna

> "The great principle of happiness consists in having a body. The Devil has no body, and herein is his punishment."
>
> Joseph Smith
>
> *The Words of Joseph Smith*, ed. Andrew F. Ehat and Lyndon W. Cook (1980), 60

Doctrine and Covenants 90:5
All they who receive the oracles of God, let them beware how they hold them lest they are accounted as a light thing, . . . and stumble and fall when the storms descend, and the winds blow, and the rains descend, and beat upon their house.

Rocks and Sand

One of my favorite Primary songs is about building houses on rocks or sand. I love singing with the hand motions. The message behind the music is made for man in mortality. When we follow a living prophet, we are following God. His prophet on earth is an oracle, a spokesman, a mouthpiece for His people.

The storms will come. Rain and wind will beat upon our homes. Making and keeping covenants and following the counsel of the prophets and apostles won't make the storms softer. But it will provide, if we heed, the inspiration and preparatory revelation needed to be a covenant shielding us from the rain. Like a beautiful umbrella of faith, if we build upon the Rock of our salvation, even Jesus Christ, by following the words of His ordained leaders, we will survive.

We may still hear the wind blow, feel the cold rain, and be unable to sleep because of the thunder, but we will be kept safe.

—Ganel-Lyn

> "We do not need to fear. The doctrine and principles that we must follow to survive spiritually and endure physically are found in the words of a living prophet."
>
> Allen D. Haynie
>
> "A Living Prophet for the Latter Days," Apr. 2023

Doctrine and Covenants 90:11

It shall come to pass in that day, that every man shall hear the fulness of the gospel in his own tongue, and in his own language, through those who are ordained unto this power.

나의 복음을 전파하라

Members of my immediate family have served as missionaries for The Church of Jesus Christ of Latter-day Saints all over the world, including South Korea, Australia, Brazil, England, Germany, Spain, and the United States. They have spoken Korean, Portuguese, German, Spanish, and unfamiliar accents in the Southern States.

As of 2021, The Church of Jesus Christ of Latter-day Saints had published portions of the Book of Mormon in 115 languages. Missionaries serve in over 150 countries, teaching in 60 different languages around the world.

What an exciting time to be alive! Our Heavenly Father cares deeply for each of His children and wants all to have a chance to hear and accept the doctrine of Christ. The good news of the gospel will continue to roll forth until everyone has heard and understood the gospel message in their own language, preparatory to the Second Coming of our Lord.

—Dru

"Fifty percent of all missionaries serve in their own homeland. That is only right. The Lord has promised that 'every man shall hear the fulness of the gospel in his own tongue, and in his own language.'"

Neil L. Andersen

"Preparing the World for the Second Coming," Apr. 2011

Doctrine and Covenants 90:18
Set in order your houses; keep slothfulness and uncleanness far from you.

Slothfulness and Uncleanness

When you hear the phrase "set your house in order," do visions of your unorganized craft cupboard or your kitchen junk drawer make you cringe with guilt?

I love the Lord's clarification. He says to put slothfulness and uncleanness far from you. So if you're working your hardest, whether raising your children, fulfilling callings, or completing worthy projects, you aren't being slothful. And by taking care of sanitary issues and keeping ahead of dirt, you are clean.

But there may be another level to this admonition. Where so much media is consumed in our homes, I wonder if the Lord knew these two standards also applied there. We should ask ourselves, Is it slothful to watch this show or play this game because I should be working on something else? Is what I want to watch unclean or inappropriate?

Perhaps the best way to keep slothfulness and uncleanness far from us is to focus on service, uplifting activities, and Christ, who can wash us clean. As we serve, teach, and share, our homes will be happy and righteous places that are in the best order ever, despite our junk drawer and craft cupboard.

—Christine

"Transform your home into a sanctuary of faith and a center of gospel learning . . . by making [Heavenly Father and Jesus Christ] the center of [y]our family life.'"

Milton Camargo

"Focus on Christ," Apr. 2023

Doctrine and Covenants 92:2

You shall be a lively member in this order; and inasmuch as you are faithful in keeping all former commandments you shall be blessed forever.

Lively

Whenever I go shopping with my son, he offers to take my purse or any items that I am carrying. He is lively in watching out for me. He takes care of me before I even realize I need the help. I never have to ask him.

The Prophet Joseph Smith was losing many of his strongest supporters to apostasy. He needed a counselor in the First Presidency whom he could count on. The Lord wanted the Prophet to have a lively helper, too. Frederick G. Williams was called upon to live the United Order, as well as to be a counselor to the Prophet. The Lord promised Brother Williams that if he was faithful and kept the commandments, he would be blessed forever.

We have the same counsel from the Lord. We are to be lively members in our ward—those who visit their ministering sisters often (more than once a month), clean up after Relief Society activities, and see the need of another sister and fill it. The lively member does not need to be asked to do acts of service. Instead, the lively member is constantly aware of other's needs and takes care of them.

—Marianna

> "Loving service to others guides us along the path to our heavenly home—the path of becoming like our Savior."
>
> Jose A. Teixeira
>
> "Remember Your Way Back Home," Apr. 2021

Doctrine and Covenants 93:1

Every soul who forsaketh his sins and cometh unto me, and calleth on my name, and obeyeth my voice, and keepeth my commandments, shall see my face and know that I am.

You Look Like Your Mom

My son, Cameron, is often told that he looks like me. I can kind of see the resemblance. We have the same eyes. He also looks a lot like his sister because they both have curly hair.

As I have gotten older, I see changes in the mirror. Wrinkles and all, I have long prayed that as my physical appearance changes, I look more and more like my Elder Brother, Jesus. I hope that as time goes on, people will look at me and see the similarities.

I believe we all want to be able to see God. To feel His love and know Him that intimately. Verse 1 of section 93 teaches that if we repent daily, forsake our sins, keep His commandments, and pray, we will know God and see His face. I don't think there is a more sacred verse of scripture in all the text.

—Ganel-Lyn

"That is what we all want—we want to see Jesus for who He is and to feel His love."

Robert M. Daines

"Sir, We Would Like to See Jesus," Oct. 2023

Doctrine and Covenants 93:12–13

He received not of the fulness at the first, but received grace for grace . . . but continued from grace to grace, until he received a fulness.

Receiving Grace

One of my sons is terrible at receiving gifts. Knowing this, I stress out every time his birthday approaches. For his last birthday I got him a flattering shirt and a game. He had read the reviews of the board game and thought it was junk. Then he went on a rant about how clothes were the worst gift ever.

When I read about the way Jesus received grace for grace, I immediately focused on the receiving part. Grace is a free gift given from God. The Savior's grace saves us, but only as we receive it in our lives. The Lord puts spiritual experiences before us that open our hearts to Him in new ways. He gives us challenges that refine us and responsibilities such as callings or community service opportunities that I believe are part of the grace that allows us to grow spiritually, step by step, until we receive a fulness.

Too often we may behave like my son and either complain about or refuse the free gifts of grace the Lord is offering us. When we do that, we will not become all we could be. Instead, I'm going to try to graciously receive opportunities in my life that I feel have been placed there by God's loving grace so I can become who He wants me to be.

—Christine

"We can be perfected by the grace of Christ and one day become like Him."

Milton Camargo

"Focus on Jesus Christ," Apr. 2023

Doctrine and Covenants 93:24

And truth is knowledge of things as they are, and as they were, and as they are to come.

Some Things Never Change

Think about this simple truth: I am a beloved daughter of my Heavenly Father. This truth brings peace and reassurance when I'm feeling overwhelmed and anxious. When the world tries to tell me I'm not good enough, the Spirit reminds me of my infinite worth. When life's trials threaten to crush my hope, I know that all things are possible with God. And when I feel alone, I can pray and know He is near.

Truth is a core principle of our faith. It gives us clarity and a solid foundation on which to build our lives. Through the gospel of Jesus Christ, we know truth is eternal and revealed through the Holy Ghost. We find stability in an ever-changing world where truth often feels up for debate. Holding on to divine truth will help us tackle life's challenges with confidence and optimistically look forward to the future, knowing that some things never change.

—Dru

> "Modern revelation defines truth as a 'knowledge of things as they are, and as they were, and as they are to come.' That is a perfect definition for the plan of salvation and 'The Family: A Proclamation to the World.'"
>
> Dallin H. Oaks
> "Truth and the Plan," Oct. 2018

Doctrine and Covenants 93:32–34

For man is spirit. The elements are eternal, and spirit and element, inseparably connected, receive a fulness of joy; And when separated, a man cannot receive a fulness of joy.

Salad Dressing

I love a good salad dressing. Using freshly infused balsamic vinegar and a pure olive oil with additional fresh herbs and spices can make a dull salad into something to be excited about.

But the problem with vinegar and oil is that they do not naturally mix together well. If the dressing is not mixed properly, the vinegar and oil naturally separate and the salad dressing does not taste as good.

This concept can be likened to our bodies. We are spiritual and physical beings and need both our spirit and body to be complete. Our eternal spirit is currently placed in a mortal body that will eventually die. At death, the body and spirit will be separated for a time, but because of Jesus Christ's supernal gift we will all be resurrected someday. Our body and spirit will never be separated again, and we will receive a fulness of joy.

—Marianna

> "We would face two main obstacles in this necessarily fallen world: (1) physical death—the separation of our bodies from our spirits . . . and (2) spiritual death—our separation from God because our sins, mistakes, and flaws as mortals distance us from His holy presence."
>
> Ahmad S. Corbitt
>
> "Do You Know Why I as a Christian Believe in Christ?," Apr. 2023

Doctrine and Covenants 93:36–37

The glory of God is intelligence, or, in other words, light and truth. Light and truth forsake the evil one.

Truth on a Shelf

One day a family friend asked us to come over so my husband could help him set up a new computer. I'd been to their house before but never in the husband's office. When I walked in, I was shocked. He had an entire wall with at least ten fifteen-foot-long shelves filled with *Star Trek* memorabilia still in their original packaging. None of it had been touched so it could retain its ultimate value.

As we drove home, I thought about some of the Lego sets of spaceships that he owned which we also had. They hardly looked the same. My boys had played with them for hours, made design adjustments, created pretend worlds, and added other pieces of Legos to them, expanding their capacity. They were well loved and well used.

Truth can be like those toys. We can have a huge understanding of gospel topics, but it doesn't do much good if we leave it on a shelf. It is the application of those truths that gives them power. Without action, energy, or light, truth never becomes intelligence and doesn't glorify God. It is by living true principles that we are able to forsake evil, which is the ultimate value of truth. So don't leave it on the shelf.

—Christine

> "God reveals doctrinal truth through prophets, and the Holy Ghost confirms those truths to us and helps us apply them."
>
> John C. Pingree Jr.
> "Eternal Truth" Oct. 2023

Doctrine and Covenants 93:40

But I have commanded you to bring up your children in light and truth.

Follow the Light

One Sunday morning in August, as my husband drove to church for early-morning meetings, he encountered a breathtaking sight along the roadside. A farmer had planted a single row of sunflowers, stretching the length of his expansive field. Each magnificent bloom, about the size of a dinner plate, faced eastward, eagerly awaiting the sunrise over the Wasatch Mountains.

As he returned home that evening, he marveled at the scene again. This time, the sunflowers had turned to face west, following the sun's descent. They instinctively knew where to turn for light, life, and warmth.

Just as these sunflowers faithfully tracked the sun's path throughout the day, we, too, must fix our gaze on the Son, Jesus Christ, the Light and Life of the World. Just as the sunflowers followed the sun to thrive, we too must keep our faces turned toward Jesus, allowing His light to illuminate our lives and guide our path.

—Dru

> "One of the fundamental needs we have in order to grow is to stay connected to our source of light—Jesus Christ."
>
> Sharon Eubank
>
> "Christ: The Light That Shines in Darkness," Apr. 2019

Doctrine and Covenants 93:53
It is my will that you should hasten to translate my scriptures, and to obtain a knowledge of history, and of countries, and of kingdoms, of laws of God and man, and all this for the salvation of Zion.

Watching Animal Planet

I asked a friend what she and her husband enjoyed watching together on television in the evenings. She answered, "We watch *Animal Planet* every night." I was surprised because she did not own any animals. I asked her why they chose that show. She said, "My husband and I figured that if we are to oversee worlds in the hereafter, then we should learn about all the animals we can." She's right!

I always think about what area of learning I would like to explore next. Gaining knowledge of history, languages, laws, and animals is an important step in our eternal progression because this knowledge will "rise with us in the resurrection" (Doctrine and Covenants 130:18).

Combining book knowledge with the Spirit also brings us additional understanding, placing our knowledge into an eternal perspective.

—Marianna

> "If we rely only on our rational mind and deny or neglect the spiritual understanding we can receive through the whisperings and impressions of the Holy Ghost, it is as if we were going through life with only one eye. But figuratively speaking, we have actually been given two eyes. Only the combination of both views can give us the true and complete picture of all truths."
>
> Mathias Held
> "Seeking Knowledge by the Spirit," Apr. 2019

Doctrine and Covenants 94:2

And behold, it must be done according to the pattern which I have given unto you.

V-Formation

You may have noticed that some birds tend to fly in certain patterns. Every fall, flocks fly south over my home in *v*-formation. I love watching these groups of migratory birds working together in a pattern that isn't just beautiful but is also the most efficient. Scientists have researched these specific patterns and discovered that the birds in the back have to work less and have lower and slower heart rates than those in the front of the *v*. The downwash, or pressure from the front of the pack, creates a higher pressure that carries those in the back.

I don't understand all the science behind this specific behavior of birds, but I love noticing divine patterns in all of God's creations. From tree growth and animal behavior to covenant making, God works with patterns and under laws. As we learn heavenly patterns, we start to better understand the nature of God.

It should be no surprise, then, that when the Kirtland Temple was revealed, the Prophet Joseph Smith received a specific pattern for its construction. God is a god of laws and patterns. Look for divine formations all around you. They are beautiful.

—Ganel-Lyn

"Besides patterns for prayer, we have direction for pondering, procedure, patience, action, and integrity. There are patterns for all worthy things if we will search for them."

Marvin J. Ashton

"A Pattern in All Things," Oct. 1990

Doctrine and Covenants 94:9

But if there shall come into it any unclean thing, my glory shall not be there.

Clean Rooms

In 1960 a physicist working for a national laboratory designed the first clean room. This room created a contaminant-free environment so that one could build sensitive electrical circuitry or work with biomedical materials without the worry of inappropriate particulates polluting the outcome. Currently, 121,000 clean rooms are utilized worldwide to create sensitive electronic parts, develop medicines, and advance new research that bless the entire world.

The Lord also utilizes a similar principle in His holy house. The temple is the ultimate clean room. In the same way that a contaminated wire won't conduct a charge properly, when blatant sin is in the temple, the Lord cannot go there.

Within the temple walls, the veil is thinned as those who have passed on have their ordinances performed on their behalf. The purity of that clean room is essential for the full power of the Lord to fill His holy temple, and its blessings, in turn, bring healing to the whole world.

—Christine

"Through temple blessings, the Savior heals individuals, families, and nations."

J. Kimo Esplin

"The Savior's Healing Power upon the Isles of the Sea," Oct. 2023

Doctrine and Covenants 95:1

Whom I love I also chasten . . . for with the chastisement I prepare a way for their deliverance in all things out of temptation and I have loved you.

It's as Easy as Riding a Bike

Have you ever watched a child learning to ride a bike? At first, they struggle to keep their balance and may even fall off. But with the help of a parent or older sibling, they can be steadied, coached, and encouraged until they can finally ride alone. Corrections, given with patience and love, help the child improve and eventually master the art of riding a bike without falling. It's the child's willingness to accept correction that leads to success.

We, too, must be willing to make changes to improve our actions and behavior. Ultimately, our lives will not be measured by how many good and bad things we have done but by who we have become. If we are to transform into what our Heavenly Father wants us to become, we must be willing to change and to be corrected from time to time when we are off course.

—Dru

> "If we sincerely desire and strive to measure up to the high expectations of our Heavenly Father, He will ensure that we receive all the help we need, whether it be comforting, strengthening, or chastening."
>
> D. Todd Christofferson
> "As Many as I Love, I Rebuke and Chasten," Apr. 2011

Doctrine and Covenants 95:6

They who are not chosen have sinned a very grievous sin, in that they are walking in darkness at noon-day.

Walking in Darkness at Noon

About sixty miles east of Seattle is the longest railroad tunnel in the United States. The old Cascade Tunnel is about four miles long and goes through the Cascade mountains. The old tunnel was abandoned in 1929, and a new longer and lower tunnel was opened. The old tunnel became a pedestrian and bike adventure for people to walk through until the winter of 2007–2008 when a section of the roof caved in.

In 2004, I decided to take my children on a bike ride through this old tunnel as a summer adventure. Everyone took their bike, a flashlight, a bottle of water, and, of course, snacks. The darkness in this tunnel is eerie. In the middle of the tunnel, there is no light for miles. You cannot see the light at either end of the tunnel, and you cannot see your hand in front of you. As we were riding our bikes, my son's flashlight stopped working. This freaked him out. I needed to calm him down and stay close to him so that he could make it to the end of the tunnel. As soon as we saw a glimmer of light at the end of our trek, he was okay.

Walking in darkness at noonday is a conscious choice. The sun is shining if you open your eyes and see the light that is there to guide you. The Savior's light is always shining upon us. We need to open our spiritual eyes to receive His guidance.

—Marianna

> "The Spirit of Christ . . . conquers the darkness that otherwise would surround us."
>
> Timothy J. Dyches
>
> "Light Cleaveth unto Light," Apr. 2021

Doctrine and Covenants 96:2

Therefore, let my servant Newel K. Whitney take charge of the place which is named among you, upon which I design to build mine holy house.

Picking Up Garbage

Since she was a little girl, my daughter, Brooklyn, has had a sweet habit. Anytime we are in public, she notices litter on the ground. But she doesn't just notice it—she picks up any trash she can see. My daughter seems to take charge as a caretaker of the earth. Her example, as an unofficial guardian of the world, inspires me to this day.

We may not be called to oversee temples, missions or large properties, but we are all called to be stewards of this earth. Section 96 was given to the Prophet Joseph for Bishop Newel K. Whitney, who was called to oversee a farm where the Kirtland Temple would be built. His stewardship extended beyond the temple construction to other properties in the area as a steward in building the city of Zion.

No matter where I go, I can't ignore garbage tossed on the ground. Because of Brooklyn, I am reminded frequently that we are all called to take charge of caring for the earth.

—Ganel-Lyn

> "As God's children, we have received the charge to be stewards, caretakers, and guardians of His divine creations."
>
> Bishop Gérald Caussé
> "Our Earthly Stewardship," Oct. 2022

Doctrine and Covenants 97:3

I, the Lord, am well pleased that there should be a school in Zion.

A School in Zion

As the early restored Church began building the first temple of this dispensation, another revelation was given—there should be a school in Zion. The School of the Prophets was started soon after, including secular and spiritual learning. Both men and women attended weekly until the Kirtland Temple was built. As the Church moved to Nauvoo, Church leaders continued to focus on education and even built a university that had to be abandoned when they were forced to flee to the West.

When the Saints settled in the territory of Utah, they continued to establish academies and universities. As they moved to statehood, the government took over many of those institutions, so the Church established the seminary and institute programs for secondary education. The Church also retained ownership of LDS Business College (now Ensign College), Brigham Young University, and Ricks College (now BYU–I).

A few years ago, the president of BYU–Idaho opened Pathway Worldwide, providing spiritually based, affordable higher education to all who want to participate. President Kim B. Clark said, "It is a miracle that we can say today that BYU–Pathway is a school in Zion, wherever Zion is" ("BYU–Pathway Worldwide: A School in Zion," October 2018).

—Christine

"The aim of all gospel learning and teaching is to deepen our conversion to Heavenly Father and Jesus Christ."

Mark L. Pace

"Conversion Is Our Goal," Apr. 2022

Doctrine and Covenants 97:8
All among them who know their hearts are honest, and are broken, and their spirits contrite, and are willing to observe their covenants by sacrifice—yea, every sacrifice which I, the Lord, shall command—they are accepted of me.

More Than It Seems

I love to go to the temple. It is a sacred space where I can feel peace and quietly seek direction from my Heavenly Father. A place where I can give my time to serve as proxy for others who cannot receive sacred ordinances for themselves. It is where I go to deepen my connection to my Heavenly Father and to seek His will in my life.

Doctrine and Covenants 97 emphasizes the significance of temples in our worship and spiritual journey. Those who approach the temple with sincerity, humility, and a willingness to obey God's commandments will find acceptance in His sight. Temple worship is not just a ritual but a heartfelt expression of love and devotion to God. When we honor our commitments and faithfully follow Him, we demonstrate our genuine affection and loyalty.

—Dru

> "Sacrifice is the crowning test of the gospel. It means consecrating time, talents, energy, and earthly possessions to further the work of God."
>
> Quentin L. Cook
> "Are You a Saint?," Oct. 2003

Doctrine and Covenants 98:1–3

All things wherewith you have been afflicted shall work together for your good, and to my name's glory, saith the Lord.

Work Together for Your Good

Why me, Lord? This might be a sentiment you have felt in your life, especially when bad things happen in triplicate. You can ask "why me" questions, or you can start asking "what can I learn from this" questions. The first will not bring you any answers that are soul satisfying. The second puts you in a mental framework to be open to the Lord's suggestions on how to improve yourself during these difficult times.

The persecution of the Saints in Missouri had reached a fever pitch with the members suffering physically and economically because people were beating them up and destroying their property. The Saints were wanting to retaliate for the wrongs they had experienced. The Lord gave these Saints a promise that all the awful things inflicted upon them would work together for their good.

Thinking celestial, rather than telestial, will help us patiently wait on the Lord for trials to strengthen us, rather than weaken us. Physical and spiritual pain takes time to heal, but it can aso make us stronger.

—Marianna

> "In our efforts to find joy in the midst of our trials, we had forgotten that having patience is the key to letting those trials work for our good."
>
> Jeremy R. Jaggi
> "Let Patience Have Her Perfect Work, and Count It All for Joy!," Oct. 2020

Doctrine and Covenants 98:8

I, the Lord God, make you free, therefore ye are free indeed; and the law also maketh you free.

Not Free

Have you ever been offered something for free only to find out later that something is actually required? "Just come to this presentation, and you can have a free cruise." Maybe you do get a "free" trip, but it requires first sitting through a four-hour, high-pressure, uncomfortable pitch.

Growing up in the Church, I often heard the phrase "free agency" taught. As I grew older, I came to understand that agency isn't free. Yes, we are free to choose, but there is always a consequence for our choices. A price to pay. When you choose light, you receive more light. When you choose darkness, you receive more darkness. Elder Randy D. Funk, General Authority Seventy, taught, "The gift of agency is not simply the right to choose; it is the opportunity to choose the right" ("Come into the Fold of God," April 2022).

The ultimate freedom comes from following God's law. The consequence of choosing to keep covenants and commandments is freedom.

—Ganel-Lyn

> "God gives us moral agency—and moral accountability. . . . The Lord promises His Atonement and gospel path can break temporal and spiritual bonds. Mercifully, this redemptive freedom extends to those who have passed from mortality."
>
> Gerrit W. Gong
> "All Nations, Kindreds, and Tongues," Oct. 2020

Doctrine and Covenants 98:14

I will prove you in all things, whether you will abide in my covenant, even unto death, that you may be found worthy.

The Proving Drawer

I love to watch *The Great British Bake Off*. Because it is based in England, many of the baking terms they use are a little different than what we use. We talk about having our bread dough rise, but their dough is *proved* in a proving drawer.

After mixing the ingredients together and kneading the dough, the bakers put their creations in the proving drawer. Then they wait and watch, often frantically. But they know they can't interfere in the process. If they open the drawer before the proving is done, it will only take longer or the change won't happen at all. So the bakers watch intently until the dough has risen to the level it needs to become the best it can be.

Like the dough, the Lord has promised He will prove the faithful to see if we "abide in [His] covenant." During those times of proving, we may feel abandoned and that our prayers aren't being answered. But I like to think of Him as the ultimate baker, waiting and watching until my dough has grown just the right amount. Then He'll lift me from the proving drawer, return me to His arms, and I will be changed.

—Christine

"In the mortal experience, we will have ample opportunity to prove ourselves, to pass tests hard enough to become ever more like the Savior and our Heavenly Father."

Henry B. Eyring

"Tested, Proved, and Polished," Oct. 2020

Doctrine and Covenants 98:40

And as oft as thine enemy repenteth of the trespass wherewith he has trespassed against thee, thou shalt forgive him, until seventy times seven.

Me Too?

Sometimes when I get discouraged, I feel overwhelmed by my shortcomings and weaknesses. The weight of my mistakes and imperfections can feel heavy, and at times I doubt my ability to measure up and become the person He needs me to be.

When we think about forgiveness, it's important to remember that extending forgiveness means embracing it for ourselves as well. Just as the Lord commands us to forgive others seventy times seven, that same principle applies to forgiving ourselves. It's easy to fall into the trap of dwelling on our mistakes, replaying them in our minds, and punishing ourselves repeatedly as if the Atonement wasn't sufficient to cleanse us completely of our sins.

The truth is that if the Lord has forgiven us, then we must also forgive ourselves. Holding onto guilt and self-condemnation only hinders our progress and diminishes the power of Christ's Atonement in our lives. Instead, we must learn to accept His forgiveness fully, allowing His grace to heal our hearts and help us move forward with faith and confidence.

—Dru

"When the Lord requires that we forgive all men, that includes forgiving ourselves."

Dieter F. Uchtdorf

"The Merciful Obtain Mercy," Apr. 2012

257

Doctrine and Covenants 99:3

And who receiveth you as a little child, receiveth my kingdom; and blessed are they, for they shall obtain mercy.

Wesley and Arthur

Two-year-old Wesley was very excited to see his new cousin, Arthur. Arthur and his parents had been living in London, so Wesley had not met Arthur during the first four months of Arthur's life. Wesley had seen him on his mother's phone and enjoyed sending sweet kisses over the internet.

Finally, Arthur was coming to visit. When Wesley arrived to see Arthur, Arthur was taking a nap. Wesley was devastated. When Arthur woke up, Wesley was so excited to hold him and play with him. When it was time for Wesley to leave, Wesley waved to him and said, "Goodbye, Arthur. I love you." His mother was surprised and said, "Wesley hasn't even said I love you to me before."

When the Lord asks us to become as a little child, I think it is the pure love of Christ that children have in their hearts for others that the Lord is referring to. Because of that Christlike love, the Spirit is with little children. We should follow their example!

—Marianna

> "Our natures change to become as a little child, obedient to God and more loving. That change will qualify us to enjoy the gifts that come through the Holy Ghost. Having the Spirit's companionship will comfort, guide, and strengthen us."
>
> Henry B. Eyring
>
> "Steady in the Storms," Apr. 2022

Doctrine and Covenants 100:6

For it shall be given you in the very hour, yea, in the very moment, what ye shall say.

Text in Sacrament Meeting

I was sitting in a sacrament meeting pondering on recent feelings of professional discouragement and disillusionment. Over the previous months, I had gone through some significant losses and endings. I was asking questions about my contributions, effectiveness as a writer, and if I had made any real impact as a speaker. I pulled out my phone to look for a scripture and noticed a text notification.

My friend and fellow public speaker, Jodi, had sent a text thanking me for my Hope Works talk about my sister's suicide. She shared some personal feelings and appreciation for the work I have done. She said, in that very moment, what I needed to hear. It was a gentle reminder that God was aware of me and my silent prayers. He used Jodi's simple words and text to touch my heart.

It was also a reminder that my imperfect offerings had indeed helped someone in some small way. That Sunday, the sacrament felt different. It was a moment of remembering that faith in Jesus Christ is the way to retain hope.

—Ganel-Lyn

> "Regardless of the size, scope, and seriousness of the challenges we face in life, we all have times when we feel like stopping, leaving, escaping, or possibly giving up. . . . Faith in our Savior, Jesus Christ, helps us overcome discouragement."
>
> Carl B. Cook
>
> "Just Keep Going—with Faith," Apr. 2023

Doctrine and Covenants 100:12

Therefore, continue your journey and let your hearts rejoice; for behold, and lo, I am with you even unto the end.

Only One

For a few years, my job required frequent travel. I vividly recall one journey back home after a series of international meetings. It was late at night, and as I sat on the plane flying over New York City, I looked out the window at the sprawling city below. The towering skyscrapers and countless lights stretched as far as my eyes could see. The sight of so many lives bustling below made me feel insignificant, realizing how many people lived their lives alongside mine, completely unaware of one another.

At that moment, a warm feeling washed over me and I found solace in a profound truth: if our Heavenly Father cares for even the smallest sparrow and knows the number of hairs on our heads, then surely He knows and treasures each of His children individually. Despite the vastness of humanity, each soul is valued and known by Him, including you and me. Like a devoted parent, our Heavenly Father lovingly watches over us. We are deeply loved and cherished. He sees us and will never leave us alone.

—Dru

> "I testify that He whom we address as our Father in Heaven is indeed our Father, that He loves us, that He knows each of His children intimately, that He cares deeply about each one, and that we are truly all alike unto Him."
>
> Christopher G. Giraud-Carrier
> "We Are His Children," Oct. 2023

Doctrine and Covenants 101:3

Yet I will own them, and they shall be mine in that day when I shall come to make up my jewels.

Becoming a Jewel

When I was a young child, my mother bought some rhinestone earrings. I thought the rainbow colors shining from the smooth plastic was the prettiest thing I'd ever seen. One day my mother showed me her diamond ring. It was much smaller than the showy plastic beads, but as I looked closer, I could see the fire inside. I was shocked the diamond was worth thousands more than the rhinestones.

One reason for gemstones' high value is their longevity. Jewels keep their value for generations. Being steadfast as we walk the covenant path is one way we can become jewel-like.

Another aspect of jewels is purity. Clarity, or having no dark inclusions, is the most significant factor in determining a jewel's worth. As we become "clean every whit" (John 13:10) through the Atonement, we become Christ's most valuable jewels.

A final factor making jewels precious is their rarity. Jewels are most often created under extreme pressure and in only a few places on earth. When we are doing our best to follow the Lord and feel as though we are the only ones, we are developing the nature of a jewel. And in the end, we will be Christ's treasure and have a place in His crown.

—Christine

> "Our Savior will polish and refine us through the merits of His atoning sacrifice."
>
> Gary B. Sabin
>
> "Hallmarks of Happiness," Oct. 2023

Doctrine and Covenants 101:16
Be still and know that I am God.

Letting Go

As a mom of six, I wanted to give my children every opportunity to grow and fully experience life. Our days were jam-packed with sports, lessons, rehearsals, performances, church, family gatherings, homework, and chores, leaving little time for rest or sanity.

Life often feels like a race with no finish line. It's easy to get caught up in the whirlwind of busyness as if the length of our to-do lists measures our worth. We fill our days with endless tasks and commitments, leaving very little time for things of the spirit or time "just to be kids." This constant hustle can leave us drained and overwhelmed, with little purpose or joy.

We often overlook the importance of slowing down and focusing on what truly matters. Sometimes, we need to step back and reassess our priorities, letting go of unnecessary burdens that weigh us down. We can find greater peace and fulfillment by simplifying our lives and prioritizing the things that bring us closer to our families and our faith. It's not about doing more but about doing what matters most, and trusting that in doing so we will find our way to the true source of peace and happiness.

—Dru

> "We would do well to slow down a little, proceed at the optimum speed for our circumstances, focus on the significant, lift up our eyes, and truly see the things that matter most."
>
> Dieter F. Uchtdorf
> "Of Things That Matter Most," Oct. 2010

Doctrine and Covenants 103:10

And inasmuch as they are not the saviors of men, they are as salt that has lost its savor, and is thenceforth good for nothing but to be cast out and trodden under foot of men.

Savory Saviors

Salt is a symbol of the covenants made between the Lord and Israel. The meat offerings that the priest would offer to the Lord were always sprinkled with salt (see Leviticus 2:13; Numbers 18:19). In the Old Testament, newborns were sprinkled with salt as a symbol of them being born in the covenant (see Ezekiel 16:4).

Salt is a pure compound that only loses its saltiness when it is diluted with water or contaminated in some other way. Similarly, we should not dilute the doctrine of Christ with worldly notions or add to the gospel the teachings of men. These would contaminate and invalidate the preservative power of gospel covenants. The destruction of our covenants' binding power would cause us to be trodden down by men. In order to keep our savor, or saltiness, we must stay away from the world and keep ourselves pure by obeying Christ.

In both Aramaic and Greek, the translation for the phrase "loses its savour" can also be translated as "becoming foolish." We do become foolish and unable to be savory saviors to others when we contaminate our covenants with God.

—Marianna

> "Focus on Jesus Christ. He is our Savior and Redeemer, the 'mark' to whom we should look, and our greatest treasure."
>
> **Henry B. Eyring**
> "Steady in the Storms," Apr. 2022

Doctrine and Covenants 103:17

For ye are the children of Israel, and of the seed of Abraham, and ye must needs be led out of bondage by power, and with a stretched-out arm.

God's Arms

I am a hugger. I mean a big-time hugger. You have been warned. I have been known to hug a few thousand strangers. I know not everyone is a hugger, but I believe in the power of a good hug. It helps improve our mental health, fostering connections and increasing hope.

I love that verse 17 in section 103 references the stretched-out arm of God leading His children out of bondage. Aren't we all in bondage at some level? Aren't we all in need of a God-shaped hug?

God will not force Himself on us. So it is with our daily choices that we can continually reach and stretch for a connection with God. This is where our ultimate happiness will come from. Remember, covenants are about connection in a relationship with God.

—Ganel-Lyn

> "The greatest happiness in God's generous plan is finally reserved for those who are willing to stretch and to pay the costs of journeying to His regal realm. Brothers and sisters, 'come, let us anew [this] journey pursue'
> ('Come, Let Us Anew,' *Hymns*, no. 217)."
>
> Neal A. Maxwell
>
> "Consecrate Thy Performance," Apr. 2002

Doctrine and Covenants 104:11–18

If any man shall take of the abundance which I have made, and impart not his portion . . . unto the poor and the needy, he shall, with the wicked, lift up his eyes in hell, being in torment.

Are We Not All Beggars?

Much of Jesus's ministry focused on feeding, healing, and clothing those around Him. He has extended this responsibility of taking care of the poor to us. This means helping those who don't have enough food, shelter, or other basic needs. It also implies taking care of those who are poor in spirit. They usually go hand in hand. We can do this by sharing what we have with others who are less fortunate. It's important to remember that everyone deserves to be treated with kindness and respect, no matter their circumstances.

One way we can fulfill this responsibility is by donating to organizations that help the poor, paying fast offerings, volunteering our time to serve those in need, or simply offering a listening ear and a helping hand to someone who is struggling. By showing compassion and generosity toward others, we can make a positive difference in their lives and help them feel loved and valued. Taking care of the poor is not only a commandment from God but also an opportunity for us to show our love for our fellow brothers and sisters and follow the example of Jesus Christ.

—Dru

> "King Benjamin says we *obtain* a remission of our sins by pleading to God, who compassionately responds, but we *retain* a remission of our sins by compassionately responding to the poor who plead to us."
>
> Jeffrey R. Holland
>
> "Are We Not All Beggars?," Oct. 2014

Doctrine and Covenants 104:78, 80

It is my will that you shall pay all your debts. . . . And inasmuch as you are diligent and humble, and exercise the prayer of faith, behold, I will soften the hearts of those to whom you are in debt.

Shopping Addiction

Spending money is a lot of fun. I love going out shopping with my daughters. I find it therapeutic to window shop and dream. Sometimes, I will buy something that I think I will love. But when I bring it home, I realize I don't need it nor do I even want it. It was just a whim or fancy.

Elder Robert D. Hales tells the story of wanting to buy his wife a beautiful dress. She refused the offer because she knew that the dress did not fit into their budget nor did it match their current lifestyle (see "Becoming Provident Providers Temporally and Spiritually," Apr. 2009).

The Lord wants us to pay off our debts. His current latter-day prophet even says being in debt can be an addiction. Using our prayers of faith to ask for the Lord's help will curb our appetite to spend and inspire us to know how the Lord wants us to use our money.

—Marianna

> "As you think celestial, you will find yourself avoiding *anything* that robs you of your agency. Any addiction—be it gaming, gambling, debt, drugs, alcohol, anger, pornography, sex, or even food—offends God. Why? Because your obsession becomes your god."
>
> Russell M. Nelson
>
> "Think Celestial!," Oct. 2023

Doctrine and Covenants 105:14

For behold, I do not require at their hands to fight the battles of Zion; for, as I said in a former commandment, even so will I fulfil—I will fight your battles.

What Goliath Are You Fighting?

As President Russell M. Nelson taught, "One of the Hebraic meanings of the word *Israel* is 'let God prevail.'" What a powerful principle. The prophet goes on to invite us to consider while studying our scriptures making "a list of all that the Lord has promised He will do for covenant Israel. I think you will be astounded!" ("Let God Prevail," October 2020). I remember when President Nelson issued that invitation. I took it seriously, going on to even write a small book about applying the principle. I considered the scripture story of David and Goliath in a new light. Young David was underestimated by many in his family but not by God. He faced the giant Goliath armed with only a sling and five stones.

I love God's economy. He accomplishes the most with the very least. Ultimately David had more than just a bag of rocks; he had a relationship with and trust in God. Each of us will be faced with our own giants. Letting God prevail means believing, really trusting, that God will fight our battles as we face everything with faith.

—Ganel-Lyn

> "My dear brothers and sisters, as you choose to let God prevail in your lives, you will experience for yourselves that our God is 'a God of miracles.'"
>
> Russell M. Nelson
> "Let God Prevail," Oct. 2020

267

Doctrine and Covenants 106:5

Therefore, gird up your loins, that you may be the children of light, and that day shall not overtake you as a thief.

Children of Light

I've always been a night owl. When I was young, I loved to sneak out of my bed and go downstairs to read while no one knew. As a mom, I'd wait until all the children were in bed to write or watch a show they didn't care for. Even now that they are grown, I sometimes find my most productive hours are after my husband is snoring. So, when I read about the importance of being one of the children of light, I grew nervous.

The New Testament makes a number of references to being children of light. Jesus told the people they were the light of the world and to let their light shine. Later, right before the Last Supper, Christ taught the multitudes, "While ye have light, believe in the light, that ye may be children of light" (John 12:36). As we believe in the light of Christ, we become children of the light.

I was still feeling unsure, until I turned to Thessalonians. Paul taught the early converts there, "Ye are all the children of light. . . . Therefore let us not sleep, as do others; but let us watch and be sober" (I Thessalonians 5:5–6). See? I can be a child of the light and not sleep. But I need to watch for Christ's coming and shine to help the world find Him.

—Christine

"Let us as a people become a true light on the hill—a light that 'cannot be hid.'"

Russell M. Nelson

"Peacemakers Needed," Apr. 2023

Doctrine and Covenants 107:1

There are, in the church, two priesthoods, namely, the Melchizedek and Aaronic, including the Levitical Priesthood.

Power from on High

My sweet granddaughter Tatum was recently given a name and father's blessing by her dad. When I see men in my family performing sacred priesthood duties, my heart fills with deep gratitude. Blessing babies, confirming new Church members, helping with the sacrament, ordaining others to the priesthood, and anointing and healing the sick are all sacred acts performed in the name of the Lord. It reminds me that these men are trying their best to serve God and raise a good family.

President Nelson has reminded us that the restoration of the priesthood matters just as much to women as it does to men. Anyone who makes and keeps covenants with God and participates worthily in priesthood ordinances has direct access to God's power, regardless of gender. When we are endowed in the temple, we receive a gift of God's priesthood power because of our covenant.

When women are set apart to serve in a calling under the direction on one who holds priesthood keys, we are given priesthood authority to function in that calling. Similarly, in the holy temple we are authorized to perform and officiate in priesthood ordinances every time we attend. As covenant women and men, we have the right to draw freely from the Savior's power to bless our family and those we love.

—Dru

> The heavens are just as open to *women* who are endowed with God's power flowing from their priesthood covenants as they are to men who bear the priesthood."
>
> **Russell M. Nelson**
> "Spiritual Treasures," Oct. 2019

Doctrine and Covenants 107:23

The twelve traveling councilors are called to be the Twelve Apostles, or special witnesses of the name of Christ in all the world—thus differing from other officers in the church in the duties of their calling.

Witnesses to the World

While we served in Brazil, both Elder Richard G. Scott and then-Elder Russell M. Nelson came to visit our mission. My missionaries were all so excited to have these Apostles come to visit. As a family, we were also excited to have them in our home.

Both times, as they spoke at the pulpit to a chapel full of missionaries, their message was the same—Jesus is the Christ, the Savior and Redeemer of the world. The Apostles are His special witnesses that His gospel is restored on the earth. After hearing their testimonies, we were all fired up to be more valiant messengers of His gospel.

Every general conference, after hearing all Twelve Apostles and the First Presidency bear witness of Christ, we should feel fire in our bones (see Jeremiah 20:0) to take His gospel message to the world.

—*Marianna*

> "The fundamental principles of our religion are the testimony of the Apostles and Prophets, concerning Jesus Christ, that He died, was buried, and rose again the third day, and ascended into heaven; and *all other things* which pertain to our religion are only appendages to it."
>
> Joseph Smith
>
> *Teachings of the Presidents of the Church: Joseph Smith (2007), 49*

Doctrine and Covenants 107:48

Enoch was twenty-five years old when he was ordained under the hand of Adam; and he was sixty-five and Adam blessed him.

My Scariest Calling Ever

Standing to speak in front of thousands of people or doing a five-minute live television interview doesn't scare me. Being asked to play the organ in sacrament meeting or lead the music scares me the most. Fearfully, I accepted a call to be the Primary chorister. I believe the Primary may be the most important auxiliary we can serve in. I didn't feel confident in teaching the songs, entertaining, or correctly leading. After a sacred experience with the sacrament and being set apart, I knew God was with me.

Enoch was also overwhelmed when called to serve. Elder David A. Bednar said, "Notice that at the time of Enoch's call to serve, he became acutely aware of his personal inadequacies and limitations. And I suspect all of us at one time or another . . . have felt much like Enoch" ("Abide in Me, and I in You; Therefore Walk with Me," Apr. 2023).

I never became a brilliant chorister, but I loved serving those children and singing about the principles of the gospel. I was magnified with God each Sunday when I walked into the Primary room.

—Ganel-Lyn

"Enoch ultimately became a mighty prophet and a tool in God's hands to accomplish a great work, but he did not start his ministry that way! His capacity . . . was magnified as he learned to . . . walk with the Son of God."

David A. Bednar

"Abide in Me, and I in You; Therefore Walk with Me," Apr. 2023

Doctrine and Covenants 107:79–80

Thus the Presidency of the High Priesthood and its counselors shall have power to decide. . . . And after this decision it shall be had in remembrance no more before the Lord . . . and a final decision upon controversies in spiritual matters.

The End of the Argument

My parents met on the debate team at BYU. As a result, our family loved to have vigorous gospel discussions at the dinner table. I remember debating where the line was between hypocrisy and reaching to improve, what constituted scripture when it came to uncanonized texts, and how to increase your faith muscle versus simply waiting on the Lord.

Every now and then our discussion became heated, and though my parents would say the discussion was over, my brother and I would continue on our own time. I don't think I ever won, not because I wasn't correct but because he was much more forceful.

The gospel is meant to be chewed up and digested. We should discuss with our family and friends the meaning of conference talks and the application of family councils. There is value in this sort of connection and group thought. But the Lord has made it clear that when the prophet makes a decision after receiving revelation, there is no more room for debate. Sometimes that is hard when we feel passionate about something. That's when we have to turn to the Lord in prayer to calm our hearts, knowing that all things will be made right in the end.

—Christine

> "As we trust in the Savior, promised miracles will occur. Whether in this life or the next, all will be made right."
>
> Neil L. Andersen
>
> "What Thinks Christ of Me?," Apr. 2012

Doctrine and Covenants 108:7

Therefore, strengthen your brethren in all your conversation, in all your prayers, in all your exhortations, and in all your doings.

Spiritual Strength Training

Lifting weights strengthens both muscles and bones. But becoming stronger does not come overnight. You start light and then gradually use heavier and heavier weights to build up your strength, muscles, and bones.

In the gospel, we also need spiritual strength training as we monitor the way we handle disagreements, the way we treat others, and the way we converse with others. We must be kinder and gentler with each other. The strength we need is in holding back unkind comments, gossiping words, or forgiving those who have wronged us or our family members.

But in spiritual strength training, we don't just exercise for ourselves. Instead, through our actions we can actually strengthen our brothers and sisters in the gospel. Their testimonies will become stronger as we are examples of His love for them. The foundation or bones of our testimony will become stronger as we strengthen our testimonies and the testimonies of others.

—Marianna

> "Through my covenants I receive the sanctifying, strengthening power of Jesus Christ, which allows me to become a new person, to forgive what seems unforgivable, to overcome the impossible. Intentionally remembering Jesus Christ always is powerful; it gives me added strength to 'keep his commandments which he has given [me].'"
>
> Joaquin E. Costa
> "The Power of Jesus Christ in Our Lives Every Day." Oct. 2023

Doctrine and Covenants 109:8

Organize yourselves; prepare every needful thing, and establish a house, even a house of prayer, a house of fasting, a house of faith, a house of learning, a house of glory, a house of order, a house of God.

House Cleaner

I love an organized house. I have always been a house cleaner. Even as a little girl, I would suggest to my mom that for fun we should clean and organize the house!

This verse of scripture talks about organizing our homes and creating a place of order. But I don't think it refers to just how our closets look or how tidy our rooms are. It is about putting the most important things first in our family culture.

Yes, the spirit of the temple is enhanced by its cleanliness and effective organizational systems. But the focus of the temple, and of our homes, should be prayer, faith, and God. So, the next time you are vacuuming, consider it time to talk to God about your loved ones. Vacuuming creates order, but when we use it as prayer time, it establishes our homes in every needful thing.

—Ganel-Lyn

> "Your love for your children creates a rich environment for teaching truth and building faith. Make your home a house of prayer, learning, and faith; a house of joyful experiences; a place of belonging; a house of God."
>
> Dieter F. Uchtdorf
>
> "It's a Miracle," Apr. 2013

Doctrine and Covenants 109:12

That thy glory may rest down upon thy people, and upon this thy house, which we now dedicate to thee, that it may be sanctified and consecrated to be holy, and that thy holy presence may be continually in this house.

Temple Glory

In section 88, the Saints were commanded to build a temple in Kirtland, Ohio. Three years and three months later, the Kirtland Temple was dedicated. What a glorious day for the Saints to dedicate the first temple of the Restoration! What a blessing that the Church now owns this temple again!

A temple dedication is a time to rededicate ourselves to God. Temple dedicatory prayers call upon the powers of heaven to devote His house to holiness and to His glory. King Solomon gave a dedicatory prayer for the temple in Jerusalem similar to the Prophet Joseph Smith's prayer. Solomon prayed, "I have surely built thee an house to dwell in, a settled place for thee to abide in forever" (1 Kings 8:13). That is the prayer for every temple around the world.

The Saints experienced angelic visitations, heavenly light, and the gift of tongues during the temple dedication. Those who prepare themselves to enter His holy house are armed with power (v. 22), have the name of Christ written on them (v. 23), bear great truth to the world (vv. 25–26), enjoy pentecostal experiences (vv. 35–37), and have their sacrifice and offering accepted by the Lord (vv. 77–78). These are the same blessings we can enjoy as we enter the temple today.

—Marianna

> "Honoring covenants arms us with righteousness and with the power of God in great glory."
>
> **David A. Bednar**
>
> "With the Power of God in Great Glory," Oct. 2021

Doctrine and Covenants 109:13

That all people who shall enter upon the threshold of the Lord's house may feel thy power . . . that it is thy house, a place of thy holiness.

Mother May I

When I was young, my siblings and I spent the majority of our summers playing in the yard with the other neighborhood children. One of our favorite games was Mother May I. After asking the child designated as the mother if you could do something such as take ten giant steps, the mother would respond, "Yes, you may" or "No, you may not." The first one to tag the mother won. It was years before I realized the winner is totally dependent on the whims of the mother.

The only good part of that game was it taught me the difference between *can* and *may*. *Can* means you have the ability to, like *can* you do ten pushups? (I can't.) But, *may* reflects permission or a possibility. In my game, the *may* is about permission, but in the above scripture, it's about a possibility.

Because I've had such powerful temple experiences, I forget that we are only promised we "may feel [His] power." It is available to all who enter the temple but remains only a possibility unless we open our hearts and ask for it. I know it is possible and will happen in the Lord's time. His power is there. I've felt it.

—Christine

"The temple lies at the center of strengthening our faith and spiritual fortitude because the Savior and His doctrine are the very heart of the temple."

Russell M. Nelson

"The Temple and Your Spiritual Foundation," Oct. 2021

Doctrine and Covenants 109:17–19

That all the incomings of thy people, into this house, may be in the name of the Lord; That all their outgoings from this house may be in the name of the Lord; and that all their salutations may be in the name of the Lord, with holy hands, uplifted to the Most High.

How to Be Happy

In his October 2022 general conference address, President Russell M. Nelson said, "I promise that increased time in the temple will bless your life in ways nothing else can."

The temple is a sacred place where we make important promises and take part in sacred ceremonies. Everything we learn and do there helps us understand the crucial role of Jesus Christ in God's plan for our happiness. All of the teachings, ordinances, and service performed in the temple point us toward Him.

The more I attend the temple, the more clearly I see where I fit in the eternal scheme of things. Being there helps me to feel more connected to heaven and understand my purpose here on earth. The veil thins as I search for answers, pray for God's power to bless those I love, and seek His guidance and blessings.

—Dru

> "The most sacred covenants and priesthood ordinances are received only in a temple—the house of the Lord. Everything that is learned and all that is done in the temple emphasize the divinity of Jesus Christ and His role in Heavenly Father's great plan of happiness."
>
> David A. Bednar
>
> "Let This House Be Built unto My Name," Apr. 2020

Doctrine and Covenants 109:22

And we ask thee, Holy Father, that thy servants may go forth from this house armed with thy power, and that thy name may be upon them, and thy glory be round about them, and thine angels have charge over them.

Angels Round About

There are no coincidences in the Lord's work—only small miracles that the world would call coincidences. The Lord's servants are armed with the power to see and act on these coincidences so that they can be where they are supposed to be to bear testimony of Him.

For example, a missionary companionship visited a family of investigators. They had been there only five minutes when the phone rang and the family was told that a close family friend had died. The family was devastated, but the missionaries were able to comfort them and teach them about the Atonement and the Resurrection. The missionaries felt that angels were present comforting this family.

The fact that the missionaries happened to be in this home when the family needed comfort and understanding of the Lord's mission on earth illustrates how angels will be on your right and on your left or round about you when you are doing His work.

As we become His servants, His angels will spiritually strengthen us and the people we minister to.

—Marianna

> "You will learn how to part the veil between heaven and earth, how to ask for God's angels to attend you, and how better to receive direction from heaven."
>
> **Russell M. Nelson**
> "The Temple and Your Spiritual Foundation." Oct. 2021

Doctrine and Covenants 109:38

Put upon thy servants the testimony of the covenant . . . that thy people may not faint in the day of trouble.

Extra Batteries

My husband likes technology, computer cords, and having extra batteries. Rob always has what you need tech-wise. When we are traveling, he is in charge of making sure our cell phones and tablets have enough power. Keeping our technology charged every day is much like the process of conversion and of overcoming the world and all its ills.

President Russell M. Nelson taught, "Overcoming the world is not an event that happens in a day or two. It happens over a lifetime as we repeatedly embrace the doctrine of Christ. We cultivate faith in Jesus Christ by repenting daily and keeping covenants that endow us with power. We stay on the covenant path and are blessed with spiritual strength, personal revelation, increasing faith, and the ministering of angels" ("Overcome the World and Find Rest," Oct. 2022).

Keeping covenants, connecting with God in prayer, and learning the gospel with scripture study are all a choice. When we make these daily decisions, we can rest in the assurance that we will have the power to not faint in the day of trouble.

—Ganel-Lyn

> "A lack of deep personal prayer and deep genuine worship also erodes our faith, and we may 'faint in the day of trouble.'"
>
> Neal A. Maxwell
>
> "Lest Ye Be Wearied and Faint in Your Minds," Apr. 1991

Doctrine and Covenants 110:1–2

The veil was taken from our minds, and the eyes of our understanding were opened. We saw the Lord standing upon the breastwork of the pulpit, before us.

I Wonder When He Comes Again

Every Sunday I get to play in Primary. I teach the ten-year-olds, and they are so smart that I sometimes don't realize what they don't know. Recently we learned the song "When He Comes Again." These children had never even heard it before. The beginning of the second verse starts, "I wonder, when he comes again, / Will I be ready there / To look upon his loving face / And kneel with Him in prayer?" We were all singing, and I thought it was sweet until I saw a tear hanging from the corner of one of my children's eyes. She was asking herself if she was ready, and so was I. I want *to want* for that day to come.

I wonder, when Jesus came to Joseph and Oliver at the Kirtland Temple, did they feel ready? They had worked so hard to prepare the temple, but even with all the other heavenly messengers, Christ had not appeared since the First Vision. Yet, right after the temple dedication, He came! He declared His divine role, forgave their sins, and ushered in the restoration of all the keys necessary for His work to roll forth.

Still, I wonder how I'll feel on the day I see Jesus's face. I'll try to live so that it is the most joyous day of my life, whether it's tomorrow or many years hence.

—Christine

> "Let us seek His loving face and then be vessels of His mercy to His children."
>
> Robert M. Daines
>
> "Sir, We Would Like to See Jesus," Oct. 2023

Doctrine and Covenants 110:14–15

Behold, the time has fully come, which was spoken of by the mouth of Malachi—testifying that he [Elijah] should be sent . . . to turn the hearts of the fathers to the children, and the children to the fathers, lest the whole earth be smitten with a curse.

Forever Yours

This past November, our youngest son got married and sealed to his bride in the Payson Utah Temple. It was the first time all six of our children and their spouses were together in the temple. As I looked around the ordinance room and saw each of their faces, I felt overwhelming gratitude for my family. Being with them and my grandchildren forever is the most important goal in my life. This was just the beginning of our eternal story.

We don't just go to temples to create personal or family memories. We go to receive essential ordinances for our salvation, which purify our hearts and prepare us to be with God again. By finding and submitting names of ancestors and doing temple work for them, we bless both them and ourselves. Serving others in this way shows our love for God and our extended family, and it brings us closer to Jesus.

—Dru

> "The most sacred covenants and priesthood ordinances are received only in a temple—the house of the Lord. Everything that is learned and all that is done in the temple emphasize the divinity of Jesus Christ and His role in Heavenly Father's great plan of happiness."
>
> David A. Bednar
>
> "Let This House Be Built unto My Name," Apr. 2020

Doctrine and Covenants 111:10–11

For there are more treasures than one for you in this city. Therefore, be ye as wise as serpents and yet without sin; and I will order all things for your good.

Finding Treasure

The Fenn Treasure was a chest filled with gold and other artifacts that Forrest Fenn hid in the US Rocky Mountains in 2010. Fenn wrote many clues in a book, *The Thrill of the Chase*, to help people know where to look. For a decade, people searched for the treasure estimated to be worth $2 million. Five people died while searching for it. Fenn was criticized for putting people in harm's way with such a stunt. Finally, in 2020 during the COVID-19 pandemic, a medical student from Michigan found the treasure in Wyoming.

We can all find eternal treasure worth so much more than worldly wealth. The clues to the treasure we seek are found in the scriptures. Through these pages, we can gain a testimony of Jesus Christ and the everlasting joy of living with Him again. He and His eternal gift to us, the Atonement, is our treasure.

—Marianna

> "Jesus Christ is our treasure. Treasure the opportunity to repent, the privilege of partaking of the sacrament, the blessing of making and keeping temple covenants, the delight of worshiping in the temple, and the joy of having a living prophet."
>
> Dale G. Renlund
> "Jesus Christ Is the Treasure." Oct. 2023

Doctrine and Covenants 112:10

Be thou humble; and the Lord thy God shall lead thee by the hand, and give thee answer to thy prayers.

Walk by Faith

Have you ever been at girls' camp and done a faith walk activity? Blindfolded, you have a leader nearby giving verbal cues where to step and turn safely. I love doing these trust-building activities. To navigate the blind obstacle course, you have to focus on the voice you know and block out all the other sounds.

Humility requires learning how to hear the voice of God and letting His Spirit lead you by the hand. Mortality is filled with detours and distractions. Pressing forward on the covenant path is about finding the iron rod and not letting go. Then, like the holiday song says, just keep putting one foot in front of the other, and soon you will be walking a God-guided life ("Put One Foot in Front of the Other," featured in the 1970 Rankin/Bass Christmas special Santa Claus Is Comin' to Town).

Just like during a faith walk, we must find our own way. Each of us is on an individual journey of praying and acting on the answers given.

—Ganel-Lyn

"We cannot just do and think what others are doing and thinking; we must live a guided life. We must each have our own hand on the iron rod."

Larry Y. Wilson

"Take the Holy Spirit as Your Guide," Apr. 2018

Doctrine and Covenants 112:11

Be not partial towards them in love above many others, but let thy love be for them as for thyself; and let they love abound unto all men.

A Self-Love Makeover

Have you heard of a love/hate relationship? I have one with myself. At times, I think I'm awesome and clean up pretty well. Other times I get frustrated with my weaknesses but hold it together, and still other times I downright hate myself and engage in some harsh self-talk.

Thomas B. Marsh's revelation warned him not to have favorites, people he liked more than others. Then he was told to love them with the same love he had for himself. If I did that, I'd be abusive to my best friends! Maybe I need a self-love makeover. We do need to love ourselves but not go overboard and love ourselves too much. In Timothy, Paul warned that in the last days men would become lovers of their own selves (see 2 Timothy 3:2)

As I focus on the Savior and feel His love for me, it is easier to love myself. At times, when I am negative, I can count my blessings or read my patriarchal blessing to remember who I am. When my self-love is secure, I'll still enjoy my besties, but I'll be confident enough to reach out to those who need love, even when they aren't their best selves, because I've loved myself when I'm not my best self.

—Christine

> "Our Heavenly Father wants us to love ourselves—not to become prideful or self-centered, but to see ourselves as He sees us: we are His cherished children."
>
> S. Gifford Nielson
>
> "This Is Our Time!," Apr. 2021

Doctrine and Covenants 112:33

Verily I say unto you, behold how great is your calling. Cleanse your hearts and your garments, lest the blood of this generation be required at your hands.

Never the Same

During my time as Young Women president in my ward, I developed a deep affection for each of the sixty young women I served. They each had their own unique personalities, talents, and gifts. While their testimonies were at different stages of development, it was evident that they were all striving to learn about Jesus and follow Him. After my release from the calling, I lost touch with many of the girls. Looking back, I realize that I distanced myself because I thought my responsibility was over and didn't want to interfere with their connection to the new presidency. Now, I wish I had stayed connected to them, offering encouragement and support along their way.

Our callings are never over. Jesus Christ needs us to care for His children, and our love should have no boundaries. He wants those who truly love Him to aid Him in His work. Once we have tasted of the sweet fruit of the love of God, our lives can never be the same.

—Dru

> "After an encounter with the living Son of the living God, nothing is ever again to be as it was before."
>
> Jeffrey R. Holland
>
> "The First Great Commandment," Oct. 2012

Doctrine and Covenants 113:6

It is a descendant of Jesse, as well as of Joseph, unto whom rightly belongs the priesthood, and the keys of the kingdom, for an ensign, and for the gathering of my people in the last days.

Deep Roots

Every spring, I try to prepare the soil by getting rid of all the roots I can from the previous year. I am amazed at how deep the roots grow. Many of the roots stretch down for at least a foot! Some roots I just give up on; they are too strong and too deep for me to remove.

The Prophet Joseph Smith's roots were deep. His entire family nurtured his testimony of his mission here on earth. Their support and understanding enabled the Prophet's conviction to be so deep that even when others tried to pull at him, his roots in the Restoration were too strong. His testimony could not be dug up. His example has become an ensign and beacon to the world

Persecution did not stop with the early Saints. Throughout the world, Saints still have to deal with negative consequences because of their faith. But if our roots are deep, even when others try to pull us out of our foundation in the gospel, we will remain steadfast and not be moved.

—Marianna

> "We should always remember the price Joseph and Hyrum Smith paid, along with so many other faithful men, women, and children, to establish the Church."
>
> M. Russell Ballard
>
> "Shall We Not Go in So Great a Cause?," Apr. 2020

Doctrine and Covenants 113:10

We are to understand that the scattered remnants are exhorted to return to the Lord from whence they have fallen; which if they do, the promise of the Lord is that he will speak to them, or give them revelation.

I Heard You on the Radio

I love being a guest on radio shows. There is something about the medium that allows listeners to connect with you in traffic, while running errands, or on a road trip. Some of my favorite radio appearances have been conversations where the host is comfortable letting God direct the conversation. It is always fun after being interviewed to hear from friends who just happened to catch my segment. I usually hear something like, "I was driving down the freeway and thought that voice sounds familiar. And then it was you!"

Does the voice of our Heavenly Father sound familiar? Are you able to recognize when He is speaking to you? Reading and studying the scriptures helps us learn the language of the Spirit. Through daily feasting on His Word, we will have greater access to spiritual power.

—Ganel-Lyn

> "These words are more than ink on a page, sound waves in our ears, thoughts in our minds, or feelings in our hearts. The word of God is spiritual power."
>
> Douglas D. Holmes
> "Deep in Our Heart," Apr. 2020

Doctrine and Covenants 114:1

It is wisdom in my servant David W. Patten, that he settle up all his business as soon as he possibly can . . . that he may perform a mission unto me next spring.

David Patten, the First Martyr

Soon after moving to Missouri, I was traveling with another sister who pointed out the window and said, "That's where David W. Patten was martyred at the Battle of Crooked River." I'd never heard of him but found two references about him in the Doctrine and Covenants. He is a true hero.

Patten was baptized by his brother and then served twelve missions. Married but childless, Patten was called as one of the original Apostles under Joseph Smith. One convert wrote, "I could at a glance see the noble spirit he possessed. . . . Before he was half through I could have borne my testimony of the truth of the gospel and doctrine he was preaching."

In 1838 three boys were taken captive by the local militia. Patten took a group to retrieve them. They met the soldiers near Crooked River. Patten charged the line and was shot. The boys were freed, but three other Saints and one militia man were killed. In retaliation, Hawn's Mill was attacked less than a week later. The next morning Joseph Smith was taken to Liberty Jail. Patten died from his injuries, but a later revelation mentioned, "David Patten . . . is with [Christ] at this time" (Doctrine and Covenants 124:19). Patten gave everything for his testimony. Are we willing to die for the truth? Are we willing to live for it?

—Christine

> "Jesus taught that our offering may be large or it may be small, but either way, it must be our heartfelt all."
>
> Dieter F. Uchtdorf
>
> "Our Heartfelt All," Apr. 2022

Doctrine and Covenants 115:4

For thus shall my church be called in the last days, even the Church of Jesus Christ of Latter-day Saints.

The Perfect Name

Before the birth of my children, I spent many months trying to find the perfect names for them. Each of my twelve children were named after one of my ancestors. I tried to read these ancestors' histories and anything I could find out about them. Then, I would think about my unborn child and try to match the qualities I felt about my child with the right ancestor. I hope that this person will be an example to my child throughout his or her life.

The name of the Church also bears another person's name—Jesus Christ. At baptism, we take upon ourselves the name of Jesus Christ. As members of His Church, we are examples of Him to the world. Whenever we say the name of the Church, we should think about Him.

We may ask ourselves, Is my life's story worthy of being associated with His name? We are blessed to belong to His Church, to be His Saints, and to take upon us His name.

—Marianna

> "As members of The Church of Jesus Christ of Latter-day Saints, may we 'gladly [take upon us] the name of Christ' by honoring His name with love, devotion, and good works."
>
> Lisa L. Harkness
> "Honoring His Name," Oct. 2019

Doctrine and Covenants 115:5

Verily I say unto you all: Arise and shine forth, that thy light may be a standard for the nations.

When You Grow Up

When I was little, I loved playing banker and teacher. When my mom took me to the bank, I took deposit slips home to pretend play. I wanted to be a lot of things when I grew up, but one dream was be a talk show host. I kind of feel like I am living the dream now. I love doing television, radio, speaking events, and podcasts because I value having important conversations. Holding space for the authentic and awkward questions makes a difference. It helps people not feel so alone. Sharing stories offers connection and hope.

When I look back on my childhood dreams and the directions given in my patriarchal blessing, I see where God has helped me grow up. We are all asked to arise and share our unique individual light in the world. Whether it is in a classroom, a boardroom, or a living room, you are called to shine.

—Ganel-Lyn

> "Your patriarchal blessing will help you know that you have a noble birthright. As you get older, you will see the prophecies in your blessing taking shape in your life. The Lord has important and exciting things for you to do."
>
> Julie B. Beck
>
> "You Have a Noble Birthright," Apr. 2006

Doctrine and Covenants 115:8
Therefore, I command you to build a house unto me, for the gathering together of my saints, that they may worship me.

Blessings Still to Come

About half an hour north of the town of Liberty, on a straight country road, lies a field with a fence around it, a bathroom, and a parking lot. All around it are cornfields and prairie grass. But as you walk up to the fence, you can feel a stark difference in the spirit of the area.

Inside, the grass is mowed, green, and lush. Flowers surround a plaque describing this place, and four cornerstones lie in the ground forty by eighty feet apart, encased in glass. In obedience to revelation, these cornerstones were laid almost two hundred years ago to build the second temple of this dispensation, the Far West Temple. But why isn't it built? Why is it still an empty field?

Many blessings we are given are not yet fulfilled. I've had friends who were told in their blessings of experiences like motherhood or callings that never came. I've had a priesthood blessing tell me of my relationship with a son who passed away. Still, I have hope of these blessings' fulfillment in the Lord's time, just like this temple which I hope will be built eventually.

The plaque says that the Far West Temple will be "for the gathering together of [the] saints that they might worship [the Lord]." I can feel the peace of the temple in this lot, but it is a blessing still to come, like so many others. That is my brightest hope.

—Christine

> "We all need to believe that what we desire in righteousness can someday, someway, somehow yet be ours."
> Jeffrey R. Holland
> "A Perfect Brightness of Hope," Apr. 2020

Doctrine and Covenants 116

Adam shall come to visit his people, or the Ancient of Days shall sit, as spoken by Daniel the Prophet.

Fireflies

I am obsessed with fireflies. When I was a kid in Tennessee, my cousins and I would chase them around our grandma's yard during summer nights. We'd try to catch them as they glowed with green, yellow, or orange light, filling the air with wonder.

Years later, after the rededication of the Nauvoo Illinois Temple, my family embarked on a three-week-long trip to explore Church history sites. One evening, as the sun was setting, we arrived at the Adam-ondi-Ahman site in northern Missouri. The senior missionaries were closing the gate, but we explained our journey, and they kindly let us in. As darkness fell, thousands of fireflies appeared, surrounding us with their twinkling lights. Overwhelmed with joy, my kids chased them, creating cherished memories in this sacred place illuminated by the magical glow of fireflies.

Adam-ondi-Ahman is near where Adam and Eve lived after they left the Garden of Eden. Three years before Adam passed away, he gathered his righteous descendants there and blessed them. In the future, Adam will return to this place as a resurrected being. There, he will meet with other resurrected beings, and prophets who held priesthood keys will give those keys to Adam. He will then give the keys to Jesus Christ. This event is important in preparing for Jesus Christ's Second Coming. I imagine it will be filled with fireflies.

—Dru

> "Here is where the human race began."
> Mark E. Petersen
> "Adam, the Archangel," Oct. 1980

Doctrine and Covenants 117:11

Let my servant Newel K. Whitney be ashamed of the Nicolaitane band and of all their secret abominations, and of all his littleness of soul before me.

Littleness of Soul

In the New Testament, the Nicolaitane band was composed of followers of Nicolas, an apostatized early Christian. Before leaving the Church, he had been one of the seven appointed to distribute food and goods to the early Christian Saints (see Acts 6:5). After leaving the Church, Nicolas started his own sect. His band believed that it was all right to eat meat sacrificed to idols and to participate in the orgies associated with such feasts. Elder Bruce R. McConkie wrote that Nicolaitans today are "members of the Church who [are] trying to maintain their church standing while continuing to live after the manner of the world" (*Doctrinal New Testament Commentary*, 3:446).

In the early days of the restored Church, Bishop Newel K. Whitney was charged with overseeing the distribution of food and goods but was becoming too involved with land speculation, rather than the weightier matters of caring for the Saints. The members were being persecuted and driven from their homes. They needed a righteous bishop taking care of the Church's needs.

We, too, have "littleness of soul" when we think more about our worldly wealth than helping those in need or donating our tithes and generous offerings to the Church.

—Marianna

> "The windows of heaven open in many ways. . . . Some are subtle and easy to overlook.
>
> Neil L. Andersen
>
> "Tithing: Opening the Windows of Heaven," Oct. 2023

Doctrine and Covenants 118:3

I, the Lord, give unto them a promise that I will provide for their families; and an effectual door shall be opened for them, from henceforth.

Is My Family Going to Be Okay?

I have talked to a lot of missionaries about the vulnerability they felt while serving full time away from home. Both of my children expressed concern and worry about me while they were serving. My son had a dream that I died. He wrote home saying he loved me and was worried. I tried to assure him that I was fine. My daughter also dealt with some big intrusive thoughts about how her family was while she was a missionary.

We tried to comfort our kids with our support and shared how our family was being blessed because of their willingness to sacrifice and serve the Lord. Having a missionary out in the world makes a difference, not only for those they teach but for the loved ones back home. Everyone deserves to know about Jesus Christ and His gospel, and as missionaries answer that call, the Lord keeps His promise to protect their families.

—Ganel-Lyn

> "We love sister missionaries and welcome them wholeheartedly. What you contribute to this work is magnificent! Your decision to serve a mission, whether a proselyting or a service mission, will bless you and many others."
>
> **Russell M. Nelson**
> "Preaching the Gospel of Peace," Apr. 2022

Doctrine and Covenants 119:6–7

And I say unto you, if my people observe not this law, to keep it holy and by this law sanctify the land of Zion unto me . . . it shall not be a land of Zion unto you.

Tithing Blessings

Let's be real. Recently, a lot of people have been upset because the Lord's restored Church has been financially blessed. But the Church hasn't always had so many financial resources. In fact, it is a relatively new development. At the turn of last century when Lorenzo Snow was prophet, the Church was over $2 million in debt. Sixty years later when David O. McKay was prophet, they were over $32 million in debt. In 1964, my grandfather who worked in finance in New York City left his career to assist the Brethren.

They decided to create a holding company for the tithing funds and other donations so that there could be some return on investment while those resources waited until they were needed. The change made all the difference.

But we have never paid tithing because the Lord needs the money. By giving our tenth, even if it is a widow's mite, we become an equal part of The Lord's great work. And the Church, which is symbolically the land of Zion, becomes holier or more sanctified in our own hearts. If this is the only blessing we receive, it is enough, but often there are so many more.

—Christine

> "The world speaks of tithing in terms of our money, but the sacred law of tithing is principally a matter of our faith."
>
> Neil L. Andersen
> "Tithing: Opening the Windows of Heaven," Oct. 2023

Doctrine and Covenants 121:1–2

O God, where are thou? And where is the pavilion that covereth thy hiding place? How long shall they hand be stayed?

Waiting

I'm not very patient when I really need something. It's tough to wait for a family member to get better when they're sick or injured. Time feels like it moves slowly when I pray desperately for help and don't receive an immediate answer.

Why does waiting play such a significant role in spirituality? Because it's during the waiting that faith becomes essential. Consider this: if God provided instant gratification, we wouldn't need faith. It's in the waiting and the quiet moments that our faith grows. The three days between Jesus's crucifixion and resurrection teach us that silence doesn't mean God is absent.

Similarly, the eight days between Thomas expressing his doubt and Christ appearing to him show us that God is present both in miraculous moments and in times of silence. The presence of silence doesn't indicate God's absence. The challenge of waiting is to let our faith develop, trusting that on the other side of the silence, our faith will be deeper and stronger than before.

—Dru

> "I pray that 'by and by'—soon or late—those blessings will come to every one of you who seeks relief from your sorrow and freedom from your grief."
>
> Jeffrey R. Holland
>
> "Waiting on the Lord," Oct. 2020

Doctrine and Covenants 121:33

As well might man stretch forth his puny arm to stop the Missouri River in its decreed course, or to turn it up stream, as to hinder the Almighty from pouring down knowledge from heaven upon the heads of the Latter-day Saints.

Our Puny Arm

My family is building a log cabin in the woods. The logs are huge! The main log that holds up the three-story roof is so big that I can barely fit my arms around it. My puny arms would never be able to lift or move the logs that built the cabin. Without a large crane, the logs would just rot on the ground rather than become a lovely home.

Our puny arms or actions cannot compare to the magnificent tool of Christ's Atonement. We cannot move our sins off the dirty ground of our lives. They are too heavy. We need the Savior's help, His figurative crane, to lift them up. Just like the workmen building my home, my Savior can turn my puny actions into something beautiful.

While Joseph Smith and other Church leaders were stuck in Liberty Jail, they must have felt weak, helpless, and hopeless. The Lord reminded them that this was His work. No man could stop the light and knowledge He was and continues to pour down on the Latter-day Saints—then and now.

—Marianna

> "The immensity of His atoning sacrifice means that . . . our puny actions approach zero in comparison. But they are not zero, and they are not insignificant."
>
> Dale G. Renlund
> "Abound with Blessings," Apr. 2019

Doctrine and Covenants 121:40
Hence many are called, but few are chosen.

Pick Me, Pick Me

I think one of the most uncomfortable moments at school is when teams are being picked. You're standing with others on the line. Two captains are staring at all their friends. You anxiously wonder who will be the last picked—and pray silently that you won't be that poor soul not chosen.

When God says that many are called, but few are chosen, He isn't playing favorites. Elder Bednar clarifies what it means to be chosen by God: "God does not have a list of favorites to which we must hope our names will someday be added. He does not limit 'the chosen' to a restricted few. Instead, our hearts, our desires, our honoring of sacred gospel covenants and ordinances, our obedience to the commandments, and, most importantly, the Savior's redeeming grace and mercy determine whether we are counted as one of God's chosen" ("Put On Thy Strength, O Zion," Oct. 2022).

Eternal life and exaltation aren't about being popular or being the fastest on the track. God isn't standing back picking His best friends to live with Him for eternity. Being chosen is about the sacrifices we make to have a relationship with God.

—Ganel-Lyn

> "To be or to become chosen is not an exclusive status conferred upon us. Rather, you and I ultimately can choose to be chosen through the righteous exercise of our moral agency."
>
> **David A. Bednar**
> "Put On Thy Strength, O Zion," Oct. 2022

Doctrine and Covenants 121:33

Reproving betimes with sharpness, when moved upon by the Holy Ghost; and then showing forth afterwards an increase of love.

Being Sharp

One of my mother's greatest talents was her ability to give a compliment. She wouldn't simply say, "You look nice today." Nope, she would look deeper and say, "That dress really makes your waist look thinner" or "It matches your eyes." She was specific and accurate. Perhaps the way my mother complimented me is the same type of sharpness that the Lord was talking about when He said to reprove with sharpness. As we correct those under our authority, either as a parent, in a calling, or moved upon by the Spirit, we should be specific and accurate.

In Primary two weeks ago, one of my students was being disruptive. I'd asked him to calm down a few times, but then I paused. He was touching the other children, getting out of his seat, and leaning back in his chair. I decided to be sharp, as in specific and accurate. I chose to correct just one thing. "Sweetie," I said, "could you keep all of your chair's feet on the floor until the end of this story?"

When he did, I smiled and told him he could get the first treat out of the reverence box. He was well behaved the rest of class. Sharpness and love worked . . . at least that week.

—Christine

> "No one can employ a sharp tongue or unkind words and still 'sing the song of redeeming love.'"
> **Jeffrey R. Holland**
> "Not as the World Giveth," Apr. 2021

Doctrine and Covenants 121:45–46

Let thy bowels also be full of charity towards all men, and to the household of faith.

Helpless

During my seventh month of pregnancy, I contracted a rare virus that left me severely ill. The virus attacked my inner ear, causing unimaginable dizziness and nausea that lasted for months. I had to spend extensive time in the hospital and was unable to care for myself or my young family. Mercifully, friends, neighbors, and extended family stepped in to help. The assistance we received was invaluable, and I will always be grateful to those who helped during that difficult time.

Charity, the pure love of Christ, is all about caring for others without expecting anything in return. When we have love in our hearts, we see others as children of God and go out of our way to serve them.

Day to day, extending the pure love of Christ also means being patient, even when others let us down. It's not getting upset but accepting people for who they are. It's about being kind and forgiving without criticizing or judging others.

When we practice charity, we become more like Jesus Christ, who showed perfect love to everyone He met. It is the most important virtue we can cultivate and brings us closer to God and each other.

—Dru

> "As we arise each morning, let us determine to respond with love and kindness to whatever might come our way."
>
> Thomas S. Monson
>
> "Love—the Essence of the Gospel," Apr. 2014

Doctrine and Covenants 122:1–4
The ends of the earth shall inquire after thy name, and fools shall have thee in derision, and hell shall rage against thee; While the pure in heart, and the wise, and the noble, and the virtuous, shall seek counsel, and authority, and blessings constantly from under thy hand.

Heads or Tails

A two-sided coin is often used to decide which team gets the ball first at a football game or who gets to pick first when deciding who is on which team. Only one side of the coin matters after it is tossed. People are often judged by one side. We may view them as either heads or tails or all good or all evil. We should always try to look at the side of people that will put them in the best light.

The Lord warned Joseph Smith that people around the world would inquire after him. Those who are fools shall hold his life in derision. Those who are virtuous and wise will seek his counsel and authority.

We should view our Church leaders with the view that will hold them in the best light. If we are too critical, we may find that "hell shall rage" against us. We need to sustain our current prophet and Church leaders with the same reverence, faith, and appreciation that we have for the Prophet Joseph Smith. As we sustain them, we will receive constant blessings from their hands.

—Marianna

> "My purpose today is to convey the Lord's appreciation for your sustaining His servants in His Church. And it is also to encourage you to exercise and grow in that power to sustain others with your faith."
>
> Henry B. Eyring
> "The Power of Sustaining Faith," Apr. 2019

Doctrine and Covenants 122:8

The Son of Man hath descended below them all. Art thou greater than he?

I Know How You Feel

I fell and shattered my left wrist in fifty-two places. It was a pain beyond any pain I had previously experienced. Once the breaks healed, I had to go to physical therapy to regain movement and use of my hand. On my first day of therapy, the therapist shared that she, too, had suffered almost exactly the same injury seven years earlier. She said it was one of the most painful injuries the body can experience. In that moment, I knew that the person taking care of my healing knew exactly how I was feeling.

Elder Neal A. Maxwell taught, "The Lord knows firsthand that mortality is hard. His wounds remind us that He 'descended below . . . all'" ("Hosanna to the Most High God," Apr. 2023). The ultimate Healer knows exactly how you are feeling at any given moment. The Savior's wounds match yours. Because of Jesus, you never have to feel alone.

—Ganel-Lyn

> "Jesus' personal triumph was complete and His empathy perfected. Having 'descended below all things,' He comprehends, perfectly and personally, the full range of human suffering!"
>
> Neal A. Maxwell
>
> "Apply the Atoning Blood of Christ," Oct. 1997

Doctrine and Covenants 124:1

For unto this end have I raised you up, that I might show forth my wisdom through the weak things of the earth.

Weak Things

Joseph Smith was an unlikely prophet. As a boy of fourteen from a poor, hard-working family, he had no prominence in the community. Like David.

His reading and writing skills were never very strong, so he needed a scribe to even accomplish the work the Lord had called him to. Like Moses needed Aaron.

In 1841, the Saints had at last settled in Nauvoo. Almost two years had passed since Joseph was in Liberty Jail and had received his last recorded revelation. Now the Lord revealed section 124 to him and said that He didn't choose Joseph in spite of his weakness but because of it.

Although the gospel can change and strengthen us, there may be struggles that even the closest relationship with the Lord won't fix. Our brains may work a little differently, or we may have physical pains or weaknesses that are not healed. Remember, the Lord "show[s] forth [His] wisdom through the weak things of the earth," so being weak at times may not be so bad.

—Christine

> "The point is that faith means trusting God in good times and bad, even if that includes some suffering until we see His arm revealed in our behalf."
>
> Jeffrey R. Holland
> "Waiting on the Lord," Oct. 2020

Doctrine and Covenants 124:15

I, the Lord, love him because of the integrity of his heart, and because he loveth that which is right before me, saith the Lord.

Money, Money, Money

Once, a man owned a beautiful piece of land. It was ideally located at the top of a gentle hill that overlooked the valley below. Although not for sale, he told an inquiring realtor that if someone offered him $250,000, he would sell it. Years later, the realtor brought an offer for the exact amount. But by then, the land was worth $400,000. It was a problem. After thinking for a moment, the man said, "A deal is a deal," and he kept his promise.

This is a true story of a beloved friend, a man of integrity and a man of God. He understood that the Lord values honesty and integrity above all else. Even when faced with a difficult decision, he chose to do what was right and be true to his commitments regardless of the cost. This act of integrity not only honored his word but also demonstrated his character and commitment to living according to the principles of the gospel, even when he could have chosen otherwise.

—Dru

> "When we are true to the sacred principles of honesty and integrity, we are true to our faith, and we are true to ourselves."
> Richard C. Edgley
> "Three Towels and a 25-Cent Newspaper," Oct. 2006

Doctrine and Covenants 124:29–30

For a baptismal font there is not upon the earth that that my saints may be baptized for those who are dead—For this ordinance belongs to my house.

Baptisms for the Dead

I was in college when I attended the first funeral where I actually knew the person who had died. This was not the case for the early Saints. Death surrounded them. In the 1800s nearly half of all children didn't live until adulthood, and the average life expectancy was in the mid-forties.

In August of 1840 at a funeral in Nauvoo, Joseph Smith restored the doctrine of baptism for the dead. The joy that brought to those new converts must have been immeasurable. Almost immediately members were baptized in rivers and streams for their dead by one holding the priesthood. Three months later the above revelation clarified that these sacred ordinances should only be done in the temple. The Nauvoo Temple was little more than a basement in October 1841 when baptisms for the dead outside the temple ended. Within the next month, the Saints put a font in that basement so they could continue blessing their family members who had passed on.

Although the names we prepare for temple work may be distantly related, we should feel that same excitement that we are able to give those in our families who have passed on the opportunity to walk on the Savior's path.

—Christine

"The Spirit will flood our hearts, awaken our faculties to do it, and guide us as we search for the names of our ancestors."

Benjamin De Hoyos

"The Work of the Temple and Family History," Apr. 2023

Doctrine and Covenants 124:60

Let the name of that house be called Nauvoo House; and let it be a delightful habitation for man and a resting-place for the weary traveler.

A Delightful Habitation

My mother was an incredible hostess. She had a flare for making any home she inhabited delightful. My parents bought a new home with white walls, and my mother painted accent walls of bright orange and green. In any other home, these colored walls may have seemed too bright or garish. But in her home, they were perfect. She worked hard to make wherever she lived beautiful and a place where others felt welcomed.

After the Saints were kicked out of their homes in Missouri, they found a refuge in a swampy land full of mosquitoes. Their new home needed a lot of work to make it livable, let alone welcoming. The Saints had the same wish as my mother—to create a lovely home where others would want to visit. In section 124, the Lord gave practical instructions to His servants on how to make this a beautiful place. One of the Lord's instructions was to build a house where weary travelers would find rest. This was to be a delightful habitation where people could "contemplate the glory of Zion" (Doctrine and Covenants 124:60).

—Marianna

> "Since becoming President of the Church, I have been amazed at how many presidents, prime ministers, and ambassadors have sincerely thanked me for our humanitarian aid to their people. And they have also expressed gratitude for the strength that our faithful members bring to their country as loyal, contributing citizens."
>
> Russell M. Nelson
>
> "The Second Great Commandment," Oct. 2019

Doctrine and Covenants 124:45

And if my people will hearken unto my voice, and unto the voice of my servants whom I have appointed to lead my people, behold, verily I say unto you, they shall not be moved out of their place.

Airport Voice

After flying into San Diego, we took a shuttle from the airport to pick up our rental car. On the bus a video was playing with a voice directing us where to go to get our car. When we arrived at the rental car agency, I thought I had heard the correct instructions. I hadn't. After going up the escalator and walking around the third level, Rob and I realized we had missed a step. So down the escalator we went to backtrack and follow the right directions instead of the ones we thought we heard.

God has made sure we have a living prophet on earth to help direct and guide us through the ups and downs of life. Sometimes we miss the directions or don't hear the voice correctly. It is then that we can all use the Atonement to backtrack and find a new way forward.

We have to be willing to not only hear but hearken. When we willingly choose to follow His prophet, we follow God.

—Ganel-Lyn

> "Listening to and hearkening to living prophets will have profound, even life-changing effects in our lives. We are strengthened."
>
> Dean M. Davies
>
> "Come, Listen to a Prophet's Voice," Oct. 2018

Doctrine and Covenants 124:92–93

From henceforth he shall hold the keys of the patriarchal blessings upon the heads of all my people, that whoever he blesses shall be blessed.

Show Me the Way

When I'm headed somewhere new, I rely on my GPS to guide me. With just a few taps on my phone, I can enter the address and get directions to my destination. It gives me confidence that I'll find my way, no matter where I need to go.

Just as a GPS helps travelers navigate their journey, a patriarchal blessing serves as a spiritual guide for each of us. It's a unique gift from God that offers direction, warnings, and encouragement for our journey through life. Unlike a physical map, this blessing is personal and tailored to our individual needs and circumstances.

In our patriarchal blessings, we receive divine insights about our family history and our life's purpose. They provide us with a roadmap to navigate challenges, make important decisions, and find joy and fulfillment. These blessings are not just words on paper—they are promises from God to guide us and protect us as we walk the path of discipleship.

—Dru

> "Your patriarchal blessing is your passport to peace in this life. It is a Liahona of light to guide you unerringly to your heavenly home."
>
> Thomas S. Monson
> "Your Patriarchal Blessing: A Liahona of Light," Oct. 1986

Doctrine and Covenants 124:98

And these signs shall follow him—he shall heal the sick, he shall cast out devils, and shall be delivered from those who would administer unto him deadly poison.

Signs

When I first received my driver's license, I studied all the road signs and what they meant for the dreaded driver's test. A stop sign was easy—I knew what that meant. But warning signs, such as falling rocks ahead, no overtaking, and no turn around were signs I did not know.

Signs will follow those who believe in the Savior. For example, the Prophet Joseph Smith healed many who were sick with malaria from the mosquitoes surrounding Nauvoo. He cast out devils from Saints and was protected from those who would kill him. But many in Missouri and Illinois refused to see those signs. They refused to study and learn from the miracles that followed those who believed.

We can also look for signs in our own life that will illustrate to us and others how close we are to our Savior. We can monitor how kind, patient, and loving we are to people, especially those who might not deserve it, as a sign that we are becoming more like Him.

—Marianna

> "One of the most evident signs that we are drawing closer to the Savior and becoming more like Him is the loving, patient, and kind way with which we treat our fellow beings, whatever the circumstances."
>
> **Ulisses Soares**
>
> "Followers of the Prince of Peace," Apr. 2023

Doctrine and Covenants 125:3

Let them build up a city unto my name upon the land opposite the city of Nauvoo, and let the name of Zarahemla be named upon it.

Let's Get Together

I love getting together for the holidays. Gathering to celebrate, catch up, and eat yummy food is good for the soul and fosters unity.

As we read in section 125, the Lord calls the Saints to gather together. In addition to the building up of Nauvoo, the establishment of two new communities was commanded: Zarahemla and Nashville in the Iowa Territory. Stakes were organized, and the gathering began.

The Lord no longer commands the Saints to move to a single location. But in the early days of the Restoration, living together and being together was what the new church needed. As you approach upcoming get-togethers, remember that connection and conversation creates community. And we all do better when we are a part of a community.

—Ganel-Lyn

"The stakes and districts of Zion are symbolic of the holy places spoken of by the Lord where His Saints are to gather in the last days as a refuge from the storm."

Ezra T. Benson

Teachings of Presidents of the Church: Ezra Taft Benson (2014), 293

Doctrine and Covenants 126:1, 3

My servant Brigham, it is no more required at your hand to leave your family as in times past. . . . Take especial care of your family from this time, henceforth and forever.

Mary Ann Angell Young

Mary Ann Angell married Brigham Young, a widower with two small daughters, in Kirtland. Brigham was away on missions for almost half of their first years together. When at last he returned in the fall of 1837, Kirtland was in conflict, and he fled to Missouri. Mary Ann followed him after a difficult winter alone, being terrorized by mobs.

Soon, the Twelve were called on a mission to Great Britain. Brigham was sick with malaria, and Mary Ann had had her fifth child ten days earlier. As she waved good-bye, Brigham and Heber C. Kimball stood feebly and shouted, "Hurrah for Israel!" trying to cheer up those they left behind.

At first, Mary Ann had to cross the river in a little rowboat with her baby to get supplies, often getting chilled and wet. When she was given a lot in Nauvoo, she built her own shelter and used blankets to hang over the doors and windows. After being gone for almost two years, Brigham returned, and Joseph received the revelation that Brigham needed "to take especial care of his family . . . henceforth and forever." Many feel this revelation was for Mary Ann. Although she would continue to serve, never again would she struggle as she had during those early years. The Lord blesses those who do all they can.

—Christine

> "In the Lord's church we served where called, 'which place one neither seeks nor declines.'"
>
> **Gerrit W. Gong**
> "Love Is Spoken Here," Oct. 2023

Doctrine and Covenants 127:4

Let the work of my temple . . . be continued on and not cease; and let your diligence, and your perseverance, and patience, and your works be redoubled, and you shall in nowise lose your reward.

The Chance of a Lifetime

On the one hundredth anniversary of the Salt Lake Temple dedication, my husband and I had a great idea. We decided to go to the temple and perform ordinances to commemorate this special occasion. Turns out, we weren't the only ones with this idea—thousands of Saints in the area had the same plan. When we got there, we found a long line stretching over three hours just to get into the chapel. But then, the temple president offered us an amazing alternative. He said that if we skipped our session, he would give us a grand tour of the temple instead. We couldn't resist!

We strolled through the priesthood assembly room and climbed the sixty-six granite steps of the spiral staircases inside the majestic temple spires. We admired the round cap where the angel Moroni stood, attached to a long rod that extended down to a room in the upper temple. Next to the rod, there was a gauge that allowed him to move when the wind blew. The gauge bore the initials PPP for Parley P. Pratt. We gazed into the council room of the Twelve Apostles, affectionately known as the Talmage Room, where James E. Talmage spent many hours writing the book *Jesus the Christ*. Even though our official temple work was postponed for a night, the memories of this historic event will last forever.

—Dru

> "When the Lord calls for us to 'redouble' our efforts, He is asking that we increase in righteousness."
>
> Ronald A. Rasband
>
> "Recommended to the Lord," Oct. 2020

Doctrine and Covenants 128:7

Another book was opened, which was the book of life; but the dead were judged out of those things which were written in the books, according to their works.

Books

I love books—the physical kind. There is something about a beautifully printed book and physically holding it in your hands while you read that makes the communication something special—something you want to save and cherish.

Sections 127 and 128 are letters from the Prophet Joseph Smith while hiding from persecutors. Originally, Nauvoo had been a reprieve from persecution. In late 1842, that all changed. Joseph was hiding, hoping to save the Saints from further trouble.

Section 128 mentions the book of life. Joseph Smith's life story is well documented, and many books have been written about him. Some have vilified him; others have extolled him. The truth about his life is found in the book of life kept in heaven.

Each of us will be able to read our story as written in the book of life. Personally, I think the book of life will be a leather-bound physical book that we can touch and hold. Writing our life's story is not a fictional project. Instead, we need to be honest in our discussions about our life. If we are not, the book of life will show us the truth.

—Marianna

> "We will be judged by our book of life."
> Camille N. Johnson
> "Invite Christ to Author Your Story," Oct. 2021

Doctrine and Covenants 128:9

It may seem to some to be a very bold doctrine that we talk of—a power which records or binds on earth and binds in heaven.

What about Me?

While doing sealings in the Mount Timpanogos Utah Temple, the sealer in our session shared an important story. He was performing sealings for a family of nine children in one family who had died many years before. Using all the patrons serving in the session that day, the altar was surrounded. But there weren't enough people to be a proxy for all the kids. The sealer placed one daughter's name card on the small temple desk and he started the ordinance.

Then he heard, so clearly, *What about me?* With tears in his eyes, the sealer stopped the sealing. He found another patron and added the final member of this eternal family to the altar.

This is what the power of the priesthood means to God's children. It is about eternal hope, eternal connection, and eternal love on both sides of the veil.

—Ganel-Lyn

> "With access to the sealing power, our hearts naturally turn to those who have gone before. The latter-day gathering into the covenant crosses through the veil."
>
> D. Todd Christofferson
> "The Sealing Power," Oct. 2023

Doctrine and Covenants 128:15

Therefore, blessed are ye if ye continue in my goodness, a light unto the Gentiles, and through this priesthood, a savior unto my people Israel.

Each Has a Name

When I think about the Savior's invitation to feed His sheep, I think of family history and temple work. Like a shepherd gazing at a vast flock, we may feel overwhelmed, unsure of where to start. We may think there are too many sheep and that this responsibility is too great. In faith, we begin by taking one small step, trusting that the Lord will show us what to do. As we come closer to those we serve, we find that they are not just a massive flock, but they each have a name. We see their faces, learn their stories, and become acquainted with their families. Each has been waiting for the day we would find them. As we come to know them individually and spend our time loving and serving them, they become precious to us. They become ours, and it becomes a sweet labor of love.

The Prophet Joseph Smith declared, "The greatest responsibility in this world that God has laid upon us is to seek after our dead" (*Teachings of the Presidents of the Church: Joseph Smith*, 475). We have been given valuable tools to succeed in this task: FamilySearch, computers, family history libraries, the internet, and temples being built across the earth. The Lord has entrusted this task to us in our day. Let's cheerfully get to work.

—Dru

> "I invite you to prayerfully consider what kind of sacrifice—preferably a sacrifice of time—you can make [to] do more temple and family history work."
>
> **Russell M. Nelson**
>
> "Open the Heavens through Temple and Family History Work," *Ensign*, Oct. 2017

Doctrine and Covenants 128:18

For we without them cannot be made perfect; neither can they without us be made perfect.

The Magnet and the Fridge

Our refrigerators have always been covered with family photos, to-do lists, bulletins of upcoming events, and my children's hand-drawn masterpieces—each held in place with a colorful magnet of fruit, donuts, unicorns, and fingerprints. So many fingerprints. I was really excited when we decided to get a new refrigerator that was fingerprint-proof.

The new refrigerator arrived. It was beautiful with a vinyl front. I was thrilled until I tried to put up my children's pictures. My magnets wouldn't stick. I was shocked and disappointed. My magnets were doing their job, but the refrigerator wasn't cooperating and would never hold the joy and beauty I wanted to lavish on it.

In like manner, proxy work for the dead takes both parties to make it effective. Even if their hearts are ready to accept the covenants, they can't do it if we don't do the work for them. That's why the Lord said that the hearts of the children need to turn to the fathers and the fathers to the children. When both work together, they create something beautiful that is connected forever.

—Christine

> "We honor our ancestors by opening the heavens through temple and family history work and by becoming a welding link in the chain of our generations."
>
> Gerrit W. Gong
> "We Each Have a Story," Apr. 2022

Doctrine and Covenants 129:1–2

Jesus said: Handle me and see, for a spirit hath not flesh and bones, as ye see me have.

Handle Me and See

The Savior's experience after His Resurrection will help us understand the nature of our bodies after we die and the nature of the body of our Heavenly Father.

In Luke, the Savior unexpectedly appeared to the Twelve. They were affrighted because they knew He was dead. He said to them, "Behold my hands and my feet, that it is I myself: handle me, and see; for a spirit hath not flesh and bones, as ye see me have" (Luke 24:39). The Apostles felt His hands and feet, but they still wondered. Then, He asked if they had any food, and He ate with them to show them that He had a resurrected, physical, functioning body.

Our physical, mortal bodies are a blessing. Joseph Smith taught, "All beings who have bodies have power over those who have not" (*Teachings: Joseph Smith*, 211). Our bodies protect us from Satan in this life and in the next. After death, we will receive the Savior's gift of a physical, resurrected body because of His resurrection.

—Marianna

> "As He cast His eyes on the multitude, He noticed that they were in tears, looking steadfastly upon Him as if they would ask Him to tarry a little longer. . . . It seems that He could see them through the eyes of His atoning sacrifice. He saw their every pain, affliction, and temptation."
>
> Peter F. Meurs
>
> "He Could Heal Me!," Apr. 2023

Doctrine and Covenants 130:2

And that same sociality which exists among us here will exist among us there, only it will be coupled with eternal glory, which glory we do not now enjoy.

The Weekend from Heck

Usually, spending time with the people we love most is wonderful. But every once in a while, on a long road trip or when someone is sick or in pain, it can be trying. Especially when contention breaks out.

One weekend my family rented a cabin at Island Park in Idaho and went snowmobiling with my daughter and her new fiancé. My newly married son and his wife came, as did our five other children. Some were angsty teenagers, and others were college students who didn't want direction. I was on edge and with good reason. It was the weekend from heck!

What should have been a joyful time was so stressful, and to make matters worse, the beds were so uncomfortable that no one could sleep. Soon raised voices and sarcastic remarks began to abound. I adored everyone I was around, but by the end of that weekend, frustrated with my children's bad attitudes and physically exhausted, I found myself in tears three times.

When we dwell eternally as families, "that same sociality which exists among us here will exist among us there, only it will be coupled with eternal glory." There won't be tired and grumpy husbands, hormonal teenagers, or stressed out young mothers, just each of the people I love most at our best. It will be heavenly. I can't wait!

—Christine

> "True, enduring joy and eternity with those we love are the very essence of God's plan of happiness."
>
> Gerrit W. Gong
> "Happy and Forever," Oct. 2022

Doctrine and Covenants 130:18–19

Whatever principle of intelligence we attain unto in this life, it will rise with us in the resurrection. And if a person gains more knowledge and intelligence in this life through his diligence and obedience than another, he will have so much the advantage in the world to come.

The Glory of God Is Intelligence

I am a first-generation college graduate. I began my pursuit of higher education at the age of seventeen but became a little distracted when I got married, had six children, and had a myriad of life experiences in between. Finally, I finished my MBA at the age of forty-nine. It's never too late to receive an education. One person in my graduating class was seventy-six years old!

Even if you don't have access to formal education, don't let that stop you from gaining knowledge. Books can be like your own personal university, always open for learning. Strive to learn about things that are good and praiseworthy. Seek knowledge with humility and faith. As you study, both spiritually and intellectually, your understanding will grow.

Don't forget to seek guidance from God. The scriptures and the teachings of modern-day prophets are valuable sources of wisdom and insight. They can help you find answers to life's challenges and lead you to peace and truth. Focus on learning about Jesus Christ and the truths that bring happiness and teach you the things of eternity.

—Dru

"If formal education is not available, do not allow that to prevent you from acquiring all the knowledge you can."

Dieter F. Uchtdorf

"Two Principles for Any Economy," Oct. 2009

Doctrine and Covenants 130:22–23

The Holy Ghost has not a body of flesh and bones, but is a personage of Spirit. Were it not so, the Holy Ghost could not dwell in us.

The Holy Ghost Dwells in Us

I still remember my baptism vividly. I was baptized on my eighth birthday, and I was so excited for that day. My father baptized and confirmed me. After the baptism, all my friends came over to my house, and we had a Hawaiian luau.

Days after my baptism, I still could feel the priesthood hands upon my head. I asked my father why. He explained that the Holy Ghost can reveal Himself through physical manifestations, such as a burning in the bosom, a peaceful feeling in your heart, and for me, the feeling of the hands of the priesthood still on my head. It was such a spiritual experience for me.

The Holy Ghost is the third member of the Godhead who will testify to our minds and hearts that the gospel of Jesus Christ is true. We are given the gift of the Holy Ghost at baptism, but we must receive it in order for it to dwell within us because the Holy Ghost cannot dwell in unholy temples or bodies.

—Marianna

"The Holy Ghost is different from the Light of Christ. He is the third member of the Godhead, a distinct personage of spirit with sacred responsibilities, and one in purpose with the Father and the Son. . . . Through the Holy Ghost, we experience 'the multitude of [Christ's] tender mercies' and miracles that do not cease."

Robert D. Hales

"The Holy Ghost," Apr. 2016

Doctrine and Covenants 131:6

It is impossible for a man to be saved in ignorance.

First Graders

I love being a teacher. I student taught an amazing group of Arizona first graders who were excited to learn. I was doing chemotherapy during that school year, and some days I had to take a nap in the teachers' lounge just to make it through the day. Some of my students came from really difficult family situations, but they came every day willing to learn.

That year changed me. I learned as much—or maybe more—from my students as I taught them. I learned that I could do hard things. I learned that kids are honest and accept you right where you are. Even when your hair is falling out.

Elder Ulisses Soares taught, "We all have to seek to learn and to teach one another the gospel of Jesus Christ" ("How Can I Understand?," Apr. 2019). I love serving in different callings in the Church. Sometimes we are the teachers, and sometimes we are the students. And sometimes we are both in the same classroom. God loves helping His children learn. We just need to be willing to show up every day.

—Ganel-Lyn

> "In the context of learning and teaching the gospel, . . . we need the help of a faithful and inspired teacher."
>
> **Ulisses Soares**
> "How Can I Understand?," Apr. 2019

Doctrine and Covenants 132:16

Which angels are ministering servants, to minister for those who are worthy of a far more, and an exceeding, and an eternal weight of glory.

The Weight of Glory

The Apostle Paul wrote about the persecutions he suffered on his mission: "For our light afflictions, which is but for a moment, worketh for us a far more exceeding and eternal weight of glory" (2 Corinthians 4:17). Although this phrase is only mentioned once in the Bible, C. S. Lewis wrote a whole book, entitled *The Weight of Glory*, that explains what he believes glory to be and how we change to accept it.

Interestingly, in a revelation given to Joseph Smith and Sidney Rigdon on the importance of treating sacred things with proper care, they are warned that if they obey they "may receive a more exceeding and eternal weight of glory, otherwise, a greater condemnation" (Doctrine and Covenants 63:66).

For me, the best explanation of the weight of glory is in Michelangelo's *The Last Judgment*, which depicts Christ at the center surrounded by throngs of people. Below Him are those being cast to hell, but above Him are only a few good souls carrying the heavy pillars of heaven. As we live our covenants, we prepare ourselves to be able to lift the weight of further responsibility in God's kingdom—even the weight of glory.

—Christine

> "I bear witness that when we pledge to follow Him, the path will, one way or another, pass by way of a crown of thorns and a stark Roman cross."
>
> Jeffrey R. Holland
>
> "The Greatest Possession," Oct. 2021

Doctrine and Covenants 132:24

This is eternal lives—to know the only wise and true God, and Jesus Christ, who he hath sent. I am he.

Are You Willing?

Alma 20–22 teaches us the story of the conversion of Lamoni's father, who was king of all the land. In a physical encounter with Ammon, the king realized he could not slay Ammon and feared for his life. In exchange for his life, the king said, "If thou wilt spare me I will grant unto thee whatsoever thou wilt ask, *even to half of the kingdom*" (Alma 20:23; emphasis added).

Later, as Aaron expounded the plan of redemption to the king, he asked, "What shall I do that I may have this eternal life? . . . *I will give up all that I possess, yea, I will forsake my kingdom,* that I may receive this great joy" (Alma 22:15; emphasis added).

But Aaron told him if he desired eternal life, he must pray, repent, and call on God in faith. So the king prayed: "If thou art God, wilt thou make thyself known unto me, and *I will give away all my sins to know thee*" (Alma 22:18; emphasis added).

Each of us has to answer these questions for ourselves. What are we willing to do to know God and have eternal life? Will we bow down before God in prayer, give away our sins, and have faith in Jesus Christ, who offers eternal life? The choice is ours.

—Dru

> "I witness and promise we can not only know about the Lord but also come to know Him as we exercise faith in, follow, serve, and believe Him."
>
> **David A. Bednar**
> "If Ye Had Known Me," Oct. 2016

Doctrine and Covenants 133:4–5

Wherefore, prepare ye, prepare. . . . Go ye out from Babylon. Be ye clean that bear the vessels of the Lord.

Be Ye Clean

When all my children were young, after I fed them, the kitchen would look like a food fight had taken place. I often commented that I would be able to feed a third-world country from the food on my floor and walls. But every night, I would sweep the floor and spot wash the walls. Making my kitchen clean again made me feel so much better and ready for the next meal.

When my house is not spotless, I do not want guests to come over and visit. I try to quickly scrub before guests arrive. But if I do not wash up every day, then the work to clean a week's worth of kitchen mess is much harder than it is for just one meal.

Keeping our surroundings clean is important, but keeping our bodies clean—inside and outside—is eternally important. Our bodies are the vessels of our spirits, similar to our homes being the abode of our physical bodies. When we are clean from the messes of the world, our eternal guest, the Spirit of the Lord, is able to abide in and with us. Keeping our surroundings clean takes daily work, just as sincerely repenting daily keeps our spirits clean. When we are clean from the messes of the world, our eternal guest, the Spirit of the Lord, is able to abide in and with us.

—Marianna

> "Our bodies are sacred gifts from our Heavenly Father. They are personal temples. As we keep them clean and pure, we can be worthy to help our Heavenly Father create bodies for His beloved spirit children."
>
> Linda S. Reeves
>
> "Worthy of Our Promised Blessings," Oct. 2015

Doctrine and Covenants 133:8

Send forth the elders of my church unto the nations which are afar off; unto the islands of the sea; send forth unto foreign lands; call upon all nations.

Share Jesus

The week after my daughter decided to serve a mission, her dear friend Lauren was unexpectedly killed in a car accident. Lauren was also preparing to serve a mission at the time of her death. The morning Brooklyn got news about the tragic crash, she said, "Mom, I want to serve even more now. I want to share Jesus with the world. Because some people don't know that there is hope after losing someone you love."

President Ezra Taft Benson boldly said to future missionaries, "You are needed in the service of the Lord today as never before. 'The harvest truly is great, but the labourers are few' (Luke 10:2)" (April 1984). Our missionary force is larger in numbers than it was in 1984 when President Benson made that statement. With more than seventy thousand now serving—the most in the history of the Church—more are needed to help prepare for the Second Coming of Jesus.

Saying goodbye to my daughter for eighteen months was hard. But there was nowhere else I would have wanted her to be. I love Jesus. I love Brooklyn. If you are on the fence about serving a mission, remember that the world needs to know what you know. Jesus is coming.

—Ganel-Lyn

"This commission to take the gospel to every nation, kindred, tongue, and people is one of the signs by which believers will recognize the nearness of the Savior's return to earth."

Ezra Taft Benson

"Our Commission to Take the Gospel to All the World," Apr. 1984

Doctrine and Covenants 133:19

Wherefore, prepare ye for the coming of the Bridegroom; go ye, go ye out to meet him.

Going Out to Meet Him

I sent all five of my sons on missions. The moment I saw my missionary in the airport after being apart for two years would get me every time. The family would stand, waiting with their signs as he disembarked and came past security. The minute he passed the barrier, our whole family would run up and shower our returning son with hugs, wanting to know how he was, looking at how he'd changed, and crying in joy at his return.

As we prepare for the coming of Christ, are we looking forward to that grand meeting with the same joy as I did on greeting my sons? Or do we feel dread? Section 133 encourages us to prepare by sanctifying ourselves and gathering to the land of Zion (see Doctrine and Covenants 133:4). Modern prophets have taught that the land of Zion is anywhere there is a temple, and the way we are sanctified is by being worthy to enter it.

That is our lamp, lit and ready, like the signs in the airport. The key is that we watch and listen so that when He comes again, we can run out to meet our Savior, prepared and filled with joy.

—Christine

> "I have learned from personal experience that spiritual preparation for the coming of the Lord is not only essential but the only way to find true peace and happiness."
>
> **Amy A. Wright**
> "Abide the Day in Christ," Oct. 2023

Doctrine and Covenants 133:56

And the graves of the saints shall be opened; and they shall come forth and stand on the right hand of the Lamb, when he shall stand upon Mount Zion, and upon the holy city, the New Jerusalem; and they shall sing the song of the Lamb, day and night forever and ever.

Songs of the Heart

Music has a unique ability to express our emotions in a way that nothing else can. We all have our favorite songs, often connected to important moments in our lives. Whether it's the hymns we sang in childhood while learning about the gospel, the tunes that played during our first crushes, or the grand orchestrations that inspire awe, music touches our hearts and reflects our innermost feelings.

One of my favorite hymns is "Come Thou Fount of Every Blessing." Nearly twenty years ago, the Brigham Young University Combined Choirs recorded an album titled *American Thanksgiving of Hymns*, featuring this hymn among others. You can still find a video of the performance on YouTube, and I've lost count of how many times I've watched it. Every time I do, I'm deeply moved by the Spirit, and tears flow freely. Its powerful message reminds me of the healing power of the Savior that comes as I strive to dedicate my life to Him.

One day, the righteous will be gathered from all corners of the earth to Zion. There, they will raise their voices in songs of everlasting joy to their eternal King, who will reign forever. What a glorious day it will be when together in unity, all of those who love Him will express their gratitude to God and the Lamb for Their infinite love and mercy.

> "Sacred music has a unique capacity to communicate our feelings of love for the Lord."
>
> **Dallin H. Oaks**
>
> "Worship through Music," Oct. 1994

Doctrine and Covenants 133:57–58

And for this cause, that men might be made partakers of the glories which were to be revealed, the Lord sent forth the fulness of his gospel, his everlasting covenant, reasoning in plainness and simplicity.

Reasoning in Plainness and Simplicity

In law school, moot court experiences teach students what a real courtroom is like before they actually work in one. A judge watches over the proceedings to make sure that no one breaks the law, and the judge determines who wins.

Many law students will try to give complicated explanations about the case or try to find loopholes in the law. But the students who win are the ones whose reasoning is plain and simple.

When we are brought before the throne of God, we, too, might want to find loopholes as an explanation of why we did not live the law of God the way we should have on earth. But living the gospel is plain and simple—keep God's commandments.

—Marianna

> "The adversary is clever. For millennia he has been making good look evil and evil look good. His messages tend to be loud, bold, and boastful. However, messages from our Heavenly Father are strikingly different. He communicates simply, quietly, and with such stunning plainness that we cannot misunderstand Him."
>
> Russell M. Nelson
>
> "Hear Him," Apr. 2020

Doctrine and Covenants 134:5

We believe that all men are bound to sustain and uphold the respective governments in which they reside, while protected in their inherent and inalienable rights by the laws of such governments.

Fourth of July Parade

I live in an area of the United States where the Fourth of July is a big deal. We have the best hometown parade and fireworks shows. I get emotional when veterans and missionaries walk in the Freedom Festival Parade.

Every country has its own laws, traditions, and history. In section 134, God declares that all of His children are called to respect the "governments in which they reside."

Not everything in my country makes sense. Our history and politics are complicated. But regardless of the imperfection, being a good Saint means also being a good citizen. Following the laws of the land, voting in elections, and paying taxes all make a difference if someone is striving to live like Christ would.

—Ganel-Lyn

"A saint is an honorable citizen, knowing that the very country which provides opportunity and protection deserves support, including prompt payment of taxes and personal participation in its legal political process."

Russell M. Nelson

"Thus Shall My Church Be Called," Apr. 1990

Doctrine and Covenants 134:9

We do not believe it just to mingle religious influence with civil government.

Not Letting Politics Divide Us

We live in turbulent times. The divide in the United States between political parties has never been more polarized in my lifetime. In many circumstances it can pull families and friendships apart. A simple comment can end relationships.

Membership in the Church is completely independent of political affiliation. Sometimes, especially when we consider movements the Church has endorsed like ERA, anti-abortion legislation, and Proposition 8, we can incorrectly believe there is a right and wrong in the political arena. This is not the case.

In the past, Zion was composed of people who "were of one heart and one mind, and dwelt in righteousness; and there was no poor among them" (Moses 7:18). Finding that oneness and unity may mean holding certain opinions to ourselves. This can be difficult, but we should remember that when Christ comes in all His glory, we will all belong to the same political party, for He will rule us.

Until then, let's respect and love each other no matter what some say. As we strive for unity and forgiveness, we can become a truly Zion people.

—Christine

> "[We] can literally change the world . . . by modeling how to manage honest differences of opinion with mutual respect and dignified dialogue."
>
> Russell M. Nelson
>
> "Peacemakers Needed," Apr. 2023

Doctrine and Covenants 135:3

Joseph Smith, the Prophet and Seer of the Lord, has done more, save Jesus only, for the salvation of men in this world, than any other man that ever lived in it.

Restoration

Growing up outside of New York City, I enjoyed visiting the Metropolitan Museum of Art, the Museum of Modern Art, the Guggenheim, the Frick, and the Whitney often. I was initially surprised when I saw a missing painting and a little card resting in the empty space reading, "Removed for Restoration." When I would return later, the old painting was revitalized in color and texture. A picture that once looked dull and worn now looked new and vivid.

The Apostasy darkened and dulled the light of the gospel of Jesus Christ. Pieces of the truth had been lost. Through the Prophet Joseph Smith, the Restoration brought back to the world those lost pieces—the covenants, the priesthood, a prophet of God. The worn and incomplete Church was brought back to the same organization and authority as the original Church of Jesus Christ.

On June 27, 1844, Joseph and Hyrum Smith were brutally murdered as martyrs of the Restoration. John Taylor's tribute to these men's sacrifice was included as the final section of the 1844 edition of the Doctrine and Covenants. As Elder Taylor expressed, "Joseph Smith . . . has done more, save Jesus only, for the salvation of men in this world." The words "praise to the man" fill my heart every time I read section 135.

—*Marianna*

> "The Restoration of the gospel and the Church is not something that happened once and is over. It is an ongoing process—one day at a time, one heart at a time."
>
> Dieter F. Uchtdorf
>
> "Daily Restoration," Oct. 2021

Doctrine and Covenants 135:4

I am going like a lamb to the slaughter; but I am calm as a summer's morning; I have a conscience void of offense toward God, and towards all men.

Answered Prayer

The first time I felt that the First Vision was real was in Primary. I was singing "Joseph Smith's First Prayer," and while all the boys were making fun of the word *bosom* in the last verse, I found myself wiping away unbidden tears. After my baptism I read the Book of Mormon and got a very clear answer to my prayer. During my tumultuous teens, I also gained a testimony that I could trust canonized scripture.

Years later, my brother left the faith and told me he thought Joseph was a fallen prophet. He still believed in the First Vision and the Book of Mormon, but they were only to bring truth to the world. Like David of old, he felt Joseph had lost his calling.

Reeling, I took this issue to the Lord in prayer. I still remember kneeling at the corner of my bed with my scriptures before me. After my prayer I opened my scriptures randomly, and my eyes were drawn to Joseph's final words before he was taken to Carthage: "I am going like a lamb to slaughter. . . . I have a conscience void of offense towards God." As I read those words, a feeling of peace filled my heart. I was so grateful these words were canonized! I knew they were true, and I *know* Joseph Smith was a true prophet until the end of his life. It's true!

—Christine

> "Jesus Christ restored His Church and the truths of the gospel through the Prophet Joseph Smith."
>
> John C. Pingree
>
> "Eternal Truth," Oct. 2023

Doctrine and Covenants 136:4
And this shall be our covenant—that we will walk in all the ordinances of the Lord.

Light Therapy

I struggle with seasonal affective disorder. The shorter, colder days during the winter months make for longer nights and less sunlight. I have to be really intentional about navigating and supporting my mental health. One of the tools I use to stay well is going to light therapy on a weekly basis.

The same is true for our spiritual health. Elder Timothy J. Dyches taught how to use your agency to add light to your life: "You will invite spiritual sunlight into your soul and peace into your life each time you repent. As you partake of the sacrament every week to take the Savior's name upon you, to always remember Him and keep His commandments, His light will shine within you" ("Light Cleaveth unto Light," Apr. 2021).

If you are going through a winter season of faith, make choices to turn up the light. Spring is coming.

—Ganel-Lyn

"A drop of sunshine is added every time you seek God in prayer; study the scriptures to 'hear Him' [Russell M. Nelson, 'Hear Him,' *Ensign* or *Liahona*, May 2020, 89]; act on guidance and revelation from our living prophets; and obey and keep the commandments."

Timothy J. Dyches
"Light Cleaveth unto Light," Apr. 2021

Doctrine and Covenants 136:11

And if ye do this with a pure heart, in all faithfulness, ye shall be blessed; you shall be blessed in your flocks, and in your herds, and in your fields, and in your houses, and in your families.

French Fries and Fortresses

When our kids were little, we made a deal with them: if they cleaned their rooms and picked up all their toys, we promised to take them to McDonald's. Throughout the day they had used everything in sight to build forts and populated their homemade cities with stuffed animals and furnishings of every kind. It looked like a tornado had swept through, with blankets and toys scattered everywhere. Motivated by the promise of Happy Meals and plastic ball pits, they were determined to earn their trip. After an hour or so, their rooms were spotless, and they proudly showed us their clean and tidy spaces. It was a victory for me and my husband, and a delicious prize for our kids.

Just as our children were blessed for their efforts to obey their parents, when we do the things our Heavenly Father has asked, we will be blessed in all aspects of our lives, including our possessions, homes, and families. When we keep the commandments with pure intent and love in our hearts, we invite the blessings of heaven.

—Dru

> "Keep the commandments! Wonderful and glorious are the rewards which are in store for us if we do."
>
> Thomas S. Monson
> "Keep the Commandments," Oct. 2015

Doctrine and Covenants 136:23–25
Cease to contend one with another; cease to speak evil one of another. Cease drunkenness; and let your words tend to edifying one another. If thou borrowest of thy neighbor, thou shalt restore that which thou has borrowed.

Rules to Follow

January 1847 must have been a devastating month for the Saints. Their prophet had been slain, and persecution continued to rage rather than slacken. In 1846, the Saints began the exodus from Nauvoo and crossed the Mississippi River, moving farther west. Winter Quarters was thrown together with thousands of people living in hastily built dwellings. Women and babies died in childbirth in these rough conditions. There was little food and little shelter from harsh winter storms.

Yet the Saints continued forward with faith in every footstep. On the west bank of the Missouri River, near Council Bluffs, Iowa, Brigham Young sought revelation from the Lord on how to organize the Saints for the trek west. In section 136, the Lord set out practical standards for the Saints to follow that would lighten their load and bring happiness..

These standards are rules for all of us to follow in our lives. We do not need to live in tents with thousands of people around us to realize the importance of not fighting, going to bed early, working hard, and being grateful. As we edify and strengthen each other, we will find happiness too.

—Marianna

> "Heavenly Father and His Beloved Son . . . want you back home with Them! They want you to be happy. They will do anything within Their power that does not violate *your* agency or *Their* laws to help you come back."
>
> **Russell M. Nelson**
> "The Love and Laws of God," BYU devotional, Sept. 17, 2019

Doctrine and Covenants 136:31

My people must be tried in all things, that they may be prepared to receive the glory that I have for them, even the glory of Zion.

I Can Do Hard Things with God

My first published book, a compilation project, was titled *I Can Do Hard Things with God*. Each chapter was a story of a woman of great faith navigating a hard thing. And choosing to do it with God. Each of us will be called to navigate adversity and opposition. One of the hardest things I have gone through is the loss of two of my sisters.

From working on the book I learned that no matter what the trials were—in my case, mental health, financial struggle, or infertility—we will all be tried. It will be through our adversities that we will be refined and qualified for all God has to give us.

If you are currently navigating a hard thing, I hope you search carefully and find God in it.

—Ganel-Lyn

> "The Lord is always quietly refining His faithful people individually anyway, but events will also illuminate God's higher ways and His kingdom."
>
> Neal A. Maxwell
>
> "Plow in Hope," Apr. 2001

Doctrine and Covenants 137:5

I saw Father Adam and Abraham; and my father and my mother; my brother Alvin that has long since slept.

Alvin Is There!

Joseph Smith admired his oldest brother, Alvin. Five years his senior, Alvin believed in and encouraged Joseph in his calling. The angel Moroni had first shown Joseph the plates only three months before Alvin passed. According to the history of Lucy Mack Smith, Alvin's last words to Joseph were, "I want you to be a good boy and do everything that lies in your power to obtain the record. Be faithful in receiving instruction and in keeping every commandment that is given you."

Imagine Joseph's bittersweet feelings when he learned of baptism by authority. Alvin had died before he could join the restored gospel. Joseph may have thought Alvin was lost. Then after the dedication of the Kirtland Temple, Joseph saw Alvin in "the celestial kingdom of God." He was there! By revelation Joseph was taught the eternal truth that "all who have died without a knowledge of this gospel, who would have received it . . . shall be heirs of the celestial kingdom"(Doctrine and Covenants 137:7). Interestingly, he was not told how this could happen at that time..

Three and a half years later, in Nauvoo, Joseph finally received the revelation about baptisms for the dead, opening the gates for the glorious work making temple blessings available to all.

—Christine

> "Temple covenants are gifts from our Heavenly Father to the faithful followers of . . . Jesus Christ."
>
> J. Kimo Esplin
>
> "The Savior's Healing Power upon the Isles of the Sea," Oct. 2023

Doctrine and Covenants 138:11

As I pondered over these things which are written, the eyes of my understanding were opened, and the Spirit of the Lord rested upon me, and I saw the hosts of the dead, both small and great.

Surrounded by Loss

In 1918, Joseph F. Smith found himself amidst a world torn apart by the devastating effects of World War I and the deadly Spanish influenza pandemic, which claimed the lives of millions. These global crises intensified the personal grief Joseph F. Smith was experiencing, having recently lost many loved ones, including his son Elder Hyrum M. Smith of the Quorum of the Twelve Apostles, as well as other family members and close associates.

Against this backdrop of widespread suffering and loss, Joseph F. Smith turned to prayer and meditation, seeking solace and answers about the fate of those who had passed away. It was during this time of deep reflection and spiritual seeking that he received a profound vision revealing insights into the spirit world and the destiny of the souls of the departed. This vision, recorded in Doctrine and Covenants 138, provided comfort, clarity, and hope amidst the turmoil of war and pandemic, offering reassurance about the eternal plan of salvation and the ultimate destiny of all God's children.

—Dru

> "I invite you to thoroughly and thoughtfully read this revelation. As you do so, may the Lord bless you to more fully understand and appreciate God's love and His plan of salvation and happiness for His children."
>
> **M. Russell Ballard**
> "The Vision of the Redemption of the Dead," Oct. 2018

Doctrine and Covenants 138:11

As I pondered . . . the eyes of my understanding were opened, and the Spirit of the Lord rested upon me, and I saw the hosts of the dead, both small and great.

Ponderize

In October 1918, just a few weeks before his death, President Joseph F. Smith was pondering Peter's description of the Savior's mission in the spirit world after His Crucifixion. President M. Russell Ballard spoke about this glorious vision in his conference talk in October 2018, one hundred years after the revelation was received: "I bear witness that every person can read it and come to know it is true."

The concept of pondering scripture, knowing truth, and receiving revelation was taught to our family by my son's mission leader, Devin G. Durrant. When my son returned from his mission, he told us about the power he felt as he pondered the scriptures daily. Elder Durrant's "ponderize" talk touched the hearts of our entire family.

Scriptures become firmly embedded in our hearts and minds as we memorize and ponder them. We can experience moments of revelation, just like President Joseph F. Smith, as we prepare our minds through intense scripture study and prayer, asking for answers to questions.

—Marianna

> "I invite you to 'ponderize' one verse of scripture each week. The word *ponderize* is not found in the dictionary, but it has found a place in my heart. So what does it mean to ponderize? I like to say it's a combination of 80 percent extended pondering and 20 percent memorization."
>
> **Devin G. Durrant**
> "My Heart Pondereth Them Continually," Oct. 2015

Doctrine and Covenants 138:12

There were gathered together in one place an innumerable company of the spirits of the just, who had been faithful in the testimony of Jesus while they lived in mortality.

Single Still

I was talking with someone I love who has been divorced twice. She is afraid that she won't make it to the celestial kingdom because she doesn't have an eternal companion. I reminded her that what matters is the efforts she is making to keep her covenants. I reminded her that the Millennium is a thousand years. So much will be worked out during those years.

Through the Prophet Joseph Smith, God has revealed so much about His nature and eternal life. But as much as we know, there is much we don't know. We are promised eternal progression and learning. Focus on what you can control: your faithfulness, your choices, and your willingness. Won't it be a beautiful gathering in eternity? Because of Jesus Christ, all will be made possible.

—Ganel-Lyn

> "Our standing before the Lord and in His Church is not a matter of our marital status but of our becoming faithful and valiant disciples of Jesus Christ."
>
> Gerrit W. Gong
>
> "Room in the Inn," Apr. 2021

Doctrine and Covenants 138:37–38

Among the mighty and great ones who were assembled in this vast congregation of righteous were Father Adam . . . and our glorious Mother Eve with many of her faithful daughters.

The Woman at the Veil

The first time I walked in the celestial room of the Salt Lake Temple and turned around, I was in awe. Above the veil was a life-sized statue of a woman with two cherubs on either side of her. I wondered how she got there and what this statue symbolized.

Don Carlos Young was the son of Brigham Young and begged his father to go east to study architecture. While there, he bought a small figurine of a woman called *The Angel of Peace* and two little cherub busts. When he returned to Utah, Don Carlos was put in charge of finishing the interior of the temple. He felt strongly that *The Angel of Peace* and the cherubs should be included in the celestial room decor and got permission to use them. *The Woman at the Veil* was installed with no other explanation.

Twenty-five years later, Joseph F. Smith had his vision of the spirits of the dead, now section 138. In this vision as he sees "the great and mighty ones" who have received celestial glory, he first sees Adam. Then, beside him is "our glorious Mother Eve with many of her faithful daughters who had lived through the ages and worshiped the true and living God." Perhaps the *Woman at the Veil* symbolizes all those great and mighty women who pass through the veil and receive the full blessings of God from Mother Eve down to you and me.

—Christine

> "The commitment to aid one another across the veil can be classified as a covenant promise."
>
> D. Todd Christofferson
>
> "The Sealing Power," Oct. 2023

341

Doctrine and Covenants 138:50

For the dead had looked upon the long absence of their spirits from their bodies as a bondage.

It's Not Perfect, but It's Mine

We all seem to have a tendency to complain and find fault with our bodies. We moan about being out of shape, too pale, or having weird toes. We joke that our hair looks like a bird's nest and our bums are the size of Texas. But hey, let's give our bodies some credit—they're pretty awesome! Just think about all the amazing things we can do with them that bring us joy.

I love indulging in Ben & Jerry's ice cream, feeling the sun's warmth on my face, and softly touching a new baby's squishy cheeks. I love breathing in the sweet scent of orange blossoms, getting warm hugs from my grandkids, and holding my husband's strong, gentle hands. I love dancing in the kitchen and seeing the majestic mountains outside my window when I wake up. These simple joys always make me happy and bring warmth to my heart.

I am overwhelmed with gratitude for the things I can physically experience and where my body has carried me so far. Instead of complaining, I want to focus on the happiness it provides.

—Dru

> "Your body, whatever its natural gifts, is a magnificent creation of God. It is a tabernacle of flesh—a temple for your spirit."
>
> **Russell M. Nelson**
> "We Are Children of God," Oct. 1998

Doctrine and Covenants 138:57–58

The faithful elders of this dispensation, when they depart from mortal life, continue their labors in the preaching of the gospel. . . . The dead who repent will be redeemed, through obedience to the ordinances of the house of God.

Continue Our Labors

Anyone who has lost a loved one knows that grief hurts; it does not matter if you have a hope of life after death. Both of the prophets who received sections 137 and 138 had questions about deceased family members and asked the Lord to help them understand. The Prophet Joseph Smith was asking about his brother Alvin and his inheritance in the kingdom of God without having received the saving ordinances restored after his death. Prophet Joseph F. Smith was pondering how the Savior could preach the gospel to so many people who had not received the gospel in the three days between His Crucifixion and Resurrection. Both revelations help us understand the connection between temple work and future missionary work to those in spirit prison after we die.

Spencer J. Condie wrote: "Mercy and justice require that those who have died without an opportunity to hear the gospel in mortality receive that opportunity in the spirit world" ("The Savior's Visit to the Spirit World," *Ensign*, July 2003). Opportunities to repent will continue after death. I look forward to continuing my labors of preaching the gospel to the people in spirit prison after I die, as well as meeting the people whom I have done temple work for on earth.

—Marianna

> "The work of salvation in the spirit world consists of freeing spirits from what the scriptures frequently describe as 'bondage.'"
>
> Dallin H. Oaks
>
> "Trust in the Lord," Oct. 2019

Article of Faith 1

We believe in God, the Eternal Father, and in His Son, Jesus Christ, and in the Holy Ghost.

God Is Real

The Prophet Joseph taught, "Could you gaze into heaven five minutes, you would know more than you would by reading all that ever was written on the subject" (*Teachings of Presidents of the Church: Joseph Smith* [2007], 419).

Because of the First Vision, we have Joseph Smith's testimony of the Godhead. I have not gazed into heaven, but I have encountered God in the face of my newborn child. I have felt the Savior hold me in the hours following my sister's suicide. And I have heard the Holy Ghost whisper warnings when I was lost and confused. Knowing by faith is knowing.

God is real. And because of this knowledge, everything that matters is possible. The hard times are made easier. The great times are made eternal. Not everyone on the planet knows that God is real. That is why our missionaries make a difference. They are taking this article of faith and that truth to all the world.

—Ganel-Lyn

> "Latter-day restoration begins with theophany—the literal appearance of God the Father and His Son, Jesus Christ, to the young prophet Joseph Smith. . . . Because the heavens are again open, we know . . . the divine Godhead."
>
> Gerrit W. Gong
>
> "Hosanna and Hallelujah—The Living Jesus Christ: The Heart of Restoration and Easter," Apr. 2020

Article of Faith 4

We believe that the first principles and ordinances of the gospel are: first, Faith in the Lord Jesus Christ; second, Repentance; third, Baptism by immersion for the remission of sins; fourth, Laying on of hands for the gift of the Holy Ghost.

The Growing Snowball

If you've ever made a snowman in really sticky snow, you know how quickly a small snowball can turn into something huge. The key is to begin with a handpacked ball of snow and then roll it on the ground in a single direction. When you've finished a rotation, turn it ninety degrees and repeat; turn and repeat again. Before you know it, you'll have a ball waist high.

The same is true of our testimonies. Often our commitment to the Lord begins hand-packed and not very big or strong. As we roll through the process of putting our faith in Christ, repenting to increase that relationship, making covenants with Him through baptism, and finally receiving the Holy Ghost, our testimony will grow, but only by a small amount.

Then turn the snowball and work on faith in prayer through Christ, repent, renew your covenant through the sacrament, and see the increased power of the Holy Ghost in your prayers. Turn again and work on the temple, missionary work, modern prophets, the scriptures, and any topic or challenge you find. Soon your testimony will be so strong it will be immovable. This is the process the Lord has set in place for us to grow. It works!

—Christine

> "The fourth article of faith is one of the greatest illustrations of gathering together in one all things in Christ."
>
> David A. Bednar
>
> "Gather Together in One All Things in Christ," Oct. 2018

Article of Faith 9

We believe all that God has revealed, all that He does now reveal, and we believe that He will yet reveal many great and important things pertaining to the Kingdom of God.

Tell Me Again

My husband is an amazing cook. He loves to surprise our family with delicious meals and fancy desserts. Once, I asked him to teach me how to make his savory chicken Alfredo pasta. Patiently, he walked me through each step, from marinating the chicken to creating the creamy Alfredo sauce. However, I got distracted and forgot some of the instructions. When I tried to replicate the dish on my own, it didn't quite turn out as expected. Determined to master the recipe, I asked for another cooking lesson. This time, I paid close attention to every detail he shared. I followed each step and made sure I didn't miss anything. As a result, my second attempt was a success.

Just as I needed instructions from my husband, receiving ongoing inspiration from heaven is essential. Heavenly Father speaks to us individually through personal revelation, which can come through prayer, scripture study, and promptings of the Holy Ghost. We can seek His guidance repeatedly, and He will answer. God also guides His people collectively through chosen leaders, like our prophet and those who serve with him. They receive inspiration for the Church, including doctrines, policies, and programs, helping us navigate life's complexities.

—Dru

> "Revelation continues to flow from the Lord during this ongoing process of restoration."
>
> Russell M. Nelson
>
> "Hear Him," Apr. 2020

Article of Faith 11

We claim the privilege of worshiping Almighty God according to the dictates of our own conscience, and allow all men the same privilege, let them worship how, where, or what they may.

Freedom of Religion

The stories behind the revelations in the Doctrine and Covenants are often full of religious persecution and apostasy. Our church was founded on the principle of freedom of belief and the rights of others to believe "how, where, or what they may." We claim that privilege, and we will fight for the rights of others to have the same privilege.

Internationally, this standard is not being upheld. In January 2024, Nazila Ghanea, the UN Special Rapporteur on freedom of religion or belief, sent a report to the UN General Assembly. She wrote: "Hateful attitudes . . . are generated through direct as well as cultural and structural means, key among which is the explicit, or thinly veiled, incitement to direct violence against targeted religious or belief minorities. However, hateful attitudes can also be spread and perpetuated through expressions of disregard or disdain found in everyday political and social discourse, both formal and informal."

We should review our communications with others, both face-to-face and electronic, to make sure we are not adding to the thinly veiled hate speech that hurts others' beliefs.

—Marianna

> "There was divine inspiration in the original provision that there should be no religious test for public office, but the addition of the religious freedom and anti-establishment guarantees in the First Amendment was vital."
>
> **Dallin H. Oaks**
> "Defending Our Divinely Inspired Constitution," Apr. 2021

Article of Faith 13
If there is anything virtuous, lovely, or of good report or praiseworthy, we seek after these things.

Have You Been to Hawaii?

My daughter, Brooklyn, had a great way to handle things when friends started gossiping about someone. She asked, "Has anyone been to Hawaii?" That simple question always changed the direction of the conversation.

President Russell M. Nelson invited us to be careful how we talk about each other. He said, "If there is anything virtuous, lovely, or of good report or praiseworthy that we can say about another person—whether to his face or behind her back—that should be our standard of communication" ("Peacemakers Needed," April 2023).

How we talk about people when they aren't around is a beautiful way to foster goodness in the world. My daughter didn't have to correct or criticize her friends. She just gently redirected with a conversation starter. That's doing good.

—Ganel-Lyn

> "How we treat each other really matters! How we speak to and about others at home, at church, at work, and online really matters. Today, I am asking us to interact with others in a higher, holier way."
>
> Russell M. Nelson
>
> "Peacemakers Needed," Apr. 2023

Official Declaration—1

The Lord will never permit me . . . to lead you astray. . . . If I were to attempt that, the Lord would remove me out of my place.

The Lord Is at the Helm

In 1890, President Wilford Woodruff drafted the first official declaration of the Church, ending polygamy. Apostle Lorenzo Snow assured members that the Lord would never allow the President of the Church to lead it astray. If he did, he would be removed out of his place. Later, this quote was canonized in the Doctrine and Covenants, verifying its truth.

In April 1982 President Spencer W. Kimball was struggling with his health. In the last session of general conference he stood to everyone's surprise. His words echoed the sentiment of President Snow: "I bear you my testimony; this work is divine, the Lord is at the helm, the Church is true, and all is well." That was the last time he spoke in conference, although he lived another three years.

Twelve years later, President Ezra Taft Benson was bedridden. His counselor Gordon B. Hinckley also said, "God is at the helm. Never doubt it." President Benson died within the month, and President Hinckley became the new prophet.

With perilous times ahead, we must trust the counsel of our Church leaders. I still remember feeling the Spirit testify to me as Gordon B. Hinckley stated, "God is at the helm." We can have confidence that Christ leads His Church, even amid change.

—Christine

> "Remember this is the Church of Jesus Christ—He is at the helm."
>
> Dieter F. Uchtdorf
>
> "God Will Do Something Unimaginable," Oct. 2020

Official Declaration–2

Extending priesthood and temple blessings to all worthy male members of the Church.

The Lord's Timing

For over a thousand years after the Savior's ministry, the world was in darkness, awaiting a final restoration. Several events paved the way. People sought spiritual truth, and religious revivals generated excitement. The United States, with its promise of religious freedom, provided fertile ground for new religious movements. Joseph Smith had personal experiences and visions that prepared him for his role. Advancements in transportation and communication facilitated the spread of ideas. Printing technology made religious texts more accessible. All these factors contributed to creating an environment ripe for the restitution of the gospel.

Some aspects of the Restoration took longer to be realized. Heavenly Father knows the beginning from the end, and though we may not always understand His timing or ways, we trust that He has a purpose for all things. He loves all His children. Due to circumstances we don't understand, some blessings were not accessible to some for a while. Praise God that priesthood and temple blessings are finally made available to everyone!

—Dru

> "He has heard our prayers, and by revelation has confirmed that the long-promised day has come when every faithful, worthy man in the Church may receive the holy priesthood, with power to exercise its divine authority, and enjoy with his loved ones every blessing that flows therefrom, including the blessings of the temple."
>
> N. Eldon Tanner
>
> "Revelation on Priesthood Accepted, Church Officers Sustained," Oct. 1978

The Family: A Proclamation to the World

Marriage between a man and a woman is ordained of God and . . . the family is central to the Creator's plan for the eternal destiny of His children. (paragraph 1)

Mawwiage

A favorite family movie is *The Princess Bride*. The scene that always gets us laughing is when Prince Humperdinck and Buttercup are being hastily married and the minister starts the ceremony with the word *mawwiage*. This one word always cracks us up. But modern marriage is not a laughing matter, nor should it be taken lightly.

"The Family: A Proclamation to the World" was first introduced at the general women's session of general conference in September 1995 by President Gordon B. Hinckley. He prefaced the proclamation by saying, "With so much of sophistry that is passed off as truth, with so much of deception concerning standards and values, with so much of allurement and enticement to take on the slow stain of the world, we have felt to warn and forewarn" ("Stand Strong against the Wiles of the World," Oct. 1995).

Marriage between a man and a woman is central to God's plan. We should be examples of these principles to the world.

—Marianna

> "I testify to you that as we—women and men—work together in a true and equal partnership, we will enjoy the unity taught by the Savior as we fulfill the divine responsibilities in our marriage relationships."
>
> **Ulisses Soares**
> "In Partnership with the Lord," Oct. 2022

The Family: A Proclamation to the World

The divine plan of happiness enables family relationships to be perpetuated beyond the grave. Sacred ordinances and covenants available in holy temples make it possible for . . . families to be united eternally. (paragraph 3)

We Are One

When I was a teenager, my parents decided that we would have a family motto and chose "The Edwards family is united as one." I had a very difficult time with the motto. I was being rebellious and did not want to think that I was exactly the same as everyone else in my family. I wanted my own identity.

But I misunderstood my parents' understanding of being one. They were trying to unite the family through covenants and gospel teachings. These would not take away my individuality.

The covenants we make in the temple, especially the crowning ordinance of eternal marriage, seal and bind us together throughout the eternities as a family.

I want to live with my family eternally and continue those precious relationships beyond the grave.

—*Marianna*

"Covenant belonging with God and each other includes knowing our spirit and body will be reunited in resurrection and our most precious relationships can continue beyond death with a fulness of joy."
Ulisses Soares
"In Partnership with the Lord," Oct. 2022

The Family: A Proclamation to the World

We declare that God's commandment for His children to multiply and replenish the earth remains in force. (paragraph 4)

Precious Blessings

Having children is a sacred gift and responsibility. As we make eternal choices, it is imperative couples openly discuss their feelings with each other and with the Lord. I almost didn't and would have lost out on one of my most precious blessings.

After having my fifth child, I was overwhelmed. My husband's career was stagnant, and every month I struggled to live within an incredibly tight budget. At that point, I felt that it was too much to have another child. I didn't want to pray about it because I'd made the decision. I even made an appointment so there would be no question I was done. The day before I was set to go to the doctor, a friend called and invited me to the temple, saying we could share a babysitter. I was thrilled to go.

While in the celestial room, I found unbidden tears streaming down my face. When my friend asked why I was crying, I responded, "I need to have another baby." The thought had never crossed my mind and only came out of my mouth.

Sarah was that baby and has been one of my greatest joys. Her children are so cuddly, clever, and adorable that I can't imagine life without them. How many precious blessings are we passing on simply because we are not trusting in the Lord?

—Christine

> "He multiplies bread and fish, and He can multiply the love and the joy in your home."
>
> Dieter F. Uchtdorf
>
> "Jesus Christ Is the Strength of Parents," Apr. 2023

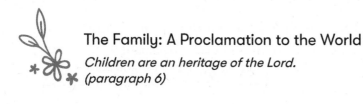

The Family: A Proclamation to the World

Children are an heritage of the Lord. (paragraph 6)

Our Wee Little Ones

I love spending time with little kids. They bless my life in so many ways. When I'm with them, I get to experience simple pleasures again, like catching a ladybug in my hand, watching an airplane fly across the sky, or the joy of eating a sprinkle-covered donut. Their innocence and zest for life are like a breath of fresh air. Their prayers are sincere, and their hugs melt my heart. They remind me of what truly matters and bring me closer to God. Their simple faith and pure love are gifts that keep me grounded in what's most important.

Jesus had an extraordinary love for little children. The scriptures tell us that He called a little child unto Him, setting the child in the midst of His disciples, and said, "Verily I say unto you, Except ye be converted, and become as little children, ye shall not enter into the kingdom of heaven. Whosoever therefore shall humble himself as this little child, the same is greatest in the kingdom of heaven. And whoso shall receive one such little child in my name receiveth me" (Matthew 18:3–5).

When we take the time to love and nurture them, we not only follow Jesus's example but also experience a bit of heaven right here on earth.

—Dru

> "You are God's agents in the care of children He has entrusted to you. Let His divine influence remain in your hearts as you teach and persuade."
>
> **Russell M. Nelson**
>
> "Salvation and Exaltation," Apr. 2008

The Family: A Proclamation to the World

Successful marriages and families are established and maintained on principles of faith, prayer, repentance, forgiveness, respect, love, compassion, work, and wholesome recreational activities. (paragraph 7)

Foundation Plus Nine

The parts of my house that bring me the greatest joy and happiness are meals served in my kitchen, the games played in my family room, and the prayers said in my bedroom. I realize that this enjoyment would not be possible without my home's structurally sound foundation.

The foundation of a happy family is living the teachings of the gospel. Yet the establishment and maintenance of happy, successful marriages and families are based on nine principles as stated in "The Family: A Proclamation to the World": (1) faith, (2) prayer, (3) repentance, (4) forgiveness, (5) respect, (6) love, (7) compassion, (8) work, and (9) wholesome recreational activities. (My favorite one is the wholesome recreational activities.) All nine are necessary to achieve that worldly elusive goal of a happy, forever family. It is not impossible to obtain; we just need to follow the blueprint outlined in this proclamation to the world.

—Marianna

> "The righteous molding of an immortal soul is the highest work we can do, and the home is the place to do it."
>
> Joseph B. Wirthlin
> "Spiritually Strong Homes and Families," Apr. 1993

The Family: A Proclamation to the World

We warn that individuals who violate covenants of chastity, who abuse spouse or offspring, or who fail to fulfill family responsibilities will one day stand accountable before God. (paragraph 8)

Warning!

I have seen firsthand the effects of abuse. It causes pain that is often carried throughout a lifetime because of the wrong choices made by others. God has made it very clear: "But whoso shall offend one of these little ones which believe in me, it were better for him that a millstone were hanged about his neck, and that he were drowned in the depth of the sea" (Matthew 18:6). God is a god of both laws and mercy.

Elder Patrick Kearon said, "He is a God of justice, and His divine justice will be served. Miraculously, the Lord is also a God of mercy to the truly repentant. Abusers—including those who were once abused themselves—who confess, forsake their sin, and do all in their power to make recompense and restitution, have access to forgiveness through the miracle of the Atonement of Christ" ("He Is Risen with Healing in His Wings," Apr. 2022).

If you have been abused, please know that God knows the pain you carry. No matter what your experience, there is hope through the Atonement of Christ.

—Ganel-Lyn

> "There is no place for any kind of abuse—physical, sexual, emotional, or verbal—in any home, any country, or any culture. Nothing a wife, child, or husband might do or say makes them 'deserve' to be beaten."
>
> Patrick Kearon
>
> "He Is Risen with Healing in His Wings," Apr. 2022

The Family: A Proclamation to the World

We warn that the disintegration of the family will bring upon individuals, communities, and nations the calamities foretold by ancient and modern prophets. (paragraph 9)

The Love of Men Shall Wax Cold

Six years ago a study of college students found them 75 percent less empathetic than college students from thirty years earlier. Researchers found a contributing factor was the overuse of technology. Violent video games and social media pressures affected behavior and mental health. But an equally large problem is the lack of face-to-face interactions, a UCLA study found. "It's where empathy is born," said Dr. Turkle.

Broken marriages are also having a huge impact on children's ability to feel compassion and love, affecting one in three children. Seventy percent of juveniles in state-operated institutions come from single-parent homes, and 86 percent of school shooters do not have a father's influence in their lives.

Focused parents can change the tide by being involved in their children's lives and curbing the unlimited use of technology. As we show love and compassion to our children, they will in turn show that love to others. But, for so many, we are seeing this sad prophecy of love waxing cold come to pass before our very eyes. Luckily, we know the antidote. It is love.

—Christine

> "Brothers and sisters, the pure love of Christ is the answer to the contention that ails us today."
>
> Russell M. Nelson
>
> "Peacemakers Needed," Apr. 2023

The Living Christ

As we commemorate the birth of Jesus Christ two millennia ago, we offer our testimony of the reality of His matchless life and the infinite virtue of His great atoning sacrifice. (paragraph 1)

Special Witnesses of Jesus Christ

In the April 1916 Conference Report, Joseph F. Smith taught: "These twelve disciples of Christ are supposed to be eye and ear witnesses of the divine mission of Jesus Christ. It is not permissible for them to say, I believe, simply; I have accepted it simply because I believe it. Read the revelation, the Lord informs us they must *know,* they must get the knowledge for themselves. It must be with them as though they had seen with their eyes and heard with their ears and they know the truth."

Just as an eyewitness provides firsthand testimony of an event, the Quorum of the Twelve Apostles serve as witnesses of Jesus Christ. Their role is to testify of Christ's divinity and share their spiritual experiences with others. Like reliable witnesses in legal proceedings, the Apostles' testimonies provide authenticity and credibility to the reality of Jesus Christ's mission and His role in the plan of salvation. Their firsthand knowledge and spiritual witness serve as a powerful testimony for individuals seeking to understand and follow the teachings of Jesus Christ.

Even though we aren't called as special witnesses, each of us can gain our own testimony of Jesus Christ through prayer, scripture study, and living gospel principles. As we continue to build simple faith and trust in Him, the Holy Ghost will confirm the truth to our hearts and minds, and we can know for ourselves that He is our Savior and Redeemer.

—Dru

> "I bear my witness that the Savior lives. I know the Lord. I am His witness."
> Boyd K. Packer
> "The Witness," Apr. 2014

The Living Christ
He taught the truths of eternity, the reality of our premortal existence, the purpose of our life on earth, and the potential for the sons and daughters of God in the life to come. (paragraph 2)

The Author and the Finisher

Paul wrote that we should look unto Jesus, "the author and finisher of our faith" (Hebrews 12:2). This phrase has always interested me. The author is the writer of words and is the means by which a book is written. The Savior is the author of the holy scriptures. He taught His words to mankind before the world was, during His ministry as Jehovah, and while He lived on earth.

John wrote, "In the beginning was the gospel preached through the Son. And the gospel was the word, and the word was with the Son, and the Son with God, and the Son was of God" (JST, John 1:1). Since His words are the basis of our faith, the Savior is the author of our faith.

In carpentry, a finisher is the person who puts on the finishing touches to make the product perfect. The Savior allows us to strive for perfection through His Atonement. We must look "to Jesus the mediator of the new covenant" (Hebrews 12:24), for He allows us to repent, thus finishing, or perfecting, our faith so that we can return to live with Him and our Father again.

—*Marianna*

> "As one of His ordained witnesses, I declare this Easter morning that Jesus of Nazareth was and is that Savior of the world, the 'last Adam,' the Author and Finisher of our faith, the Alpha and Omega of eternal life."
>
> **Jeffrey R. Holland**
> "Where Justice, Love, and Mercy Meet," Apr. 2015

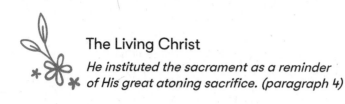

The Living Christ

He instituted the sacrament as a reminder of His great atoning sacrifice. (paragraph 4)

Saturday Night Baths

My grandmother grew up on the plains of western Canada with no indoor plumbing. As a child, I remember her telling me about Saturday night baths. She came from a family of eleven, and the work of filling the galvanized tub was so arduous they would only do it once. First in were the parents. Then the oldest children. My grandmother was the third child, fifth to bathe. Imagine how dirty the water was for the babies!

My grandmother said in the winter, the bath would begin warm, but by the time she got in it was always cold. Even though the water wasn't ideal, she said the feeling of going from dirty to clean was amazing. That was their only day to bathe all week. My grandmother said that because we can simply turn on a warm shower whenever we want, we don't appreciate how wonderful being clean is.

The same could be said of the sacrament. Because we have it so readily available each Sunday, it is easy to simply go through the motions. Instead, we should remember the sacred power of turning to Christ. Through His sacrifice and Atonement, we can be made clean every week as we use that time to repent and renew our covenants, just like a Sunday morning bath.

—Christine

> "Sins are cleaned by the power of Jesus Christ through His atoning sacrifice as we make and keep the baptismal covenant."
> Dale G. Renlund
> "Jesus Is the Treasure," Oct. 2023

The Living Christ

As Risen Lord, He visited among those He had loved in life. He also ministered among His "other sheep" in ancient America. In the modern world, He and His Father appeared to the boy Joseph Smith. (paragraph 5)

He Lives!

On the dark Friday when Jesus was crucified, the earth trembled and storms raged. His enemies rejoiced, thinking they had won. The temple veil tore, and Mary Magdalene, Mary, and the Apostles were overwhelmed with grief. It seemed like the darkest day in history, filled with despair and sorrow.

But the darkness didn't last. On Sunday, Jesus rose from the dead, victorious over death. His Resurrection brought joy and praise, replacing tears with hope. Jesus showed that death is not the end but the beginning of new life.

When Jesus rose from the tomb, He accomplished something unprecedented. He broke the chains of death, not just for Himself but for everyone who has ever lived—both good and bad. His Resurrection brought comfort to those who mourned the loss of loved ones and the possibility of eternal life to all.

—Dru

> "The atoning sacrifice and Resurrection of Jesus Christ changed each of our lives forever."
>
> **Russell M. Nelson**
>
> "Christ Is Risen; Faith in Him Will Move Mountains," Apr. 2021

The Living Christ

We declare in words of solemnity that His priesthood and His Church have been restored upon the earth. (paragraph 8)

His Church and His Priesthood

I grew up during the era when I called myself a Mormon and declared myself a member of the Mormon Church. I am so thankful for the change of focus on the name of Jesus Christ. Since revealing section 115, the Lord has emphasized the importance of His name being part of His Church. The world's nickname of Mormon sidetracked members from focusing on the true importance of the Church's name.

In 2018, President Russell M. Nelson made a statement to reaffirm our commitment to use the correct name of His Church: "The Lord has impressed upon my mind the importance of the name He has revealed for His Church, even The Church of Jesus Christ of Latter-day Saints. We have work before us to bring ourselves in harmony with His will" ("The Name of the Church," Official Statement, August 16, 2018). This statement led to a change in the way we labeled ourselves. We were no longer Mormons, but members of Christ's Church. Because this is His Church, He has given us His priesthood power to conduct His business here on earth through temple ordinances. His Church and His priesthood are restored on the earth today to prepare us for His Second Coming.

—Marianna

"We testify that those who prayerfully study the message of the Restoration and act in faith will be blessed to gain their own witness of its divinity and of its purpose to prepare the world for the promised Second Coming of our Lord and Savior, Jesus Christ."

Russell M. Nelson
"Hear Him," Apr. 2020

The Living Christ

We testify that He will someday return to earth. "And the glory of the Lord shall be revealed, and all flesh shall see it together" (Isaiah 40:5). (paragraph 9)

I Am Ready for Jesus to Come

I am grateful that the last thing I get to write about for this book is Jesus coming again. I am ready for Him to come. Until that day arrives, we can look for Christ everywhere. I hope you have found Him in your study of the Doctrine and Covenants this year. I hope you have found Him in signs of the season. Most of all, I hope you have found Him in the answers to your prayers.

When I look at the heartbreaking headlines, the hurt in families, and the lack of hope in the world, I don't have solutions. But I know Who does. Jesus is the answer to all the problems. And someday we all will kneel and praise Him. I am ready for Jesus to come. I can't wait!

—*Ganel-Lyn*

> "Look for Christ everywhere—I promise He is there! True joy rests on our willingness to come closer to Christ and witness for ourselves."
>
> **Bonnie H. Cordon**
> *"Never Give Up an Opportunity to Testify of Christ," Apr. 2023*

The Living Christ

He is the light, the life, and the hope of the world. His way is the path that leads to happiness in this life and eternal life in the world to come. (paragraph 10)

Snow Blind

My husband and I had to drive to the airport very early one December. The sunrise was lovely, but the light hit the windshield in a way that made visibility more difficult. It had also snowed during the night, a light powder, and there was a breeze that made the blowing snow act like a fog that was only a few feet off the ground. We were almost blind.

Although we knew the way, the road was almost completely covered. The only consistent thing we could see was the solid white line on the right edge of the asphalt, often called a fogline. Having faith it would guide us correctly, we kept our eyes squarely on that line all the way to the airport. Though it was slow going, we made it safely, and oh, how happy we were!

Like that fogline, the words of Christ will guide us when things are so dark and confusing that we just want to turn around and give up. Whether we receive His voice through scripture, His authorized servants, or the whisperings of the Holy Ghost, Christ will lead us if we turn to Him and hold fast. And the joy doesn't only happen at the end of the journey but all along the way. Even when we can barely see, for then we can feel His loving power the most.

—Christine

> "No matter the heaviness of our story or the current course of our path, He will invite us to walk with Him."
>
> Emily Belle Freeman
> "Walking in Covenant Relationship with Christ," Oct. 2023

The Living Christ
God be thanked for the matchless gift of His divine Son. (paragraph 10)

God Be Thanked

No words I could ever write or speak would be enough to convey the immense suffering our Lord endured—nor His limitless love for us. My heart aches to think of the weight of sorrow Jesus bore in Gethsemane and on Calvary. To grasp the depth of His love and sacrifice, and the countless tears He shed for my sake, overwhelms me with humility and gratitude. He paid the price for my sins, bore my pains and afflictions, and carried my burdens.

After enduring incomprehensible suffering in the Garden of Gethsemane, Jesus was taken to Golgotha, where He was crucified, experiencing again the mental anguish, emotional grief, and physical pain of Gethsemane. But through His literal and glorious Resurrection from the tomb, He shattered the chains of death and hell, ensuring that I will live again. This knowledge fills my heart with profound love for Him. On Calvary, He was the dying Jesus, but from the tomb, He came forth as the Living Christ.

Jesus brings indescribable joy to my heart. Knowing Him gives purpose to everything I do. With other faithful believers throughout time, I testify that Jesus Christ is my Savior, the healer of my soul who redeemed me from sin and death with His infinite love.

—Dru

"The atoning sacrifice and Resurrection of Jesus Christ changed each of our lives forever."

Russell M. Nelson

"Christ is Risen; Faith in Him Will Move Mountains," Apr. 2021

Doctrine and Covenants 1:39
For behold, and lo, the Lord is God, and the Spirit beareth record, and the record is true, and the truth abideth forever and ever.

The Beginning and the End

As mentioned in the introduction of this book, the Doctrine and Covenants is a peculiar treasure that we as members of The Church of Jesus Christ of Latter-day Saints should cherish and study. President Ezra Taft Beson called the Book of Mormon the keystone of our religion, but the Doctrine and Covenants is our capstone. From the Lord's preface in section 1 to the Lord's appendix in section 133, the Lord has cried out His message to all the world that "the voice of the Lord is unto all men, and there is none to escape" (Doctrine and Covenants 1:2).

Section 1 and section 133 have similar themes and commandments to the world. Elder John A. Widtsoe explained that the "two sections together encompass the contents of the book in a condensed form" (Message of the Doctrine and Covenants, 17). We are told to hearken (1:1; 133:1), prepare (1:12; 133:4, 17), arm ourselves against Babylon (1:14–16; 133:3–7), be true to His everlasting covenant (1:15, 22; 133:57), and follow His commandments (1:24, 37; 133:60).

The Savior is our Alpha and Omega. His voice is the voice we should hear as we read the words of the Doctrine and Covenants from beginning to end.

—Marianna

> "The Lord has placed His stamp of approval on both the keystone and the capstone."
>
> **Ezra Taft Benson**
>
> "The Book of Mormon and the Doctrine and Covenants," Apr. 1987

About the Authors

Marianna Richardson's two great loves are the gospel of Jesus Christ and her family. She and her husband served as mission leaders in São Paulo, Brazil. She currently shares her love for the gospel with UVU institute students. Her second great love is her family. She is the mother of twelve children and a growing number of grandchildren. Marianna's thirst for knowledge has compelled her to finish four graduate degrees, including a doctorate in education and a juris doctorate degree. She is an adjunct professor at Brigham Young University in the area of business communication.

About the Authors

Christine Thackeray grew up as a middle child in a large Latter-day Saint family and went to BYU but hated it. Life would have been so much easier if she could have simply walked her own path, but she knew the Church was true, and the Spirit seems to scream at her louder than most. She served a mission in London and has seven remarkable children and a husband as patient as Job himself. One of her greatest gifts was teaching all seven of her children in early-morning seminary for over ten years in three different states. Today you'll find her playing with her fourteen grandchildren, prepping for the *Women Read Scripture* podcast, or typing away on some new fiction project. She co-authored *C. S. Lewis: Latter-Day Truths in Narnia* and wrote *Crayon Messages*, *Lipstick Wars*, *Could You Be an Angel Today*, and *He's Got Her Goat*. She's served as Relief Society president, Young Women president, Primary counselor, and chorister. She was just got called as a Primary teacher, and she can't wait.

About the Authors

Ganel-Lyn Condie knows all is possible with God. She is a popular motivational speaker known for inspiring others with her unique honesty, authenticity, and spirit. She is dedicated to her family, faith, and inspiring others. As a graduate from Arizona State University, with a BS in elementary education and psychology, she became an award-winning journalist and was editor of *Wasatch Woman* magazine. She is the mother to two miracle children and loves growing older with her supportive husband, Rob. Ganel-Lyn lives with an open heart and feels passionate about sharing principles that will empower others to live life with more joy. She is a regular television and radio guest. Her YouTube channel, shows, talks, and books have now encouraged thousands of people all over the world. Ganel-Lyn's faith and family have helped her overcome and appreciate a myriad of challenging stewardships. Learn more about Ganel-Lyn at her website, www.ganellyn.com.

About the Authors

Dru Huffaker is a convert to The Church of Jesus Christ of Latter-day Saints and is passionate about her love of Jesus Christ and the restored gospel. She is married to her best friend, Mel, is the mother of six beautiful children, and is known as Honey to her eighteen grandchildren.

Dru completed a master of business administration and is the Executive Vice President of Sales and Marketing at Cedar Fort Publishing & Media, the largest independent LDS publisher. She is currently a co-host of the podcast *Women Read Scripture*. One of her greatest joys is teaching institute at Brigham Young University. She is an avid family history buff, an enthusiastic supporter of musical theatre, and a foodie at heart.

Notes:

Notes:

Notes:

Notes:

Notes:

Notes:

Notes: